Accounting for Value

ACCOUNTING

—∞— FOR

VALUE

STEPHEN PENMAN

Columbia University Press
Publishers Since 1893
New York   Chichester, West Sussex
Copyright © 2011 Columbia University Press
All rights reserved

Library of Congress Cataloging-in-Publication Data
Penman, Stephen H.
Accounting for value / Stephen Penman.
p. cm.
Includes bibliographical references and index.
ISBN 978-0-231-15118-4 (cloth : alk. paper) — ISBN 978-0-231-52185-7 (ebook)
1. Investment analysis—Accounting.   2. Accounting.   I. Title.
HG4529.P45 2010
332.63'221—dc22
2010042335

Columbia University Press books are printed on permanent
and durable acid-free paper.
This book is printed on paper with recycled content.
Printed in the United States of America

c 10 9 8 7 6 5 4 3 2 1

References to Internet Web sites (URLs) were accurate at the time of writing.
Neither the author nor Columbia University Press is responsible for URLs that
may have expired or changed since the manuscript was prepared.

Contents

Introduction

IT IS PROBABLY WITH mixed feelings that you find yourself holding a book on accounting in your hands. Apprehensive: Isn't accounting complex? Deflated: Isn't accounting boring? Amused: Remember all those accounting jokes? Your interest may occasionally be piqued when accounting is called into question, usually during a crisis—in the Enron collapse or the recent financial meltdown—but the discussions of revenue recognition, fair value accounting, variable interest entities, and so on that ensue quickly dissolve into technicalities beyond the common man. Or worse: Babel and confusion. Leave it to the nerds, it is not for me.

I hope to persuade you otherwise.

First understand that, while this book deals with accounting, it is primarily a book on valuation, written for investors and those to whom they trust their savings: investment advisors, analysts, and portfolio managers. The book explains how to employ accounting to estimate share value. It embraces the fundamental investing approach identified with Benjamin Graham, adapted to incorporate pertinent principles of modern finance. Fundamentalists distinguish price from value—the two can be different—and it is accounting, executed independently of price, to which the investor refers to determine the difference. This book shows how the investor handles accounting to identify value and challenge stock prices.

In this book the investor will see that accounting and valuation are so intertwined that valuation is actually a matter of accounting; valuation involves performing an accounting on a firm, an accounting for value. Accordingly, a valuation is only as good as the accounting underlying it. There is thus a question for the accountant to answer: What is good accounting for valuation? Do generally accepted accounting principles (GAAP) fit the bill, or does the investor look for an alternative accounting for valuation? The book is a conversation with the investor about valuation, but a conversation that accountants—particularly accounting regulators and standard setters—are most welcome to sit in on. Like investment advisors, analysts, and portfolio managers, they also serve the investor. Just as poor valuation can harm an investor's savings, so can poor accounting. And there is considerable room for improvement in today's accounting.

The Importance of Accounting

If you have ever purchased a stock, you understand the importance of valuation, but let me persuade you of the importance of accounting.

In most endeavors, whether a household, a club, a firm, or a government, one needs to keep track. Indeed we account all the time as a matter of instinctive behavior. In personal relationships, one "keeps account" of the pros and cons—assets and liabilities, debits and credits—of the relationship, often instinctively. We do so in more formal arrangements, but more formally. With corporate accounting, owners keep track of their investments and the stewards who manage them, and with government accounting citizens keep track of their politicians. Without accounting to tell us where we are, where are we?

To function well, market economies require defined property rights enforced by independent courts, along with minimal restrictions on contracting. But of equal importance are accounting systems of high integrity that track our rights and obligations to each other. For our common wealth, accounting is critical for directing capital to firms that will use it most productively, and for the efficient functioning of capital markets where those firms are valued and where our savings are at stake. It is no wonder that in almost every crash—whether it be the 1929 crash, the recent financial crisis, or corporate debacles like the Penn Central failure in the 1960s or Enron more recently—the finger is pointed at the accounting (among other suspects). Accounting is boring when all is well, but critical when one needs it most. Accounting can be complex—often unnecessarily so—but accounting is no joke. (But, still, let's keep those accounting jokes in inventory.)

Accounting defines reality. It does so by bringing specificity to what would otherwise be speculative generalities. Economists work with concepts of "revenue," "cost," "income," "assets," and such; concepts that are very helpful for economic reasoning but have no manifestation until someone puts a number on them. The rubber hits the road with measurement and measurement falls to the accountant. "Cost of production," in reality, is an accounting measure and that reality is determined by how one does the accounting. "Economic profit" is a useful concept, but no one has seen it until a number is put on it; consultants market "economic profit" measures but their products are simply accounting measures with "economic profit" a mere label (and a pretentious one at that). Accounting gives expression to "profitability," "financial position," "growth," and so on. Indeed, as we will see, accounting gives expression to "value." Without accounting, these various concepts are simply in the mind of the beholder, open to speculation. Accounting forces concreteness, not just concrete numbers but also concrete thinking.

In the heyday of strong "efficient market" views, the accounting that fundament investors so rely on was dismissed: accounting does not matter, it was said, for the market can see through the accounting. What then, one might ask, does the market see? The standard answer is that the market sees through to the future cash flows. But one cannot, of course, see the future. The market must see something observable, something real, and that reality must be some form of information that forecasts future cash flows. We, of course, do see factories, employees, the movement of goods and delivery of services, but accounting produces a representation of these realities appropriate for valuation.

It is popular to dismiss accounting as unconnected to reality, an archaic system unrelated to cash flows. This is a gross misconception. One must always reserve criticism of any particular form of accounting—GAAP, indeed—but this is not the way to look at accounting as a matter of first order. Accounting forces managers to face the numbers in reporting to shareholders rather than deliver platitudes about plans and prospects. It forces them to come to grips with reality. Sound government accounting forces politicians to be straightforward in reporting to taxpayers—to view borrowing as debt rather than revenue, for example. It forces reality. And sound accounting for valuation forces investors to come to terms with reality rather than speculate. That opens the question: What is sound accounting for the purpose at hand?

Accounting expresses our reality for another reason. You and I don't need a behavioral scientist to tell us that our ability to process information is limited, but behavioral research has told us that people adapt to this limitation by developing heuristics that focus on a few pieces of summary information. Investors do so when they multiply just one number, earnings, by a multiplier (the P/E ratio), to estimate the value of a share. Economists do so when they appeal to one economywide "earnings" number, gross domestic product (GDP), to summarize the performance of an economy. Both know they are taking shortcuts and glossing over the imperfections in the two numbers (the P/E heuristic is particularly suspect, as we will see). One should always be skeptical of any accounting measure, but the demand for summary numbers from the limited information processors of the planet is strong. They have straightforward questions, such as "What did I earn this year?" and "What did my firm earn?" They seek accounting summary numbers, like earnings, to treat as real numbers, to be relied upon. But again, the question is: What is a good summary number for the purpose at hand?

The cynic claims "There is more than one earnings number, it depends on how you measure it." Possibly so, for measurement is difficult; perhaps we cannot hope for one number to capture all the texture of a firm's operations. But summary numbers we must have, a limited few that limited information processors can handle—perhaps sales, book value, and cash flow along with earnings. While applying a P/E ratio to one number, earnings, may be a bit too simple, reducing valuation to a form that deals with just a few numbers holds out the promise of reducing the scale of the equity valuation task to something akin to applying a simple formula in bond valuation. But this depends on how the accounting is done. Earnings should mean a lot, otherwise the accounting should indeed be dismissed.

Add to the cynics those who dismiss accounting with the claim that modern computing and the emerging XBRL technology for corporate financial data allow quick access to a huge array of information without summary financial reports. But computer information consists of many millions of bits and the XBRL taxonomy is a huge array (which, in turn, typically aggregates millions of transactions). The user of these technologies—the valuation analyst, for example—is left with the task of handling the information and summarizing what it means. That process cannot be avoided and that process is accounting. Those with limited information processing ability might also take issue with the cynic's advice: "Don't worry about accounting, just disclosure; there is no issue if we just have full disclosure." Disclosure is said to make things "transparent." Transparency is a virtue, of course, but a core dump is not what they are looking for. Disclosure is a cop-out. We simply have too much data these days; data need to be assembled in a compact way. Lengthy disclosures are often supplied when the accounting is doubtful— when there are off-balance sheet entities permitted by the accounting rules or fair value "guesstimates" on the balance sheet, for example. Better accounting would be more transparent than disclosures that are often rendered as boilerplate.

Investors like accounting numbers for another reason. We understand that investing is risky and that risk cannot be eliminated. Modern finance has given us ways to measure risk and ways to reduce it— diversification and hedging, for example—but modern finance does not deal with a primary source of risk: the risk of paying too much for an investment. This, of course, is the concern of the fundamental investor, and that investor needs an accounting that supplies assurance in this regard, an accounting that helps to distinguish value from price. That brings us to valuation.

Accounting and Valuation

I trust that this apology for accounting is compelling, but persuasion comes from actually seeing accounting work in practice. This book focuses on getting the accounting to work for us in valuation. The book's title, *Accounting for Value*, signals the orientation but we will see that something deeper is involved. Valuation itself is actually a matter of accounting. When one values a business one accounts for value. This is not just a turn of phrase; the choice of a valuation method is the choice of a particular accounting method and that choice determines the confidence one derives from the valuation. Indeed, we shall see that the same principles underlie both accounting and valuation. One thinks about valuation in the same way as one thinks about accounting, and it is that thinking that is embraced to get insights about risk, growth, and value. With this practical focus, we are in a position to ask: What is good accounting? What is good valuation? What is good accounting for value?"

With valuation and accounting much the same thing, valuation is very much anchored to the accounting. The book thus harks back to the era of Benjamin Graham and his Defensive Investors (who merely protect against paying too much for a stock) and Active Investors (who exploit mispricing to their advantage). Both grounded their valuations in the fundamentals represented by the accounting. Those were the days before efficient markets theory displaced fundamental analysis as the prevailing paradigm. The view of "efficient markets" rationally pricing investment assets has come under significant challenge in recent years, not the least by investors who followed the advice that "the price is right," buying stocks passively, without investigation, and holding them "for the long run," only to be disappointed. Their experience during the bursting of the equities bubble of the late 1990s and the more recent financial crisis was sobering. They might well return to fundamental analysis and for that they need accounting numbers to anchor on, to protect them from the risk of paying too much. How does one account for value, to invest with some confidence?

The efficient markets view has come under challenge from academics as well. Not only have many market "anomalies" been documented that are seemingly inconsistent with rational pricing, but behavioral economists have also challenged the model of the "rational man," who is supposed to govern rational markets. Those of us on the planet with limited information processing abilities are capable of being moved by impulses— "animal spirits"—that result in irrational prices. We follow herds, we are moved by fashion, we are reluctant to realize losses, and we are hampered by overconfidence and a host of other psychological problems (that academics can recognize but we can't! The kids never learn!).

The field of behavioral finance is in its infancy, and many explanations for irrational markets are conjectural, but the behavioralists' idea of "bounded rationality" is appealing. Behavioralists are quick to say that the problem may not be so much with the "rational man" but with the demands placed on the rational man by the "rational model" of man. The demands placed on our information processing abilities by the rational model flies in the face of considerable evidence suggesting that investors, individually and in aggregate, do not handle information well. To deliver efficient prices, modern investment theory requires investors to mentally visualize a myriad of covariances, risk factors, risk premiums, and expected returns, all of which vary randomly through time according to some "stochastic process." Quite demanding; my head hurts. Sorry, I failed the rational man test. What is needed is an accounting for value that reduces the dimensionality of the problem.

We are indeed in conjecture land here, but might not the deviant traits that behavioral economists attribute to us be due to our failing to process information appropriately? Might market "irrationality" be a matter of failure to account for value? Accounting, governed by principles invariant to ourselves, supplies the rationality that escapes us, a counterweight to the limitations of our mental accounting with its tendency to speculate. Effective accounting supplies a check on our behavioral biases. It promotes the idea that one trades on a book—an accounting book—not on emotions, conjecture, or speculation. If the accounting is also invariant to prices, it serves to challenge prices affected by emotions, conjecture, and speculation. With this view, the idea that accounting is important to efficient capital markets becomes compelling, and the idea that "accounting does not matter" becomes objectionable. Accounting, appropriately executed, anchors investors and it anchors prices.

Accounting in the Present and the Future

To be clear, when talking of accounting, I do not necessarily refer to GAAP accounting or its recent variation in International Financial Reporting Standards (IFRS). GAAP and IFRS have some features that enhance valuation and some that frustrate it (as we will see). Rather, the focus is on the appropriate accounting for valuation, and that accounting may differ from GAAP. The Financial Accounting Standards Board (FASB) that regulates U.S. GAAP and the International Accounting Standards Board (IASB) that regulates IFRS are currently engaged in an extensive "Conceptual Framework" project to provide a foundation to govern the accounting standards they issue. Where the two boards will end up is not clear at this point, but the project to date appears to be appealing to ambiguous accounting concepts like "recognition," "measurement," "balance-sheet focus," and "exit value"—ideas far from the investor's mind—rather than focusing on the issues that investors face. "Fair value accounting" sounds good—like ice cream and apple pie—while "historical cost accounting" sounds, well, dated. But does fair value accounting actually help me to value my shares, or does it frustrate me? Could it be that historical cost accounting gives me a better way of accounting for value? This book aims primarily to lay out an architecture for accounting for valuation, rather than a critique of GAAP and IFRS, but in doing so a critique is implicit. Indeed, Chapters 8 and 9 have some explicit complaints about U.S. GAAP and IFRS and where they appear to be headed.

In recent years, the quality of valuations by professionals has come into question, particularly during the bubble of the late 1990s. Analysts and investment advisors did not stay anchored to the fundamentals. But if the accounting is suspect, the anchor drifts. Important achievements have been made in developing GAAP (and now international accounting). The Securities and Exchange Commission (SEC) has expanded disclosure, despite the clutter of too many detailed regulations. But I fear that we are in losing our way. We are losing our sense of what is good accounting and what is bad accounting, and even the ability to sort it out. To be sure, many analysts are engaged in the diagnosis of "earnings quality," the financial press is as vigilant as ever, and the SEC and similar agencies in other countries strive to enforce accounting rules. However, I am not thinking of the ability to detect violations of GAAP or IFRS, or to see through a firm's attempts to arrange its affairs to be within the rules in form but not in substance, important though such efforts are. Rather, I am thinking of the ability to visualize and implement accounting that might be different from GAAP, accounting that serves its users. Commentators snipe at GAAP, at the details, but redemption is in the broader scheme of things.

Investors, analysts, accountants, politicians, accounting regulators and, yes, many accounting academics have lost the ability to think constructively about accounting design. Fifty years ago, partners at leading accounting firms wrote papers on a whole array of accounting issues and held themselves out as thought leaders in accounting. Numbered among them are George O. May at Price Waterhouse and Leonard Spacek who led Arthur Andersen from 1947 to 1963. Accounting firms were populated by such thinkers, but now the thinking has been delegated to regulators and their bureaucracies, with accounting firms functioning as little more than compliance cops. It seems that Leonard Spacek's successors at Arthur Andersen had little idea of what good accounting and bad accounting for Enron would look like (or with too little conviction to stand up for it). To be fair, accounting firms are very sensitive to litigation and their job is to certify compliance with GAAP. Indeed, the fair value accounting that built the Enron house of cards was sanctioned by the SEC. The role of enforcing compliance is not to be underrated if we desire accounting with integrity but, in failing to tackle issues of accounting principle, accounting firms underrate themselves. A sense of professionalism has been lost. Universities that train the "professionals" once taught "accounting principles." Now they largely teach rules and regulations. A sense of inquiry has been lost in the classroom, and inquiry is what universities are supposed to be all about.

Did the SEC have a sense of good accounting when it approved fair value accounting for Enron? Does it today? Accounting regulators seem to be flailing around on many issues, without firm goalposts. Again to be fair, the FASB and IASB are subject to political influence—observe the directives from U.S. Congressional committees and the European Commission in the fair value accounting debate during the financial crisis—and politicians rightly have influence in democracies. But clarity in thinking should dominate, bringing persuasion to both regulators and politicians and a higher hurdle for lobbyists to surmount.

The folks at the FASB and IASB appear to be dedicated to the goal of forging a set of quality accounting standards. They do so not autocratically, but with broad input from many sources. However, that input comes with the baggage of special interests, and deferring to a consensus of special interests is no way to develop a long-lived, robust accounting system. In launching their Conceptual Framework project, the FASB and IASB appear to be quite conscious that good accounting flows from good concepts, not consensus, but the direction they are taking is not promising. The ghost of Orwell rises. Regulators are proceeding to build one monolithic, worldwide set of accounting standards under the banner of harmonization but a doubtful Conceptual Framework. If universities and colleges just teach the rules dictated by this regime, without challenge, a profession will have been lost and society will be the weaker for it.

How does one discriminate between good accounting and bad accounting? This can only be sorted out on the ground, at the point where accounting is employed. Just as a new drug is tested, with side effects noted, so must accounting be judged by how it helps or hinders its users. In this book I focus on equity valuation, and so will ask: When using accounting for valuation, what do we want the accounting to look like?

To the Reader

The book is pitched in the simplest terms your author can contrive. From Chapter 1 onward, the book has the ordinary investor "on Main Street" in mind, with the conviction that the financial system becomes more efficient when the investor whose money is at stake keeps an eye on the store. However, the "moms and pops" of investing have other things to do—being a mom or a pop is an absorbing task after all—so the book is probably of most relevance to the professional investor "on Wall Street" who manages the store for those on Main Street. The book presumes some familiarity with investing, though demands little accounting knowledge beyond an appreciation of what a balance sheet and income statement look like.

To those who manage the store, I trust that the book will help you to differentiate price from value—to help deal with the risk of paying too much for an investment—and so help you to be a worthy custodian of the people's savings.

To those involved in accounting standard setting, I trust this book will be of some help at this important juncture as you rework your Conceptual Framework to guide the development of accounting standards in the future.

To accounting academics, I hope this book will help put us on a common platform as we apply ourselves to think about how accounting should proceed in the future.

To academics in finance, you may not appreciate the skepticism about efficient markets. But you will see how other principles of modern finance are relevant to fundamental investing and accounting. Modern finance and fundamental analysis have for too long been seen at odds. The first two chapters go to some length to establish accounting and valuation in a way that is consistent with the principles of modern finance. I hope you will see how the accounting lens on valuation yields solutions to problems encountered in asset pricing and equity valuation.

Most important, to the investor, I hope, first and foremost, that this book will help make you a more intelligent investor (to appropriate Benjamin Graham's term). But I also trust that the book will provide you with an appreciation of what good accounting looks like. The pressures on accounting should not be underestimated. Corporate managers, trade organizations, financial engineers, bankers, and politicians—even professional accountants—want accounting that serves their purposes, and are quite vocal in their demands. They do not necessarily have your interest at heart. Issues of power and hierarchy come to the fore when markets are organized by rules and regulations. At best, the confusion of voices leads to unfocused accounting standards. I hope that you will see in this book the type of accounting that is needed for intelligent investing, the type of accounting that provides you with some security as you engage in risky investing.

A Road Map to the Book

To remove you as far as possible from the feeling of grinding through a textbook, this book reads rather like a novel. It does not provide the excitement of a potboiler perhaps, but the plot develops and thickens (not impenetrably, one hopes) as the book proceeds, with a gradual resolution that shows how to "account for value" as a practical matter. Along the way, the conclusion to each chapter, after the first, summarizes the main takeaways at that point.

Here is the plot line (that still leaves some suspense for the reader). Chapter 1 lays out the investing principles under which fundamentalists of Graham's ilk operated and compares them with the principles of modern finance. In so doing, it provides a brief history of investment ideas of the last century. The chapter identifies those ideas that provide the foundation for fundamental valuation and for the design of accounting that supports it. Chapter 2 applies these principles to a valuation approach based on accounting. It is here that one comes to understand "accounting for value." Chapter 3 then goes active, taking the accounting to the task of challenging market prices. The fundamentalist is particularly concerned about paying too much for growth, so the focus is on understanding the growth expectations implicit in the market price and the value that the market is placing on growth. With that understating, Chapters 4 and 5 bring accounting into play to evaluate growth and protect the investor from paying too much for growth. Chapters 6 and 7 evaluate risk, particularly risky growth, and offer the active investor a method for determining the expected return from an investment that finesses the need to determine a "cost-of-capital." The issue of "value" versus "growth" investing comes to the fore. Chapters 8 and 9 turn directly to the accounting, to ask how accounting might best be designed to aid valuation, engaging (among other things) the current debate over fair value accounting. Chapter 10 is a brief summary, pulling together the ideas of the book for the investor who wishes to be counted as one of Benjamin Graham's "intelligent investors."

Accounting for Value

CHAPTER ONE

Return to Fundamentals (and an Accounting for the History of Investment Ideas)

VALUATION IS A SET of methods for determining the appropriate price to pay for a firm. Accounting is a set of the methods for producing the information for that determination. Both are man-made constructions; they are a matter of design. This book asks: What is an effective design for valuation and how should accounting be designed to support valuation? These, of course, are perennial questions for both analysts and the authorities who lay down accounting standards. The book explains that valuation and accounting are very much the same thing: Valuation is a question of accounting for value. Accordingly, the valuation design question and the accounting design question are resolved in tandem.

As architects and engineers well know, safe and effective design rests on firm underlying principles (of the physical sciences). Otherwise, the house or bridge falls down. This chapter examines the principles on which a valuation architecture and an accounting architecture might be securely built. Architects and engineers also appreciate an overarching principle: The endeavor is utilitarian, the design must serve the users. So let's first focus on you, the investor, and ask: What are the principles under which you operate? Although the accounting rules of today are influenced by corporate management, investment bankers, bureaucrats, accountants, lawyers, and politicians and their lobbyists—with or without your interest in mind—my focus is on you. You, after all, are the owner of corporations, or seek to become one, and there are many of you.[1] How may you best be served? To answer that question I will review the history of investment ideas, ask how well those ideas serve you, and embrace or replace them as needed to get accounting and valuation on a firm footing.

Let's suppose you are an investor who is moving money from the safe haven of a money market fund into the stock market. You understand that the stock market is how wealth generated by corporations is shared in a capitalist economy, and you want a part of it; you want to be an owner. But you are apprehensive; you are cautious. You understand that stocks have significant upside potential over a money market fund, but there is also a downside. Witness the devastation to investors' retirement accounts in recent years. Is the stock market just a casino? You are not a gambler going for the jackpot, for you know that, just as the house on average wins against the gambler, so the agents in the stock market—the brokers, the investment managers, and other middlemen between you and your investments—are keen to take "house money" in the fees they charge you. You are willing to pay appropriate fees, but you want some comfort, some assurance that the game is not against you. You are concerned that you may be playing against professional investors. You can't protect yourself against inside information (though insider trading laws are on your side here), but you are worried that those on the other side of your stock trades may be doing their homework. So you want to make sure you have an investing approach that protects you, even one that gives you an edge. If you do surrender your money to the care of professionals, you want to be assured that they have an edge.

Now you may be an investor who draws your confidence from faith in your fellow investors. They have far more information than you, you perceive, so you take the price they set as a fair price and buy and sell at that price. You "free-ride" on their efforts to value stocks. You are not concerned that their expertise in valuation puts you at a disadvantage. In the parlance of modern finance, you believe that "efficient markets" yield rational prices that summarize all available information, and this belief is where you get your comfort. There is nothing for you to add by doing additional work. You take the advice to "invest for the long run" for (we are told) stocks reward the investor for the added risk over money market funds "in the long run." You heed the warning that you take on unnecessary risk if you don't diversify, so a broad-based market index fund is appropriate for you. (It also has lower fees!) You are a passive investor. If so, this book is not for you, and we wave goodbye with a cordial "best of luck." You do not need to understand valuation. You do not need accounting. You will not be lonely, for there are many money managers who simply "allocate" investors' funds to stocks and bonds without much investigation. But remember that, to make the market efficient for you, someone must be doing the accounting and someone must be doing the valuation. And that someone expects to get a reward for his or her labors, possibly by trading with you or your money manager at your expense.

Alternatively, you may be an investor who sees the appeal of the efficient market hypothesis but, with so many assailing the idea these days, you come to the game with some skepticism. On the one hand, you ask yourself: How can a market with many, presumably sophisticated, investors be grossly inefficient? How can prices be so wrong when there are so many keen traders working daily (and even minute by minute) to arbitrage away any obvious profit opportunities? Surely their information gets impounded in prices quite speedily. That, after all, is what economics teaches us about markets, particularly ones like the stock market, where there are few "barriers to entry." On the other hand, with the skepticism learned from life (some reserved for economists), you take the view to trust but verify. The market may be efficient, but it pays to investigate; one kicks the tires before buying a used car, and one inspects the goods before buying a used stock, for the previous owner might have a reason for off-loading it on you. After all, buying stocks at the high multiples of earnings, book values, and cash flows of the late 1990s was not such a good idea, at least after the fact. Nor was the purchase of stocks at the height of the housing and credit bubble in 2006–2007. You are cautious; Benjamin Graham, the father of fundamental investing would call you a "defensive investor." This book is for you.

Finally, you may be an investor who comes to the game with the conviction that prices are not rational. You cannot see any good economic explanation for momentum pricing, the tendency for prices to continue to rise or fall. You saw the stock prices of the late 1990s as bubble prices. You saw Cisco Systems trading at well over 100 times earnings as folly. You recognized Dell Computer as a very good firm, but trading at 88 times earnings in 1999 seemed a bit rich. Indeed, with the S&P 500 trading at 33 times earnings against a historical average of 15, you questioned the entire market at the time.[2] Recalling the Japanese price bubble a decade before and the "Nifty-Fifty" pricing of the 1970s in the United States only reinforces your view.[3] Share prices in China today seem crazy. In answer to the seeming economic imperative of efficient market theory, you may have your own pop psychology idea as to why animal spirits—to use Keynes's term—overtake stock markets. Or you might be a reader of the new "behavioral economics" that attempts to explain in more scientific terms why prices appear irrational: Investors follow the herd, whether optimistic or pessimistic; they follow fashion and pursue "glamour" stocks; overconfidence overrides common sense; humans ignore information or cannot process information adequately; humans overreact to information; humans' judgments are biased. These attributes bring "noise traders" to the market. You think you can "beat the market" by being a more "rational" human; you can gain by trading at "irrational" prices. You are one of Benjamin Graham's "active investors." This book is also for you.

It is clear that you, the investor, are in the middle of the efficient market debate, a debate that has engaged both investors and academics for almost fifty years. The efficient market view of the stock market has dominated modern finance and the academic view of the investing landscape for many years. But the mention of Benjamin Graham reminds us that this was not always the case. The efficient market view, associated with the University of Chicago in the 1960s and 1970s (and Eugene Fama in particular), was a departure from the ideas of the fundamentalists associated with Columbia University in the 1930s and 1940s (and Benjamin Graham in particular). Just as efficient market theory assailed fundamental analysis in the 1960s, the efficient market view has been assailed in recent years in academic debate but also from stark investor experience.

Here we return to fundamentals, to review what was learned then and what can be further learned. We do so in order to think about how we should face the investment task and how we might build the accounting and valuation tools that will aid that task. But we do so with an appreciation of the significant contributions of modern finance to investment theory and practice. Some of the principles of modern finance may need to be rejected, but some may depose fundamentalist principles. We examine fundamentalist principles and the principles of finance in turn, to ask what needs to be discarded and what is to be embraced, and so establish a foundation on which valuation and accounting can be designed.

First, the principles espoused by fundamentalists. These are principles of "sound investing" but are also principles to forge the accounting and valuation methods used in sound investing. Fundamentalists refer to "value justified by the facts." I hope to show you in subsequent chapters that value justified by the facts is a matter of accounting. That accounting challenges the market price, validates it as "efficient" for the defensive investor (or not), and (if not) provides a tool for the active investor. These investing principles morph into valuation principles and accounting principles in subsequent chapters, and we will hark back to them continually. At this point I mention just a few implications for accounting and valuation—to give a taste of what's to come.

Fundamental Principles

If you read Graham's *The Intelligent Investor*—and one is advised to do so—there is not much in the way of techniques or calculations.[4] Rather, Graham instructs us how to think about investing. He writes as a sage, he offers wisdom. Investing, he says, is first about attitude and approach rather than technique. Modern finance, as befits modernism, is about technique; formulas and models are at the fore. Just as engineers construct bridges and spacecraft using mathematical equations, so do modern financial engineers, whether it be models of risk and return like the Capital Asset Pricing Model (CAPM), models to price credit default swaps, models to price options (Black-Scholes and the binomial option pricing models), or, closer to home, discounted cash flow models to value equities. These models are part of the remarkable contribution of financial economics over the past fifty years. Yet these same models have been called into question, particularly during the recent financial crisis, so we do well to reconsider the more "soft" principles of yesteryear.

Here are 10 principles distilled from years of practice by fundamentalists. Most of them are familiar. I remind you of them to establish a foundation on which to build an accounting for value. Most are just plain common sense. But it is plain common sense that provides the antidote to the animal spirits against which we are warned, and it is plain common sense that questions the supposed sophistication of a mathematical model.

1. One does not buy a stock, one buys a business
2. When buying a business, know the business
3. Price is what you pay, value is what you get
4. Part of the risk in investing is the risk of paying too much
5. Ignore information at your peril
6. Understand what you know and don't mix what you know with speculation
7. Anchor a valuation on what you know rather than on speculation
8. Beware of paying too much for growth
9. When calculating value to challenge price, beware of using price in the calculation
10. Return to fundamentals; prices gravitate to fundamentals (but that can take some time)

Let's consider each principle in turn.

ONE DOES NOT BUY A STOCK, ONE BUYS A BUSINESS. This point reminds us that, when buying stocks, one buys not paper, but claims on a business. Impressive amounts of paper are traded on our exchanges each day, not only equity claims but also corporate debt, not to mention the derivative instruments tied to these claims.[5] Do these traders trade businesses or do they trade paper? Efficient market investors buy paper, without investigation of the business. Day traders buy paper, or even just a ticker symbol. But fundamental investors buy a business.

WHEN BUYING A BUSINESS, KNOW THE BUSINESS. Equity research reports open with a discussion of the business before they get to the numbers. And so they should, for to value a business one has to understand the business. That amounts to understanding the idea behind the business—the business model—and managements' execution of the idea. Successful business rides on a good entrepreneurial idea and the translation of that idea into value through business operations. Valuation, in turn, is a matter of translating one's knowledge of the business model and its execution into a price for the business. That translation is a matter of accounting. One observes factories, mines, farmers' fields, inventories, customers, suppliers, sales and purchase prices, and the many transactions in which a business engages. What to make of it? Accounting pulls these many features together to make sense out of them for the investor. Accounting, and the financial statements it produces, is the lens on the business, but only if the accounting is done well. The accounting designer seeks to focus the lens.

PRICE IS WHAT YOU PAY, VALUE IS WHAT YOU GET. Unlike the efficient market investor, fundamental investors do not accept price as necessarily equal to value. Price is what the market is asking the buyer to pay, value is what the share is worth. Fundamentalists entertain the notion that prices can "deviate from fundamentals." So they approach prices skeptically and they challenge prices to understand whether prices are justified by value received. They understand that one buys a business and the business can be a very good business—like Cisco Systems and Dell Computer—but they also know that good businesses can be bad buys—like Cisco and Dell in 1999.

PART OF THE RISK IN INVESTING IS THE RISK OF PAYING TOO MUCH. Modern finance supplies models, like the CAPM, to help us understand the risk of holding a stock. Business school students are drilled on beta, in an exercise they refer to as "beta bashing." Beta measures the investor's susceptibility to price movements. The fundamentalist sees it differently. As a matter of first order, the risk is in buying a stock rather than holding it, and that risk is the risk of paying too much. To fundamentalists, knowing a firm's beta ranks rather low on the list of things they would want to know. They are buying value, so, although they are concerned with fundamental risk—the risk from competition, poor management, and too much debt that can damage value—they are less focused on the price fluctuations that are the concern of those who buy just on price alone. Indeed, they may see a price drop as presenting an opportunity rather than inflicting damage. Buying at less than value is low risk, in fact providing a "margin of safety." [6] They emphasize the need for a model to detect the risk of paying too much rather than a beta model.

IGNORE INFORMATION AT YOUR PERIL. Equity investing at its core is a matter of dealing with uncertainty. Information reduces uncertainty, so this principle is indeed pure common sense, to be dismissed only if one is persuaded that efficient prices already contain all the information required. However, the point begs the questions "What information is relevant?" and "How do I pull that information together?" That is a matter of accounting, of accounting for value.

UNDERSTAND WHAT YOU KNOW AND DON'T MIX WHAT YOU KNOW WITH SPECULATION. In evaluating climate change and its effects, the rationalist holds to the adage "Let's understand what we know—the science—and separate that from fear and speculation." Only then can one develop persuasive scenarios and design corrective action. The adage also applies to investing: Don't contaminate what you know—your reliable information—with conjecture. Knowing a firm had sales of $150 million this year is different from a forecast that sales three years hence will be $250 million. Don't mix them. Focus on "value justified by the facts," and so be better prepared to challenge speculation. If current sales are $150 million, what would cause them to climb to $250 million in just three years?

The fundamentalist operating under this principle has a request to make of the accountant: Tell me what you know, but don't add too much speculation to the financial statements. Keep to the facts and leave the speculation to me. Accounting is defined by what it includes, but also by what it leaves out. I don't want the accounting to be based on guesses about fair value (says the fundamentalist). Don't let us go back to the 1920s, when accountants "put water in the balance sheet" only to see the "fair values" that had been booked evaporate in the 1929 crash. I want solid, even conservative, accounting on which U.S. GAAP (Generally Accepted Accounting Principles) has largely been based ever since. I understand that some estimation is required—to discount receivables for the uncertainty about bad debts or to estimate pension liabilities—but keep it within bounds and based on solid evidence. The fundamental analyst is very glad that the accounting authorities did not succumb to booking speculative "intangible assets" to the balance sheet during the speculative 1990s. They were harassed for adhering to "accounting for the industrial age," where value came from tangible assets, rather than adapting to the "information age," where (it was said) value comes from intangible assets. "Value reporting" was advocated. Fortunately, the accounting authorities were largely unmoved by calls from those who pointed to the high (speculative) price-to-book (P/B) ratios at the time as evidence that the accounting was deficient. Those high P/B ratios subsequently evaporated, as they had in 1929.

ANCHOR A VALUATION ON WHAT YOU KNOW RATHER THAN ON SPECULATION. Having separated what is known from speculation, the fundamentalist anchors on what is known. Indeed, fundamental analysis is really a matter of sorting out what we know and applying it to challenge speculation. So, in the 1990s, amid all the hype about the prospects of the dot.coms, the fundamentalist observed that those firms were reporting continuing losses. He or she gave considerable weight to that observation and, as it turned out, those losses were a good indicator of most of those firms' demise.

Investing, of course, involves speculation about the future, so speculation must be entertained. But particular weight should be given to what is known, to discipline speculation, to keep it in check. Accounting, based on "what we know," anchors a valuation. Indeed, the valuations in subsequent chapters take the form

Value = Anchoring accounting value + Speculative value.

That is, the investor identifies value implied by the accounting and then thinks of adding extra value for speculation. The accounting must be of such quality that the investor can anchor with confidence, of course, so that poses the question of the appropriate accounting.

BEWARE OF PAYING TOO MUCH FOR GROWTH. Wall Street loves growth and markets tend to get overexcited about it, particularly in boom times. Visions of growth stimulate all sorts of fortune-telling. Fundamentalists are aware that growth is the most speculative part of any valuation, so they are disciplined about buying growth. Graham saw growth as not worth paying for: In most cases, other than a firm with a clear, protected franchise, growth will be competed away. That may be a bit extreme, but growth surely is a risky bet. We have another call on the accounting: Account in a way that protects us from paying too much for growth.

WHEN CALCULATING VALUE TO CHALLENGE PRICE, BEWARE OF USING PRICE IN THE CALCULATION. If one seeks to challenge price, one must refer to information that is independent of price; price is not value, so do not refer to price in calculating value. An investor who estimates a value by applying a P/E (price-earnings ratio) observed in the past or from "comparable" firms is using price to calculate price. Analysts who increase their earnings forecasts because the price has gone up are on a slippery slope if they use those same forecasts in their valuations. And accounting that introduces prices into the financial statements—by marking to market, for example—is in danger of basing value on price. The analyst craves an accounting that is independent of price, an accounting that gives insights about value that can be used to challenge price.

RETURN TO FUNDAMENTALS: PRICES GRAVITATE TO FUNDAMENTALS (BUT THAT CAN TAKE SOME TIME). Active fundamental investing rests on the notion that prices can deviate from fundamentals but ultimately return to fundamental value. The idea is that fundamental value will ultimately be revealed and become obvious to the market through credible information arriving at the market. If the accounting is nonspeculative, as the fundamentalist desires, the correcting information comes through firms' financial statements. Earnings drive stock prices, so the fundamentalist focuses on "long-run earnings power" with the recognition that prices will adjust to earnings information as it arrives. Thus one can think of valuation as asking, "What will the financial reports look like in three, four, or more years?" The answer involves speculation, of course, but the focus on the future financial statements disciplines the speculation if those statements—and the quality of the earnings they report—are determined by an accounting discipline that eschews speculation.

The warning that the return to fundamentals may take some time is often coupled with the advice, "Be patient." This warning is often directed to short-term traders: Fundamental analysis is not for you. For the long-term trader: Patience is required, for prices that deviate from fundamentals can deviate even more before they gravitate. As in life, patience is always tested, particularly if the trader takes uncomfortable short positions during bubbles. Fundamental investors of the 1990s know this well: They could see that the expectations implicit in the prices of dot.com firms were unreasonable, but their sell positions in 1997 seemed increasingly foolish as the momentum continued. Patience was ultimately rewarded, however, as the sales and earnings anticipated by market prices failed to materialize in financial reports.[7]

What dictates these 10 principles? Well, there is no formal model to explain them, though perhaps one day a behavioral scientist might develop one. The principles are distilled from human experience in dealing with uncertainty, presumably embedding the instincts that we humans have developed through our socialization over time. They simply fall into that category of "common sense," those unmodeled ideas that our very being tells us are worthy to accept, even to cling to. They are broad principles, and the issue is how to make them operational. The next few chapters take up the task.

But, first, let's compare the fundamentalist principles to the principles of "modern finance." Modernists might claim that fundamentalists are dealing with old-fashioned notions of yesteryear, a cult of prudence formed by overly conservative practitioners scarred by the 1930s Depression. Traditional fundamental analysis is ad hoc, more a liberal art than a science, they might say. The fundamentalist principles are too glib, making investing look too easy, even smelling of easy money. Modern finance has moved on. Indeed, modern finance has a model of the rational man, supplied by neoclassical economics, and that model explains how the rational investor should handle risk. Bring in Samuelson, Arrow and Debreu, and Modigliani and Miller. And we might do well to do so, for economics has taught us much. Financial economics, in particular, has made major contributions to economic theory and the practices of Wall Street over the last fifty or so years. Let's challenge the fundamentalist principles with the insights from finance. Those insights may indeed be helpful in refining the fundamentalist's guiding principles before we attend to accounting and valuation issues.

Principles of Modern Finance

There is some sorting out to do. Modern finance substitutes models and machines for the art of analysis; the "quants" supply algorithms that replace investor judgment. Such is modernism. But, on the heels of the financial crisis, modern finance is much denigrated these days. Challenges have been made to efficient market theory and the whole asset pricing apparatus. Some financial engineering products have failed, and the automatic execution of mathematical strategies may have caused prices to cascade together (some claim), exaggerating the crisis. But let's not throw out the baby with the bathwater. Some of the achievements of modern finance have been astounding. The proliferation of products for practice is exemplary of what a social science (indeed, any science) should deliver. Let us examine the principles of modern finance and sort out which to retain and which to discard. Let us review the products that have flowed from those principles, to see how useful they may be to you, the investor, concerned with the risk of paying too much. Much of the critique that follows has been well aired; my aim is to apply the critique to our endeavor of accounting for value.[8]

The No-Arbitrage Principle

The no-arbitrage principle is the cornerstone of modern finance; prices are set in relation to each other such that there is no profit to be gained from selling at one price and buying at another. Prices cannot be arbitraged. Oil should trade in Rotterdam and New York at the same price, adjusted for transportation and other transaction costs. Oil futures trade relative to spot prices such that there is no advantage to arbitraging the two. And the price of a call or put option on a stock must bear a no-arbitrage relation to the stock price.

The no-arbitrage principle was seen as a momentous innovation because it meant that theorists could get to insights with much less baggage. At one time financial theorists made dubious assumptions about the form of investors' utility functions—the shape of investors' likes and dislikes—to derive their propositions. The need for such abstractions was swept aside by the no-arbitrage principle: Rational prices must be set relative to each other on the basis of their different risk, so the investor is rewarded only for the risk born. Any difference in prices not so explained must be due to "limits to arbitrage" such as the transaction costs of arbitraging. Almost every proposition in finance depends on no arbitrage. The idea has led to a huge array of products designed to enhance risk sharing in the economy.

Lately, however, behavioral economists have come to view the dismissal of utility functions as too dismissive; investors bring their very selves to their investing. Fundamentalists have always seen the no-arbitrage principle in a different way. They uphold the principle when it comes to value, but not to price. Fundamental value is a no-arbitrage price with respect to information and, if prices obey the no-arbitrage condition, they do so not because of their relationship to other prices, but because of their relationship to information. If price differs from a no-arbitrage value, fundamentalists see information as the arbitraging mechanism in the market. Prices gravitate to fundamentals as information on which value is based is recongnized by the market.

Efficient Market Hypothesis

In the recent financial crisis, efficient market theory was blamed for all manner of sins more likely attributable to inefficient incentives in the financial system, inefficient risk management, interest rate regulation, and easy money. A "dogma," a "failed creed," an "intellectual Zeitgeist." It's a bad rap. One must distinguish efficient pricing in capital markets, about which the theory was originally concerned, from the efficiency of the economic system in general and it is efficient capital markets with which the investor is concerned. Unfortunately, both sides to the efficient market debate have come at it with passion, and there is nothing more dangerous to serious inquiry than passion.

Efficient market theory is an expression of the no-arbitrage idea, and indeed is a statement of no arbitrage with respect to information: One cannot arbitrage prices with information because prices already reflect that information.[9] It probably was never intended to be taken as literally true—it was originally stated as a hypothesis, subject to testing. Like most economic concepts, it is a point of departure for our thinking. It is usually conceded that prices may not be efficient with respect to private information. And it is generally acknowledged that there must be some mispricing to reward investors and their advisors for going about the task of information gathering and analysis that make prices efficient. If no one evaluated information market prices would indeed follow a "random walk," but it would be a random walk that reflected uninformed prices rather than informed prices.[10] However, the efficient market idea has a certain imperative to it, if one accepts the standard assumptions about economic behavior: How can significant mispricing survive for long if profit-seeking investors can quickly exploit the mispricing and, in doing so, drive prices to the value justified by the fundamentals? Further, with so much mandated disclosure these days, considerably more public information is available than in Graham's time, suggesting more information-efficient prices.

On the other hand, the theory is challenged by the stark evidence of a history of bubbles and associated momentum investing of which the 1990s dot.com bubble and the 2005–2007 credit bubble are only recent examples.[11] The experience of investors buying at prices higher than indicated by accounting fundamentals is a brutal reality. The stock market crash in 1987, apparently in the absence of any determining information, gives pause. And when academics, as early as the 1970s, began to view the efficient market theory as a falsifiable hypothesis rather than an inviolable precept of economics, the weight of evidence they produced cast significant doubt on the theory.[12] The fundamentalist view that price and value can be different is still on the table.

Fundamentalists are not moved by fads, however, and that includes the current fad of rejecting market efficiency outright. They anchor on what they know. And they know that study after study shows that "active" managers of equity funds, despite the representations in their advertising, typically earn the same return for their investors (after subtracting the costs and fees) as one would earn from just passively buying a market index fund. Experienced fundamentalists know that bargains are hard to find; the quick-buck, "get-rich" scheme is just not there. It is hard to "beat the market."[13]

Fundamentalists thus respect prices; they accept the notion that prices contain information. Fundamentalists admire Hayek's great insight about the price system aggregating dispersed information in the economy and accept that they, like Hayek's central planner, cannot hope to pull all this information together.[14] They also accept, as Robert Lucas would later model, that rational expectations require that one learns from the information contained in price.[15] However, they do not accept that the expectations of others that go into the price are necessarily those of a rational accounting. Indeed, they worry that deferring to price for one's "rational expectations" can be like joining a chain letter: A feedback loop sets prices on the basis of prices, so bubbles form. *When calculating value to challenge price, beware of using price in the calculation.* Fundamentalists will not anchor on prices, as efficient market theory would have them do, but rather seek an autonomous accounting for value. They first understand the information in market prices and then challenge that information with their own pricing. If market prices are efficient, they so confirm; if prices are inefficient, they see a trading opportunity. In confirming that prices are efficient, they are behaving like the defensive investor doing due diligence, kicking the tires. If their investigation indicates prices are inefficient, fundamentalists have an opportunity as an active investor. In either case, they stay grounded to the notion that they are playing against the information in price; in Benjamin Graham's words, they are negotiating with Mr. Market about value, and Mr. Market's asking price needs to be understood and then challenged.

Thus for fundamentalists, passivity is not a strategy, for that bears *the risk of paying too much*; they check to see whether the price is right. But that puts the onus on detecting when prices are wrong so, if one is to get an edge, one must get an edge in this discovery. That edge may come from garnering fresh information about firms, but with insider trading illegal, Regulation FD (Fair Disclosure) requiring firms to disclose information to the public broadly, and most of that information now available at one's fingertips electronically, there may be little advantage here. Rather, the advantage is likely to come from handling the information insightfully.

The efficient market hypothesis leaves big open questions: "How does the market become efficient?" "If investors believe in market efficiency and just buy an index, how does information come to the market?" and "If in the belief in market efficiency pension fund managers and other professional investors just do 'asset allocation,' how does information come to the market?" Rather than seeing information as a generic, undefined substance that nature provides to oil the efficiency of markets, the fundamentalist looks at information as a commodity that must be assembled and analyzed as a matter of rational design. If prices are efficient, it is the rational analysis of information that produces rational prices rather than something that flows by nature. If prices are not efficient, it is a failure of the supposedly rational man in handling information, a failure to account for value appropriately.

Behavioral scientists insist that human beings are limited in their ability to process information, a point that our self-awareness readily confirms. We need a deliberate accounting, outside of our mental schemes, intuition, and self-delusions to bring us to the level of rationality that is assumed for the rational man with "all available information." Our mental accounting is just not up to the task, so our view of price is very much dependent on the quality of the formal accounting we add as a remedy. Accordingly, fundamentalists embark on a disciplined, detached analysis of the information. It is not just a matter of temperament or self-discipline. An accounting for value, built on a rational foundation and governed by principles and rules that are immutable, invariant to fashion or fad and other aspects of human behavior (including management manipulation), supplies the detachment. It is that accounting and valuation about which this book is concerned.

But a rational foundation is required for that accounting. Let us explore the principles of modern finance further to see whether they supply that foundation. After all, financial economics is the science of rational investing.

Value Is Based on Expected Cash Flows

Drummed into every business school student, this principle recognizes that one invests to get cash payoffs, so the value of an investment is equal to the present value of the expected future cash flows from the investment. The idea ties back to a fundamental idea in economics that human happiness comes from consumption. Cash buys consumption so if one surrenders current consumption by investing cash, one expects to get (hopefully more) future consumption in return. Thus the value of an investment is determined by the expected cash it will return to buy that future consumption. But it is also determined by how much the future cash, and thus future consumption, are at risk.

This idea is usually expressed in the form of a model. For equity investments, the cash return is in the form of dividends so, applying the model to calculate value now (date o):

$$\text{Value}_0 = \frac{\text{Dividend}_1}{1+r} + \frac{\text{Dividend}_2}{(1+r)^2} + \frac{\text{Dividend}_3}{(1+r)^3} + \cdots.$$

where r is the discount rate (the required return for risk) and the ellipsis points indicate that, for a going concern like a business, the forecasts continue indefinitely into the future. This is the "dividend discount model."[16] There is no controversy about this idea: It is a principle on which sound valuation must be based, and it is the principle on which the accounting for value in the next chapter will build.

Dividend Irrelevance: Value Does Not Depend on Dividend Payout

Investors typically do not hold going-concern equity investments for-ever, but rather liquidate them after some time, perhaps at retirement. Suppose shares were to be sold three years hence, so that your cash pay-offs would be three years of dividends and a liquidating dividend from selling the stock at the price at the end of three years, P_3. Then, accord-ing to the dividend discount formula, you would see your value as

$$\text{Value}_0 = \frac{\text{Dividend}_1}{1+r} + \frac{\text{Dividend}_2}{(1+r)^2} + \frac{\text{Dividend}_3}{(1+r)^3} + \frac{P_3}{(1+r)^3}.$$

Clearly, this is not going to help us with a valuation because, to get the value now, we have to know the price at the end of year 3, and we cannot get value by using price in the calculation! But the exercise is instructive. When a firm pays out a dividend, the share price drops as one would expect; paying out a dollar means the firm is worth a dollar less. But the shareholder is no worse off; he or she has a dollar less of value in the firm but a dollar in hand. This is sometimes referred to as the dividend displacement property: Paying dividends displaces (re-duces) value in the firm but leaves the shareholder no worse off. Now consider the payment of future dividends. If a firm pays dividends for three years, the price at the end of three years is displaced by the divi-dends; if a firm pays no dividends, the price is not displaced. But a lower price with higher dividends does not change the present value of the cash flows from lower dividends but a higher price.[17]

This property is called the dividend irrelevance property. It is also called the Miller and Modigliani (M&M) proposition, after the pro-fessors who had the insight.[18] The idea was awarded a Nobel Prize, and it stands as one of the foundational principles of modern finance. Value is not affected by dividend payout policy. But it leaves us with a conundrum: The value of a share is based on expected dividends to shareholders, but the dividends that a firm pays up to the liquidat-ing dividend are irrelevant (and going-concern firms are deemed not to liquidate).[19] The conundrum points to the need for an alternative valuation approach to dividend discounting. We require a valuation that accounts for value generated in the firm rather than the distribution of value through dividends. But that accounting must honor the principle that the value, so calculated, is independent of the expected payout.

The idea cuts across the ideas of the fundamentalists of old. They thought that a firm paying more dividends should be worth more. In their words, "A bird in the hand is worth two in the bush" (a saying more acceptable to the hunters of that time than the conservationists of our time).[20] Miller and Modigliani showed them to be wrong.

Diversification and Risk

Harry Markowitz had a celebrated insight in 1952: The risk in holding a stock is based not on the variance of the stock price or even its downside volatility, but rather on the variance that cannot be diversified away by holding a portfolio of stocks.[21] If stock returns are less than perfectly correlated, one can reduce risk by diversification. This Nobel Prize-winning idea is a formalization of the commonsense notion: Don't put all your eggs in one basket. The ultimate diversification strategy is to invest in the broad market portfolio. It is a central tenet of modern portfolio theory.

The fundamentalist who sees risk primarily as the risk of paying too much might not put a lot of weight on the point. Buying at value below price provides the margin of safety one needs.[22] Diversification, fundamentalists sniff, is a strategy for those who do not know much about their investments, a protection from one's own ignorance. *One ignores information at one's peril,* and buying the market portfolio to diversify leaves one exposed to risk that might be reduced by some examination of stocks in the portfolio. Buying the market portfolio might mean that one is overpaying for some stocks, while missing out on the underpricing of other stocks that might be exploited for safety. In return, one is exposed to mispricing of the market as a whole (as in a bubble), or to shocks to the whole system (as in the financial crisis). Value, and indeed risk, lies in the businesses that make up the market portfolio, so examine those businesses. *One does not buy a stock, one buys a business* and *when buying a business, know the business* (and the risks involved). To quote Keynes, "to suppose that safety first consists in having a small gamble in a large number of different companies where I have no information to reach a good judgment, as compared with a substantial stake in a company where one's information is adequate, strikes me as a travesty of investment policy."[23] Why leave stock selection to the folks at Standard and Poor's or the designers of the FTSE (Financial Times Stock Exchange) index? They weight stocks in the index according to price rather than fundamentals, and stocks with a higher price get a higher weight!

Nevertheless, the idea of protecting against risk cannot be ignored; we are indeed ignorant of the unexpected shocks that might hit our investments. So, while maintaining a focus on value versus price, don't take on the risk of the unexpected that you can protect against. The fundamentalist asks whether the margin of safety indicated by value over price is sufficient protection or whether additional protection should be added. Risk management (for which diversification is just one tool) provides protection against what we don't know. In seeking return, know your risks, understand what you wish to be exposed to, and protect yourself from what you do not wish to be exposed to. (Diversification may not be the appropriate risk-management tool, for you might seek protection from marketwide shocks that diversification pushes you toward.) In the words of the "constrained optimization" methods of financial engineers, maximize exposure to your value-to-price insight ("alpha") while minimizing your exposure to factors that put your alpha at risk ("beta").

Borrowing Does Not Add Value

Fundamentalists of Graham's time, with their common sense, recognized that leverage is risky; borrowing magnifies gains, but also magnifies losses. Modigliani and Miller, in a second proposition, went further: Leverage does not add value.[24]

This M&M proposition applies to all investments, but it is particularly directed to equities: Firms cannot increase value for shareholders by borrowing. They can increase shareholders' expected return, but in so doing add risk, and the two cancel. M&M came to this conclusion as an implication of no arbitrage: If the sum of the value of the debt and equity of a levered firm were higher than that for the same firm without debt, there would be an arbitrage opportunity. Simply put, if a firm borrows in the debt market at fair value (to change its debt-equity mix), the transaction is a zero-net-present-value transaction (it does not add value). Similarly, if a firm uses the proceeds from the borrowing to repurchase stock (and so increases leverage further), it cannot add value if the stock is fairly priced (again, transactions at fair value are zero-net-present-value transactions). In short, value comes from the firm's business, not from the composition of the claims on the business.[25]

The fundamentalist, buying at a margin of safety with value greater than price, might lever up what is seen as a sure bet with borrowing, but surely with extreme care. When it comes to analyzing firms, the fundamentalist takes particular care; value is added by the business activities and not from zero-value-added financing activities. Focus on the business and understand that leverage just adds canceling risk and return. There is also instruction for the accountant to account in such a way to distinguish between business activities and financing activities. Sadly, GAAP and IFRS (International Financial Reporting Standards) do not do this cleanly, though the accounting authorities are taking steps toward a remedy. Accounting for value in the next few chapters comes clean.

The Products of Modern Finance

The principles of modern finance have not only provided important theoretical insights, but have also spawned a large number of financial products. Alas, if you have a product focus, you inevitably have some product failures, particularly in the social sciences where laboratory testing is difficult.[26] Here I review a few financial products and ask whether fundamental investors would do well to incorporate them in their tool kit.

An Investment Strategy: Stocks for the Long Run

In 1998, the Church of England created a pension fund for its clergy. The fund invested 100 percent in equities, at the height of the bubble. That turned out to be unfortunate. Shaun Farrell, chief of the Church of England Pensions Board, says that the fund invested in equities because retirement payouts are made in the long run and "equities will give you the highest returns over the long run." By 2009, the fund had a "huge great hole."[27]

The Church was taking its chapter and verse from the text of modern finance; buy stocks and hold them for the long run, for history shows that stocks outperform bonds over the long term.[28] The Church of England fund was not the only investor to place faith in this doctrine; many individual investors who also clung to it in their retirement accounts faced a similar demise to the clergy. Regrettably, the advice is just another invitation to speculate, an invitation to put information aside, this time in the guise of academic respectability. The advice should come with a product warning label: The higher average return to stocks is a risk premium and risk means the investor can be hit badly. Indeed, the recommendation is a misinterpretation of efficient market theory, which says that in buying at an efficient price, one just gets the expected return for the risk born. And risk means that pain is possible. No free lunch.

The 100-year history of stock returns in the United States does indeed show that stocks have yielded higher returns than less risky bonds. But that was the American century; those returns were for a country that after the fact was very successful, without revolutions, famines, plagues, and with victory in (almost) all of its wars.[29] Equity returns in Japan, Germany, and China—to name just a few countries where outcomes were different—were far lower.[30] And even experience in the United States brings pause. We are often reminded that it was not until 1954 that stocks regained the level of 1929 (in nominal terms, before adjusting for inflation). We are told that, if we bought stocks in the 1920s and held them through to the end of 2007, we would have earned about a 10 percent annual return (before adjusting for inflation). The subsequent drop in prices up to the end of 2008 would have reduced that return by only 1 percent, to about 9 percent. But if you had bought in 2007, you would have lost half your money by the end of 2008. Stocks performed worse than bonds in the twenty years through 2008. For baby boomers hoping for a retirement nest egg, this was risk in action.[31]

These historical returns clearly depend on the end point (the price of one's stocks at retirement, say). But they also depend on the starting point; your return depends on the price at which you bought. Buy value, not price. Fundamentalists buy stocks for the long run—principle number 10 gives them this orientation—but they do so with an appreciation of where value will be in the long run, with the expectation that prices will gravitate to value in the long run. Fundamentalists see the long run as risky, not secure, and are particularly wary of long-term growth: *Beware of paying too much for growth*. They are aware of the tendency of the market to overprice growth. So they do some accounting for the future. They then have some confidence, under the tenth fundamental principle, to be patient and wait. But that confidence is not a matter of faith in "stocks for the long run," but an assurance developed from their accounting.

The Method of Comparable Multiples

Pricing on the basis of comparable multiples is perhaps the most common valuation method on Wall Street. It certainly is simple: Price a target firm on the basis of the multiples—P/E, price-to-book, price-to-sales ratios, and so on—at which "comparable" firms are trading. It is justified by efficient market theory; read the value of one firm from the price of another because that price is value.

But of course the method violates the fundamentalist notion that price is not necessarily value. And it violates the ninth principle: *When calculating value to challenge price, beware of using price in the calculation.* The spectacle of IPO (initial public offering) bubbles tells the tale. Investment bankers base floatation prices on the price of other firms in recent IPOs. Firms float at an opportune time, when they view stocks prices as high. Basing price on other prices in a hot IPO market is akin to joining a chain letter. Bubbles form and burst, just as a chain letter ultimately collapses. Witness the Internet IPOs of the late 1990s and the earlier theme-restaurant and teleservicing IPOs. As a tool for the investment banker trying to get the best price for an offering, the method is appropriate. But investment bankers are on the sell side, pushing stocks; investors are on the buy side and *caveat emptor* applies.

Diversification in Real Time

A fundamentalist who views value over price as protection from risk may have little use for diversification. But risks remain. If one seeks further protection through diversification, experience has delivered a warning, however: When things go really wrong—when one is most desirous of protection—returns tend to become more highly correlated, so diversification becomes less effective.[32] In the 2008 financial crisis, investors fled all risky assets for the safety of cash, so prices fell together. Liquidity pressures hit investors in many markets, inducing correlated selling. Investment funds that had diversified out of stocks into investments with supposedly low correlation with stocks—foreign exchange, emerging markets, and commodities—found that those investments fell along with stocks as the economy worsened. A perfect storm, it was called, with no place to shelter. Oil and equities typically move in opposite directions (as higher oil prices hurt firms) but in 2008–2009, they moved closely together; U.S. and non-U.S. stocks moved in unison. In the words of the finance theorist, correlations are "nonstationary," but predicting their variation is not an easy task. This lurking danger, along with the considerable uncertainty about stock returns "in the long run," raises considerable doubt about whether modern finance has really come to grips with understanding risk. Indeed, the idea that some risk—so-called unsystematic or diversifiable risk—is not risk at all reeks of a free lunch.

Asset Pricing Models

That assessment may come as a surprise, for hasn't finance developed well-used models that help us understand and handle risk? Well, yes. Markowitz's diversification property led directly to the development of asset pricing models. The term is really a misnomer; asset pricing models do not deliver an asset price, but rather the required return (for risk), otherwise known as the cost-of-capital. That is, these models deal with the denominator of the dividend discount model, the discount rate, not the numerator, so supply only part of the picture.

The CAPM, another staple of the business school curriculum, started it all (and garnered a Noble Prize for Bill Sharpe, one of its creators). The CAPM sees the market portfolio as providing the ultimate in diversification—one cannot diversify beyond the portfolio of all investment securities—so risk other than that related to movements in the market as a whole is diversifiable (indeed, not risk at all). Accordingly, the risk for a specific investment is determined by how its return varies with the market return, that is, its beta.

Products fail because of design problems—faults in their conception—or problems in implementation. The CAPM certainly has conceptual problems; it assumes return outcomes follow the bell-shaped normal distribution—whereas history tells us that those distributions have "fat tails"—or gets personal and attributes a particular "utility function" to the investor. Further, the implementation problems are overwhelming. The investor has to estimate a beta and beta measures contain considerable error. Betas presumably are not constant, so applying a beta estimated from the past to the future is problematical, and particularly can get us into trouble when correlations move toward one in down markets. To magnify the problem, the CAPM multiplies the estimated beta by an estimated market risk premium—the expected return for the market in the future over the risk-free rate—and this is anyone's guess. Textbook estimates of the market risk premium range from 3 to 10 percent (though some of that is variation over time). Estimating the market risk premium is a very speculative task. Implementing the CAPM is largely playing with mirrors. The fundamentalist is at once on guard: *When challenging speculative prices, separate what you know from speculation.* Inserting a CAPM estimate of the required return into a valuation model (like the dividend discount model), is building speculation into the valuation. The discount rate in these models is supposed to accommodate our uncertainty, not to compound it.

It is fair to say that, despite the enormous effort of asset pricing research, we cannot measure the cost-of-capital. Indeed, the goal may be elusive. Although you and I may each have our own hurdle rate for investment (and that's a personal matter, varying according to our disposition toward risk), it may be misguided to pretend that a cost-of-capital exists in nature (as it were), to be discovered by researchers. The model requires us to measure expectations of future covariances and the future return on the market. As expectations, these are in the mind of the beholder. Even if they were constants, they would be hard to estimate.

But betas, risk premiums, and expected market returns are time varying, as those who propose a "conditional CAPM" recognize. That just
compounds the problem; now we have to measure expectations and
numerous covariances, with these expectations and covariances themselves as random variables. An elusive task indeed.

Not that there haven't been attempts to do so. Under the rubric of
arbitrage pricing theory (APT), researchers have offered "multifactor"
asset pricing models adding additional risk factors to the market portfolio. As the name suggests, these models are invoked from the no-
arbitrage principle. The idea is good (in theory) for, if investors bear
risk (beyond that in the overall market) that cannot be diversified away,
prices will be set such that they are compensated (by the no-arbitrage
principle). The problem is in the implementation. We now must estimate additional betas for the additional risk exposures along with risk
premiums for those exposures. The measurement problems with the
CAPM are magnified. And, although the market portfolio in the
CAPM can be roughly identified, we have no idea what the additional
factors are! Now we are really speculating. As a practical matter, this is
verging on the absurd.

The Fama and French model is one notable attempt to deal with the
problem.[33] Fama and French take a strictly empirical approach. They
observe in the data that firm size and book-to-price (B/P) predict stock
returns, even better than beta over the last fifty years. As adherents to
efficient market theory, they then say that size and B/P must be risk attributes for, in an efficient market, predictable returns must be reward for risk. The consequent pricing model has three factors: the
market portfolio, a size factor, and a B/P factor for which risk premiums and individual security betas must be estimated. The same implementation problems that beset the CAPM are present (and magnified),
but the distressing aspect is that there is no theory as to why size and
B/P might represent risk (though conjectures abound). The model simply comes from data dredging. And, of course, declaring that predictable returns must be a reward for taking on risk cuts across fundamentalists, for they see predictable returns from comparing value to price.
Indeed, B/P (or P/B) is often seen as an indication that the market
is mispricing book value; buy low price-to-book and sell high price-
to-book. As if that were not enough speculation in attributing B/P to

risk, enhancements to the Fama and French model add a "momentum factor," horrifying to an investor who sees momentum pricing as bubble pricing.

The vacuous nature of the Fama and French asset pricing model, the leading successor to the CAPM, highlights the sorry state of asset pricing. Asset pricing researchers are attempting to redeem the situation, [34] but there has to be another way. In this book I will show that insights can come from accounting. Indeed, as book-to-price is, in part, an accounting phenomenon (it incorporates book value!), I will show how B/P is involved in the accounting for value and the accounting for risk.

Growth and Value

"Growth" and "value" investing are two investing styles so popular that benchmark indexes have been developed for both. History shows that "value stocks" (priced with low multiples of book value, earnings, sales, etc.) yield higher returns on average than "growth stocks" (priced with high multiples). Active investors see the difference as due to mispricing, but adherents to efficient market theory attribute the return spread to risk.

Modern asset pricing theory has bent over backward to rationalize why growth should be less risky (and so requires a lower return). Growth means firms have flexibility during recessions (they conjecture); growth is an option that works like a hedge against bad times. The idea comes as a shock to fundamentalists, for they have traditionally viewed growth as risky. Growth can be competed away. Growth presents additional value, and additional value must have risk around it. Growth means more expected earnings and surely earnings are at risk. Growth is in the long term, and the long term is risky. Leverage increases expected growth but also adds risk. Fundamentalists see that the only way one can earn lower returns to growth is by overpaying for growth, by not understanding the risks involved: *Beware of paying too much for growth.*

Here, then, is an important difference to sort out: Do I buy growth to lower my risk or do I see risky growth as something to protect against? For the answer, I will turn to accounting for value, and in doing so will draw a different picture from the standard value versus growth split.

Financial Engineering

The recognition of the no-arbitrage principle was a breakthrough in financial engineering. Black, Scholes, and Merton developed their option pricing formula on the principle: The price of an option on a stock must bear a no-arbitrage relation to the underlying stock. With this principle, financial engineers can now price calls, puts, warrants, convertible debt, the prepayment feature on a mortgage, and a credit default swap. Indeed, corporate debt can be priced as an option to become the owner of a firm in default, and some even imagine valuing equities as an option. Financial engineers have been able to develop a huge variety of hedging instruments tied to prices of stocks, stock indexes, commodities, mortgages, and house prices (among many). These products are not a result of "physics envy" (as some claim) but rather an acknowledgment of the no-arbitrage principle. With the ability to determine no-arbitrage prices, markets develop to trade the instruments, so enhancing risk sharing in the economy and thus (economics tells us) human welfare. And, with a better understanding of how prices might change under different scenarios, we have gained a better understanding of risk.

How do fundamental investors greet these innovations? Surely they welcome the risk-sharing opportunities that financial engineering products offer, for now (in the language of active investing) investors can be exposed to "alpha" (where the profit opportunity lies) while buying insurance against risk factors to which they do not wish to be exposed. But fundamentalists have reservations. They see arbitrage opportunities, so no-arbitrage engineering goes against the grain. Indeed, they may see the margin of safety in the difference between price and value as sufficient insurance. Although they may see the financial engineer's instruments as an opportunity to off-load some risk (at a price), they also understand that the instruments can be used not only for hedging but also for speculation, so the price at which insurance might be bought could be speculative. And speculative prices can be dangerous, especially when the financial system provides incentives to off-load risk to the taxpayers in bailouts. The contemporary fundamentalist, Warren Buffett, saw this early in calling derivatives "weapons of mass destruction."

The criticisms of financial engineering products during the recent financial crisis are well worn: The engineers based their simulations of possible outcomes on what happened in the past ("objective probabilities" indicated by historical frequencies) rather than what might happen in the future (the rationalist's "subjective probabilities"); they failed to understand risk in the tails of outcome distributions; they modeled prices as evolving smoothly rather than in jumps; they failed to see that, when investors rely on the same models and crowd into the same positions, they increase systemic risk.[35] The securitization of mortgages and other debt in the 2000s (along with the associated credit default swaps), was designed to spread risk throughout the economy. Instead for many it turned out to be a disaster, with risk shared by innocents.

The fundamentalist has a more basic problem, however. Although an option on an equity share can be priced if one knows the value of the underlying share, the question of how to value the share is left open. As assumption of efficient market pricing of the share satisfies the question; Black-Scholes valuation works well if one assumes that stock price equals value (issues of estimating volatilities aside), and the pricing of a credit default swap on a mortgage-backed security works if one ignores the possibility that the prices of the underlying mortgages may be affected by a real estate price bubble that is likely to deflate. But fundamentalists do not equate price with value. In approaching the question of the value of a share, fundamentalists see no-arbitrage pricing as no help at all, indeed exactly wrong. Buying a business rather than a piece of paper, they understand that businesses are actually in the business of arbitrage. A business is a matter of trading in input markets (for assets, materials, labor, and so on) and in output markets (with customers). Business models are conceived to sell high (to customers in output markets) and buy low (from suppliers in input markets), adding value (profits) from the spread. In short, entrepreneurs arbitrage input and output markets. Entrepreneurs can be wrong in their judgment about the probability of success, but the idea that there are no arbitrage possibilities is certainly not a good starting point.

With this understanding, a no-arbitrage financial engineering model is of no use to the fundamentalist. What is needed is a model of value added from arbitraging markets, an accounting model that accounts for how the shareholder's value is increased (or diminished) in a firm by the arbitraging input and output markets. An accounting model reports the success of the business in the past but, importantly, also serves as a tool for forecasting future outcomes and examining the sensitivity of outcomes to varying conditions.

American International Group (AIG), the worldwide insurance company, serves as a lesson. Alongside more traditional insurance products, AIG was in the business of insuring debt and securitized debt packages in the 2000s, earning considerable fees for the service. Credit default swaps (CDSs) were the primary insurance instruments. Financial engineering models simulate prices under the worst of outcomes so a limit might be set by management on the exposure. Here inputs become important, as always: Are the engineers assuming normal (bell-shaped) distributions of outcomes to the gamble when more extreme outcomes are more likely? From press reports, it appears that AIG had the expertise for applying these models, some of it from academic consultants, and surely they were aware that return outcomes are typically "fat-tailed." But a more critical question arises; the engineering problem is not a question of the value of the net market position in these instruments under different scenarios, but one of modeling the effect on the firm as a whole, as a business unit. AIG is in the business of arbitraging insurance markets rather than the trading of default swaps in isolation. Under an extreme outcome, the firm may lose a lot on the position; what then are the ramifications for the firm as a whole? As it turned out, second- and third-order effects—indeed cascading effects—were very damaging. As the prices of mortgage-backed securities and other insured debt crashed in the financial crisis, the call was made on AIG for the insurance. Doubt about its inability to honor the call led to a crisis of confidence in the company—whether it could work through the difficulties or not—such that few would trade with it. Its precious investment-grade credit rating was lost. The consequent liquidity crisis meant certain death for the firm, saved only by a government bailout. In such a scenario, what is called for is not an engineering model for credit default exposure but a model to simulate the outcomes for shareholders under all scenarios, that is, an accounting model of the business that is rich enough to entertain the effects on the whole business when something goes wrong in one of its parts.

Fundamental analysts rely on such a model in accounting for the shareholder's interest and the risk in that interest. In designing such an accounting model, they understand another tendency of financial engineers. They understand that, for a given accounting system—the GAAP accounting system, for example—financial engineers will oblige when asked to structure transactions to get around the requirements of the accounting. Structural engineers, so-called, can arrange lease transactions to take lease liabilities off the balance sheet (labeling them as operating leases rather than capital leases), take both assets and liabilities off the balance sheet into "special investment vehicles" or "special purpose entities," and restructure borrowing to look like an option on the stock. A structural engineer can hide the cost of borrowing through convertible securities and indeed the cost of compensating employees with stock options. The fundamentalist looks for an accounting that finesses this activity. It may not be GAAP or IFRS accounting.

Accounting for Value

Financial economists have added significantly to our understanding of the economics of investing. But the outcome, after fifty years of hard work, is somewhat disappointing. Rationality, efficient markets, and no-arbitrage thinking have their insights but also have their limits. When it comes to valuation, we are in particular distress. The notion that value is based on expected dividends, uncontroversial in theory, is taken out from under us as a practical matter by the M&M insight that produces the dividend conundrum. That leaves us with an open question of how to escape the conundrum: What can replace the dividend discount model? As for the denominator in that model, asset pricing has been unsuccessful in determining the discount rate. Without a specified numerator or denominator, we are left stranded. Resorting to diversification as protection from risk we cannot quantify is rather doubtful.

Regrettably, the promise of modernism has not been entirely realized in finance. Although architects and engineers have developed formulas and models to bring precision to building structures, the formulas and models of finance, mathematically sophisticated though they are, lack the precision investors crave. At best they come with serious product warning labels. Unfortunately, an orthodoxy has developed around these products, with textbooks conveying to business students a certainty that is not really there. An economist might say that the models possess considerable specification uncertainty and low empirical content.[36] The fundamentalist might state it more colloquially as "These products are not something to 'anchor on' in valuation. They do not separate what we know from speculation."

What is the reason for this state of affairs? The problem may be in the assumption of rational behavior and the no-arbitrage principle that it implies, as behavioral economists contend; we humans are just hopeless and are born to suffer for our folly. We simply cannot live up to the rationality required of the "rational man" in the economist's models, either individually or collectively. But that is just too discouraging. The following points are also worth considering, and set the stage for the rest of this book.

First, modern finance has not developed structures for handling information. Why would one do so if all the information one wants is in the (efficient) traded price? The condemnation (in the early days of efficient market theory) that "accounting does not matter" has now been retracted somewhat, but market efficiency ideas have been a distraction from the question of how one might pull information together to establish what the efficient price should be. That question is the accounting question.

Second, modern finance is an endeavor in relative pricing. Relative pricing determines the price of an asset by reference to the price of another asset, with the two connected by a no-arbitrage relationship. To a fundamentalist, determining price by reference to price is circular, a no-no. Rather, price is determined by reference to fundamentals. The no-arbitrage principle holds with respect to information, not prices.

Third, the failure of products like asset pricing models might be attributed to the difficulties of measurement and implementation, but we have to ask ourselves if the real problem is not one of conception. Most product features involve parameters of return distributions, like means, variances, and covariances, but the idea that uncertainty can be put into the straight jacket of an assumed statistical distribution (like the normal distribution) is suspect. Although the reduction of risk to a few parameters is a seemingly admirable simplification (that enables quantification), the reduction is too simple. Further, most of the product features, whether they be correlations, betas, the market risk premium, or factor loadings are expectations of the future, and implementation involves estimating these expectations. That is difficult, if not misguided. The pretense is that there is something in nature to be discovered, a "true beta," an observable risk premium, so that the investigation can proceed in the way it does in the natural sciences. This is not so. The question "What is the market risk premium?" is not a good one, for the premium is in the mind of the beholder, it does not exist in observable reality. In short, models are built on elusive, speculative notions. This is the reason for the "fake precision" of which the models are accused. In terms familiar to the fundamentalist, they do not separate what we know from speculation. Indeed, they build in speculation. An alternative for handling uncertainty is needed, and that involves methods for handling information, for information reduces uncertainty.

Fourth, finance has fallen into the trap of labeling. Science develops propositions with empirical content and takes those propositions to the data for validation. Pseudoscience merely puts labels on things. Modern finance is founded on the scientific method, but of late the game has often become one of labeling. Book-to-price is called a "distress factor" by fiat, or "risk of assets in place," or "growth opportunities" (to mention a few), a proliferation of names that take a stab in the dark but does not sort things out. These labels are not concrete, leading us wandering off into speculation. Book value is an accounting number and to be concrete one must deal with it as such. If book-to-price indicates risk, it must have something to do with how the accounting for book value handles risk and uncertainty. So later in this book I address the question: What does the accounting for book value imply for risk and return? "Value" versus "growth" are simply labels with little meaning, giving no insight into the "value versus growth return spread" and leaving the investor in danger of proceeding without any understanding as to what he or she is doing or of the risk involved. Valuation is described in textbooks as "value of assets in place plus the value of growth opportunities." These notions are too vague. They invite speculation. They need to take on reality with concrete accounting. The book puts such an accounting on the table, and in doing so sorts out "value" versus "growth" among other things.

This having been said, the drive toward quantification in modern finance, though sometimes unsuccessful, is an instinct to follow. Fundamentalist principles leave a lot to judgment. One looks for quantification without the product flaws I have just highlighted. Accounting is the quantification of business activities that, if applied appropriately, leads to valuation and practical investing tools that not only aid judgment but protect against poor judgment.

Accounting amounts to keeping a book on the firm. The fundamental investor is then seen as trading on that book. Keeping a book is just a way of organizing thinking for a task. Just as we might keep a diary or a shopping list behind a refrigerator magnet for organizing tasks, so we might keep a book on a firm to organize the task of valuation. Just as a shopping list is a response to our limited ability to keep track of the task mentally, so an accounting book on the firm responds to our limits to intuiting value mentally. That, of course, confronts us with the question of how to keep the book, how to do the accounting that we cannot do mentally.

The following chapters seek to answer this question. They do so under the fundamentalist principles of this chapter, but not with the abandonment of the principles of finance. If accounting is to be the rationalist's system to challenge price, it must honor the rationalist principles of modern finance. So the appropriate principles are embraced, albeit with a different product focus; the development of a practical accounting for value. The idea that value is based on the present value of expected cash flows is something to anchor on. So are the notions of dividend irrelevance and the principle that borrowing does not add value—as least as starting points against which exceptions might be entertained. And, indeed, the no-arbitrage idea, such a source of friction between modern finance and fundamentalist ideas, survives in valuation; (intrinsic) values obey the no-arbitrage principle, even if prices don't. A no-arbitrage valuation is needed to challenge prices, for a price that differs from value is one that does not honor the no-arbitrage principle.

CHAPTER TWO

Anchoring on Fundamentals (and How Accounting Supplies the Anchor)

THIS CHAPTER SHOWS HOW accounting works in a way that upholds the fundamentalist principles of the last chapter and, in so doing, supplies the anchor that the investor seeks to challenge speculation in market prices. The chapter also shows how the appropriate accounting incorporates those principles of modern finance that we decided to hang onto in the last chapter. The next chapter then goes active to show how one employs accounting to challenge market prices.

The last chapter surely left you with the impression that developing robust products from ideas in economics and other social sciences is exceedingly difficult. Even though we might start with good ideas, we often end up playing with mirrors (as with the CAPM). Unfortunately, the demand for products is so strong that they tend to be accepted too readily, taking on a life of their own with users pretending they have a precision, which they in fact lack. Nowhere is this more so than in valuation. Valuation is quite an uncertain endeavor but when we "assume" growth rates and apply the CAPM to plug in a guess at discount rates, we have uncertain valuation indeed. There is plenty of room to play with mirrors, as the investment banker seeking to justify a transaction price with "due diligence" well knows. Can we bring some concreteness to the exercise? Can we develop methods that give us some security? Can we avoid playing with mirrors and the self-deception that comes with it? To do so, we must be honest in what we can do in handling uncertainty and what we cannot do.

An Accounting Prototype

Accounting can be complicated, often more than is necessary, so let's keep it simple to start in order to see the relevant principles unclouded by detail. The principles that we will embrace for equities can be seen in the valuation of a simple savings account. Indeed, the savings account is a simple instrument on which to test any valuation method; if it does not work for a savings account, it will not work for equities.

Suppose, at the end of 2010, you invest $100 in a savings account earning at a rate of 5 percent per year, and (to make it similar to a going-concern firm) you plan to hold this account indefinitely, to pass it on to your grandchildren. The accounting for this account is in the first panel in exhibit 2.1.

You notice that at the end of 2010 you have book value—the balance on your bank statement—of $100, representing assets deployed and ready to earn. You decide not to withdraw anything from the account in the future (for you wish to pass on the accumulated wealth in the account to future generations); in words appropriate for the corporate world, you have a zero-payout dividend policy, like Cisco Systems and Dell Computer at the time, and a myriad of other firms. You expect the bank to report earnings of $5 at the end of 2011 and with those earnings added to book value, you forecast a book value of $105. Forecasting further into the future, you expect earnings growth of 5 percent per year as a result of your payout policy. And you also expect book value growth of 5 percent per year (the miracle of compound interest!).

The accounting numbers for future years (2011 onward) are referred to as pro forma numbers (to differentiate them from actual reported numbers in the past). Although a bank statement keeps the reporting

EXHIBIT 2.1 Accounting for Two Savings Accounts with Different Payout

2010 Payout Account

		Forecast Year				
		2011	2012	2013	2014	2015
Earnings reinvested each year (zero payout)						
Earnings		5	5.25	5.51	5.79	6.08
Dividends		0	0	0	0	0
Book value	100	105	110.25	115.76	121.55	127.63
Rate-of-return on book value		5%	5%	5%	5%	5%

Full-Payout Account

		Forecast Year				
		2011	2012	2013	2014	2015
Earnings withdrawn each year (full payout)						
Earnings		5	5	5	5	5
Dividends		5	5	5	5	5
Book value	100	100	100	100	100	100
Rate-of-return on book value		5%	5%	5%	5%	5%

For both accounts,

Value = Anchor + Extra value for speculation
Value = Anchor + 0
Value = Book value = $100
$P/B = 1$
$$\text{Value} = \text{Forward earnings capitalized} = \frac{\$5}{0.05} = \$100$$

$$\text{Forward P/E} = \frac{\$100}{\$5} = \frac{1}{0.05} = 20$$

simple, in a corporation the earnings would be the bottom-line number from a pro forma income statement and the book value would be the bottom-line number (the book value of equity) from a pro forma balance sheet. As this is a savings account, the forecasted numbers are certain; the account is government guaranteed. Accordingly, the required return for the investment (or the discount rate)—to use terms out of modern finance—is the risk-free rate, which must be the certain earnings rate in the account, 5 percent.[1]

You probably understand that the value of this account is $100. This is what you would pay for the account in 2010, and $100 is the price at which it should trade if a market for savings accounts (or certificates of deposits) were efficient. But what is the valuation approach that gives us that number? Well, one of the principles of modern finance in the last chapter says that *value is based on expected future cash flows,* and I have noted that this is noncontroversial, for cash flow means consumption and it is consumption we are after. But we have a problem here. For this zero-payout asset, we do not expect to have any cash flow to the owner—dividends—until two generations hence and forecasting cash flows sixty years ahead makes our head hurt. This is what we would have to do with zero-payout firms like Cisco and Dell, but forecasting the dividend that they may or may not pay fifty or more years hence is most certainly a very uncertain task. Our valuation would ride on forecasts of the long term and that gives us serious psychological problems! Speculation about the long term is just hard to handle. In short, it's not practical. Can we develop a valuation approach that focuses on the present—what we see now—rather than on the distant future? Can we respect the fundamentalist principle of the last chapter: *Anchor on what you know rather than speculation?*

Forecasting and discounting future cash flows is the standard finance model of valuation. Every business school student knows this. But it does not work for something as simple as this savings account. Now look at the second account in exhibit 2.1. This account has the same investment (and book value) at the end of 2010, but it pays dividends; it is a full-payout account (all earnings are paid out in dividends each year). It is also worth $100, but has very different dividends.[2] The same value for the two accounts illustrates a principle of modern finance that we decided to embrace in the last chapter: *Value does not depend on payout.* Value is indeed based on expected cash flows over the life of an investment, but the timing of the payout is not important; the value is independent of whether the firm pays out dividends in the short term or only pays dividends on liquidation of the firm. (And, a going concern is deemed to go on indefinitely, without liquidation.) That's dividend irrelevance; that's Miller and Modigliani. And that gives rise to the dividend conundrum: Value is based on expected dividends but forecasting dividends typically does not give us much of a handle on the value.

If we cannot latch onto dividends as the fundamental of interest, what can we latch onto? The accounting for the saving account without dividends provides the answer. Look at the book value of $127.63 forecasted for 2015 in the first savings account. Take the present value ($127.63/1.05^5) and you get $100. You have just done some accounting for value! That is, you have prepared an accounting pro forma that runs through the accounting for where book value will be in five years:

Accounting Principle 1

Future book value = Current book value
+ Future earnings – Future dividends.

$$\$127.63 = \$100 + 27.63 - 0.$$

The $27.63 is the total earnings added to book value over the five years (and there are no dividends). This principle says that earnings add to book value, while dividends reduce book value. Thus, ending book value for any period is beginning book value plus earnings minus dividends.

This accounting equation is sometimes referred to as the "stocks-and-flows" equation: Successive stocks (levels) of book value are explained by the flows in and out of book value, as for levels and changes in any physical, engineering, or indeed, economic system. Earnings in, dividends out. In accounting terms, earnings (from the income statement) are "closed" to book value—accountants actually refer to it as the closing entry—and then dividends are paid out of book value resulting from the accumulated earnings.[3] (This equation is also referred to as the "clean surplus" equation.)

Having done the accounting for future book value, the expected book value is then employed in valuation (by discounting the future book value to the present, as we have seen). By doing the accounting, we have accounted for value. And we have a valuation principle:

Valuation Principle 1

To get a handle on value, think of what the book value is likely to be in the future.

As *Accounting Principle 1* says that future book value is determined by current book value plus future earnings, one can equivalently state this valuation principle as follows: Think of current book value and the earnings likely to be added to book value in the future. The data indeed confirms the principle that stock returns over five- and ten-year periods are largely explained by earnings that firms add to book value.[4] This of course is appreciated by the fundamental investor investing under the slogan, "Buy earnings." One buys (future) earnings and the success of the investment depends on the actual earnings a firm delivers.

This valuation principle honors the principle of modern finance that value is based on expected cash flows. Under *Accounting Principle 1,* dividends, the cash flows to shareholders, are paid out of book value, so future book value indicates the dividends a firm can pay (even if that firm does not pay dividends). It makes a lot of sense, for when one thinks of it, dividends are not the source of value, rather just the distribution of value (that's at the core of what Miller and Modigliani said). Accordingly we have to look for where dividends come from—they are paid out of book value—and that requires an accounting for book value. By doing so, we finesse the dividend conundrum while still being consistent with the principle that value is based on expected cash flows. We have done so by doing some accounting, an accounting that yields a forecast of dividends even if there are no dividends. And accounting for dividends is accounting for value.

We can summarize all of this in a convenient form; a valuation model. For both of these savings accounts,

$$
\text{Value}_0 = \frac{\text{Dividend}_1}{1+r} + \frac{\text{Dividend}_2}{(1+r)^2} + \frac{\text{Dividend}_3}{(1+r)^3}
$$
$$
+ \frac{\text{Dividend}_4}{(1+r)^4} + \frac{\text{Dividend}_5}{(1+r)^5} + \frac{\text{Book value}_5}{(1+r)^5}.
$$

For the zero-payout account, dividends are zero, so the value of \$100 is just the present value of the year-5-ahead book value, \$127.63. For the full-payout account, dividends are received but they also reduce book value to \$100 in year 5, so the value is

$$\text{Value}_0 = \frac{\$5}{1.05} + \frac{\$5}{1.05^2} + \frac{\$5}{1.05^3} + \frac{\$5}{1.05^4} + \frac{\$5}{1.05^5} + \frac{\$100}{1.05^5} = \$100.$$

You can clearly see how the valuation is dividend irrelevant: Both dividends and future book value are in the calculation but any dividends are offset by a reduction in the book value. To put it a little differently, value is based on expected dividends but those dividends may come as actual payout or be represented by future book value from which dividends can be paid. You should also appreciate that a valuation model is not only a compact way to give directions about how to calculate value, but something more important; it directs how the accounting is to be done. A valuation model is really an accounting model, a model of how to account for value.

It has probably not escaped you that the valuation principle requires us to speculate, with the speculation directed at future book values rather than at dividends. For a government-guaranteed savings account, there is no uncertainty about the future book value, but that is not the case with an equity investment. Where is the anchor that fundamentalist principles call for, something that we can hold onto that is not speculative? The savings account gives us a clue, for here the current book value (in 2010) gives the $100 value for the asset. When introducing the anchoring principle, the previous chapter stated the form our valuation should take:

Value = Anchoring accounting value + Speculative value.

Suppose we anchored on the current book value, something we can observe in the balance sheet:

Value = Book value + Speculative value.

For the savings account with certain payoffs, speculative value is zero, so it is worth its book value of $100. Following fundamentalist principles, we have separated what we know from speculation, and have anchored on what we know. In doing so, we have found that the anchor has supplied the value. In the parlance of equity analysis, the price-to-book (P/B) ratio is 1. And so it must be; there is no uncertainty with a savings account and no speculative value. The accountant can get the balance sheet right. This points to an intriguing accounting feature that I will come to later: A P/B different from 1 has to do with uncertainty. And it is uncertainty with which we are particularly concerned as equity investors.

Note that we have not violated the no-arbitrage principle of modern finance; indeed, we have invoked the principle but have applied it differently. Although fundamentalists question no-arbitrage in prices (that is, they do not take on board the efficient market version of no-arbitrage), they do recognize that value (as opposed to price) is a no-arbitrage valuation with respect to information. In our example, the value is a no-arbitrage valuation with respect to the accounting for value; value is the present value of expected book values such that if one buys at that value of $100, one expects only to earn the required return for the risk born, here 5 percent. If the savings account were to trade at $90 in contradiction to the accounting, the investor would see an arbitrage opportunity (and thus would earn more than the required return).

There is one more feature of these two savings accounts that gives us a further insight into valuation. Although their dividends differ, you will have noticed that both accounts earn a rate-of-return on book value of 5 percent per year. That is equal to the required rate-of-return of 5 percent. This configuration underscores a principle that also applies to equities and indeed to any investment asset:

Valuation Principle 2

If one forecasts that the rate-of-return on book value will be equal to the required rate-of-return, the asset must be worth its book value.

This principle ties another accounting measure, book rate-of-return, to valuation. It follows that an asset that is expected to earn a book rate-of-return greater than the investor's required return must be worth more than book value (and one where the book rate-of-return is expected to be less than the required return must be worth less than book value.) We now have a principle under which to add value to book value:

> Value = Book value + Speculative value, and
> Value = Book value + Value for speculation about
> future book rate-of-return.

I will develop this valuation later in the chapter. But first a digression into another, popular form of accounting for value.

Cash Accounting for Value

The accounting for the savings account focuses on earnings and book values, and thus the income statement and the balance sheet. But a popular technique—discounted cash flow (DCF) analysis—focuses on free cash flows. This technique is often heralded under the banner of "Cash Is King!" And with the claim: Accounting numbers are suspect, so let's stick with the real cash flows!

Free cash flow is the difference between cash flow from operations and cash investment in operations, as in the cash flow statement. So rather than forecasting future income statements and balance sheets, DCF analysis forecasts what will flow through future cash flow statements. The cash flow statement employs what accountants call cash accounting. The income statement and balance sheet employ what they call accrual accounting. DCF analysis is indeed accounting for value, but it is cash accounting for value. So we have a clear accounting choice: For valuation, do we want cash accounting or accrual accounting?

The DCF model is familiar to every business school student. Calculate the value of the firm from the free cash flows (FCFs) the firm is expected to generate in the future, and then deduct the value of the net debt to arrive at the value of equity. In model form,

$$\text{Value of equity}_0 = \frac{\text{FCF}_1}{1+r} + \frac{\text{FCF}_2}{(1+r)^2} + \frac{\text{FCF}_3}{(1+r)^3} + \frac{\text{FCF}_4}{(1+r)^4} + \frac{\text{FCF}_5}{(1+r)^4(r-g)}$$
$$-\text{Value of net debt}_0.$$

Following this formula, the student is told to forecast FCFs up to a "forecast horizon" (here, five years ahead), calculate a "continuing value" (or "terminal value") with a growth rate, and discount the FCF forecasts and the continuing value to present value.[5] The value is for a going concern, so the continuing value is an estimate of the value of the FCFs that continue after the forecast horizon.

This model has been a standard for valuation for a long time. It preserves the notion that value is based on expected cash flows but attempts to finesse the dividend conundrum by focusing on cash flows generated within the firm rather than cash flows paid out of the firm to shareholders. Good idea, for it focuses on the generation of value rather than the distribution of value (in dividends), which Miller and Modigliani (and our savings account valuation) show is irrelevant. But is this good accounting for value?

Note, first, that the valuation does not anchor on anything in the present (unless one counts the net debt!); the value is based entirely of expectations of the future. Second, the valuation involves the daunting task of estimating a continuing value, and that estimation rides on a growth rate for the long term. That is a speculative task indeed, one that confounds the student: "What long-term growth rate do I assume, professor?" Practitioners know how sensitive their valuations are to the growth rate but often feel they don't have much of a grasp on it. This is uncertain valuation, so much so that investment bankers carrying out due diligence on a valuation for an IPO can use the model to rationalize just about any price for the offering! Benjamin Graham's words echo once again:

> The concept of future prospects and particularly of continued growth in the future invites the application of formulas out of higher mathematics to establish the present value of the favored issue. But the combination of precise formulas with highly imprecise assumptions can be used to establish, or rather justify, practically any value one wishes, however high, for a really outstanding issue.
> —Benjamin Graham, *The Intelligent Investor*,
> 4th ed., 1973, 315–316.

Graham was skeptical of the "formulas out of higher mathematics" that modernists defer to. He saw a valuation model like the DCF model as speculative because it puts too much weight on speculation rather that what we know. Just as the CAPM is based on speculative inputs, so is this model.

Can we do better?

Here now is an important point: The answer to that question turns on the accounting. DCF valuation employs cash accounting, and cash accounting leaves us with speculation; it is not something we can anchor on. To see this, consider the cash flows in exhibit 2.2 reported by Wal-Mart and Home Depot, the two big retailers, during their growth stage, and General Electric (GE), the industrial conglomerate with a finance arm.

You can see that all three companies have healthy cash flow from operations. However, they have mainly negative FCFs after subtracting cash investments ("Cap Ex"). Suppose you were evaluating these firms at the beginning of the years indicated here and were told what the cash flows were going to be, for sure. With this privileged information (low

EXHIBIT 2.2   Free Cash Flows for Wal-Mart Stores, Home Depot, and General Electric (in millions of dollars)

Wal-Mart Stores Inc.

	1992	1993	1994	1995	1996
Cash from operations	1,553	1,540	2,573	3,410	2,993
Cash investments	2,150	3,506	4,486	3,792	3,332
Free cash flow	(597)	(1,966)	(1,913)	(382)	(339)
Earnings	1,608	1,995	2,333	2,681	2,740
EPS	0.70	0.87	1.02	1.17	1.19

Home Depot Inc.

	1998	1999	2000	2001	2002
Cash from operations	1,055	1,894	2,439	2,977	5,942
Cash investment	1,376	2,273	2,620	3,521	3,406
Free cash flow	(321)	(379)	(181)	(544)	2,536
Earnings	1,160	1,614	2,320	2,581	3,044
EPS	0.80	1.10	0.73	1.11	1.30

General Electric Co.

	2000	2001	2002	2003	2004
Cash from operations	30,009	39,398	34,848	36,102	36,484
Cash investments	37,699	40,308	61,227	21,843	38,414
Free cash flow	(7,690)	(910)	(26,379)	14,259	(1,930)
Earnings	12,735	13,684	14,118	15,002	16,593
EPS	1.29	1.38	1.42	1.50	1.60

uncertainty!) you expect to be in good shape to come up with a valuation. But, by applying the DCF model, you would come up with a negative present value from these negative cash flows, and prices cannot be negative. You recognize, of course, that you have to add a "continuing value" to solve the problem. But here your problem is compounded; the continuing value (based on the long-term cash flows) is greater than 100 percent of the value (as we must have a positive price) and yet we have no idea about how to calculate it because a growth rate applied to a negative amount will not do. More than 100 percent of the value rides on forecasts for the long term and it is the long term that is most uncertain. A speculative valuation, indeed. If "Cash Is King," his subjects are not well served. Are cash flows really real?

One can show mathematically that the DCF model gives the same value as the benchmark dividend discount model if both are applied over very long (strictly infinite) forecasting horizons. So we could predict cash flows further into the future until the cash flows from investment turn positive, but now we are venturing into never-never land. A valuation that relies on a determination of the long run is problematical. In the long run we are all dead.

Graham did not like valuations that depend on long-term growth rates (as the quote above indicates). Growth in a continuing value is speculative. Indeed, Graham and his fellow fundamentalists were apprehensive about paying for growth at all. It is a guess; growth can be competed away unless there is a clear protected franchise. A valuation that rides on estimated growth is a risky valuation.[6] It is better to anchor a valuation on something we can observe now or can predict fairly confidently in the short term. We want value justified by the facts. For that we need an alternative, less speculative accounting.

Accrual Accounting for Value

The problem with DCF valuation is an accounting problem. Cash flow from operations (the first line of cash flows in exhibit 2.2) is the net cash from selling to customers and of course adds to value, but the FCF calculation then subtracts cash investment. This is odd because investments are made to add value, not reduce it (the notorious corporate jet aside). Firms consume cash to generate value (that's fundamental!). Firms reduce FCF when they increase investments (reducing value in the DCF calculation) and increase FCF when they reduce investments (increasing DCF value). Using FCF in valuation is not only odd, it's perverse. As firms increase FCF by liquidating investment, FCF is more a liquidation concept than a measure of added value from increasing investments. In short, FCF is not good accounting for value. Wal-Mart, Home Depot, and GE have negative FCF because they invest. In 2003, GE had positive FCF, but only because it reduced investment. Is this a value-adding move? Home Depot had a large, positive FCF in 2002, but only because it delayed paying suppliers. Such a one-time event is hardly something on which to base a continuing value.[7]

How might the accounting be improved? Well, as every first-year accounting student knows, the alternative to cash accounting is accrual accounting. Students are taught that cash accounting might be OK for the tennis club, but not for businesses. Yet, when they go across to their first-year finance course, students find that DCF has been maintained as a valuation method. The disconnect is striking. When they go out into "the real world," they find that analysts focus on earnings, not cash flows.[8]

Accrual accounting reports earnings rather than cash flows, but is accrual accounting better accounting for value? Accrual accounting has two enhancing properties. First, investments typically are not allowed to affect the value-added measure, earnings. Rather than being "expensed" against cash flow from operations, investments are booked to the balance sheet, to book value. As assets, they are seen as something that produces value in the future rather than as a detriment to value. Second, cash flows from operations are modified by additional "accruals." Revenue is booked when the firm has a claim on a customer (a receivable), not when cash is received, and expenses are booked when a liability is incurred to suppliers, not when cash is paid. Both bring the future forward in time. So, for example, if a firm remunerates employees with pension benefits to be paid thirty years in the future, a DCF valuation will have to forecast cash flows thirty years hence, in the long run. But accrual accounting includes the value affect as an expense in earnings immediately (and books a corresponding pension liability to the balance sheet). That brings the future forward, reducing our reliance on speculative forecasts of the long term. And it produces a number, book value, which one can potentially anchor on. Accrual accounting even recognizes value when there are no cash flows: If a firm pays employees with a stock option, accrual accounting records wages expense even though there is no cash flow. A DCF valuation misses that.

This feature of bringing the future forward in time is so important when it comes to valuation that it warrants a statement as an accounting principle:

Accounting Principle 2

Accrual accounting brings the future forward in time, anticipating future cash flows.

An accounting student is taught that accrual accounting reassigns cash flows to periods. Total earnings and total cash flows are the same over the life of a firm, accrual accounting just changes the timing. But what is often not appreciated is that the timing of accrual accounting results in recognition ahead in time such that accounting numbers anticipate future cash flows before they actually flow. We have seen this in the accounting for the savings account, where book value forecasts the future stream of dividends. One also sees this with a business firm, where investments that produce future cash flows are placed on the balance sheet (rather than reducing the flow measure). A receivable booked to the balance sheet forecasts cash inflows. And the accrued pension liability forecasts very distant cash outflows.

Accrual accounting is applied as a straightforward "correction" to cash flows. Accrual earnings from a business (before interest) is calculated as

$$\text{Earnings before interest} = \text{Free cash flow} + \text{Investments} + \text{Added accruals.}$$

In calculating earnings, investments are added back to FCFs to correct the investment problem, and then additional accruals are added.

Investments and additional accruals are placed on the balance sheet so that book value consists of cash, debt, and business assets made up of investments and accruals.[9] Returning to exhibit 2.2, you can see that while FCFs are negative for the three firms, earnings and earnings per share (EPS) are positive and indeed growing at a fairly steady rate. That is the effect of the accounting for investment and accruals. These earnings look like something we can introduce to an accounting for value.

It may sound strange to abandon cash flows as a basis for valuation as we are tempted to think of cash flows as "real" and accounting numbers as concocted. That cynicism is indeed warranted, for one must be concerned about how the accounting is done. Under GAAP accounting, for example, R&D (research and development) expenditures are usually expensed immediately against earnings rather than placed on the balance sheet as investments so that earnings are reduced by R&D investments, making the firm look less profitable. The problem is that GAAP uses cash accounting for R&D investments, and we know that cash accounting is not good accounting for value. As another example, some analysts try to solve the investment problem in DCF valuation by subtracting (in the FCF calculation) "maintenance capital expenditures" from cash flow from operations rather than all investment. (Maintenance capital expenditures is investment to maintain the cash flows from the current business, so excludes investment to grow cash flows.) Buffett calls the resulting number "owner earnings." This is a form of accrual accounting (that adjusts cash accounting). In contrast, GAAP accounting subtracts a number called "depreciation" on existing investments rather than full investment expenditures (R&D aside). So it is a question of whether maintenance capital expenditures or GAAP depreciation is a better measure to charge against earnings.

I will return to the question of appropriate accrual accounting in later chapters. The overriding consideration is to produce an accounting that we can anchor on. Accrual accounting brings the future forward in time but one would not want to bring too much speculation about the future into the accounting. *Understand what you know and separate it from speculation.* Resolving this tension between bringing the future forward (nearer the present time) and eschewing speculation is at the core of accounting for value. Is maintenance capital expenditures too much of a subjective notion to enter the accounting? Is GAAP depreciation, with its need to estimate useful lives of assets, too speculative?

Adding Speculation to Book Value

If valuation amounts to anchoring on book value and then adding speculation, we need some direction for adding speculation. Speculation is where we can go wrong, so we need a discipline that guides, indeed constrains, our speculation. Accounting supplies that discipline.

An accrual accounting model instructs us how to handle speculation about the future earnings to add to book value. The model embeds *Valuation Principle 2* that we saw in the savings account: One adds value to book value only if the expected rate-of-return on book value is greater than the required return. Suppose we anchor on the current book value, B_0, then forecast earnings and book value over the next three years. Then,

$$
\begin{aligned}
\text{Value of equity}_0 &= B_0 + \frac{(\text{ROCE}_1 - r) \times B_0}{1 + r} + \frac{(\text{ROCE}_2 - r) \times B_1}{(1 + r)^2} \\
&\quad + \frac{(\text{ROCE}_3 - r) \times B_2}{(1 + r)^2 (r - g)} \\
&= B_0 + \frac{\text{Residual earnings}_1}{1 + r} + \frac{\text{Residual earnings}_2}{(1 + r)^2} \\
&\quad + \frac{\text{Residual earnings}_3}{(1 + r)^2 (r - g)}.
\end{aligned}
$$

For each future year, t, $\text{ROCE}_t = $ Expected earnings$_t$/Expected book value$_{t-1}$ is the book rate-of-return on common equity. The numerator number that is discounted to present value, $(\text{ROCE}_t - r) \times B_{t-1}$, is so-called residual earnings, which of course compares the rate-of-return on book value, ROCE, with the required return. Residual earnings is sometimes referred to as excess earnings or abnormal earnings and is alternatively (but equivalently) calculated as Earnings$_t - (r \times B_{t-1})$, that is, earnings less a charge against book value to cover the investor's required return (or the "cost-of-capital").[10] The growth rate, g, is the rate at which residual earnings is expected to grow after year 3. The savings account is just a special case where ROCE = r (and there is no growth), so Value = Book value.

The ideas here are little different from those of the fundamentalists:

> It is essential to bear in mind that a private business has always been valued primarily on the basis of the "net worth" as shown by its statement. A man contemplating the purchase of a partnership or stock interest in a private undertaking will always start with the value of that interest as shown "on the books," i.e., the balance sheet, and will then consider whether the record and prospects are good enough to make such a commitment attractive. An interest in a private business may of course be sold for more or less than its proportionate asset value; but the book value is still invariably the starting point of the calculation, and the deal is finally made and viewed in terms of the premium or discount from value involved.
> —Benjamin Graham and David L. Dodd,
> *Security Analysis*, 1934, 306.

By *Accounting Principle 1* that connects dividends to book values and earnings, this model is equivalent to the dividend discount model for going concerns, so the valuation is consistent with the principle that value is the present value of expected dividends.[11] But the valuation does not ride on dividends—it works if the firm pays no dividends—so it finesses the dividend conundrum, just like our valuation of the savings account. The valuation is payout insensitive, so also honors the Miller and Modigliani principle of dividend irrelevance: Dividends do not affect the discounted value of residual earnings.[12]

Readers of Warren Buffett's annual letters to Berkshire Hathaway shareholders understand that he tracks book value. How much did book value grow this year and to what level might it grow in the future? The valuation of the savings account took this focus, as stated in *Valuation Principle 1*: To value a firm, think of where the book value will be in the future. We are in fact doing this here. By rearranging the residual earnings model above we have an equivalent valuation:

$$\text{Value of equity}_0 = \frac{\text{Dividend}_1}{1 + r} + \frac{\text{Dividend}_2}{(1 + r)^2} + \frac{B_2}{(1 + r)^2}$$
$$+ \frac{(\text{ROCE}_3 - r) \times B_2}{(1 + r)^2 \, (r - g)}.$$

That is, value is based on the present value of expected book value at the forecast horizon (here book value is two years ahead, B_2) plus the present value of any dividends paid out of book value up to that point, as with the savings account.[13] In the savings account, book value earns at the required return, so this is all that is needed. But here we see an extra term for the case where we forecast that the return on book value at the forecast horizon, ROCE, will be different from the required return. So we have a modification to the valuation principle:

Valuation Principle 3

To get a handle on value, think first of what the book value is likely be in the future and, second, what the rate-of-return on that book value is likely to be.

So valuation accounts for the future book value (as with the savings account), but also for future earnings on the book value, the ROCE at the forecast horizon. If ROCE is forecasted to be equal to the required return, the accounting has brought all value to be recognized into the book value (as with the savings account). If book value is not a complete accounting for value, further value is added by forecasting earnings on the book value (expressed by the last term in the model).[14]

Exhibit 2.3 takes us back to GE, the firm so hard to value using DCF valuation. The accounting numbers cover the same years as before, 2000–2004, but now the focus is on earnings and book value, with a pro forma in the same form as that for the savings account. The numbers are per share, and each book value per share (BPS) in the sequence is the prior BPS plus the earnings per share (EPS) minus the dividends per share (DPS), according to *Accounting Principle 1*.

EXHIBIT 2.3   Earnings per Share (EPS), Dividends per Share (DPS), and Book Value per Share (BPS) for General Electric, 2000–2004, with Associated Valuation Metrics

	1999	2000	2001	2002	2003	2004
Earnings (EPS)		1.29	1.38	1.42	1.50	1.60
Dividends (DPS)		0.57	0.66	0.73	0.77	0.82
Book value (BPS)	4.32	5.04	5.76	6.45	7.18	7.96
Book rate-of-return (ROCE)		29.9%	27.4%	24.7%	23.3%	22.3%
Residual earnings (10% charge)		0.858	0.876	0.844	0.855	0.882
Change in residual earnings			0.018	−0.032	0.011	0.027

As with the DCF analysis, suppose at the end of 1999 you had been given these numbers as forecasts in order to value a share of GE. Your required return is 10 percent—the risk-free rate (for a ten-year U.S government bond) of 5 percent at the time plus a premium for risk of 5 percent—so residual earnings are calculated with a 10 percent charge. Applying the valuation model with a three-year forecast horizon (up to 2002),

$$\text{Value of equity}_0 = \$4.32 + \frac{0.858}{1.10} + \frac{0.876}{1.10^2} + \frac{0.844}{1.10^2 \,(0.10 - 0.0)}$$
$$= \$4.32 + 0.780 + 0.724 + 6.975$$
$$= \$12.80 \text{ per share.}$$

Just to be clear that this valuation is the same as that from forecasting book value at the forecast horizon and the ROCE it generates (along with the intervening dividends), this recalculates as

$$\text{Value of equity}_0 = \$\frac{0.57}{1.10} + \frac{0.66}{1.10^2} + \frac{5.76}{1.10^2} + \frac{(0.247 - 0.10) \times 5.76}{1.10^2 \,(0.10 - 0.0)}$$
$$= \$0.519 + 0.545 + 4.760 + 6.975$$
$$= \$12.80 \text{ per share.}$$

Yes, value is the present value of book value expected at the forecast horizon (plus the value of any intervening dividends), but with added value for the ROCE at which book values are expected to be earning at that point, in accordance with *Valuation Principle 3*.

It should be clear that we have a better handle on the value of GE than we had with the DCF valuation. At least the value is positive! While DCF valuation would work if we had long forecasting horizons, we have just observed the property that accrual accounting, with its treatment of investment and accruals, moves the valuation forward in time. Accordingly, we can work with shorter forecasting horizons and with more assurance than we can with speculative long-term cash flows (provided the accounting is good accrual accounting). This is so, not just for GE, but for firms generally.[15]

"Hold it" (you say), "there is something missing here!" For the "continuing value," the last component of $6.975, the calculation has set the growth rate, g, to zero; this is a valuation without growth. Well, that is just what we want. Fundamentalist principles warn us not to include speculation in a valuation and are particularly wary of speculative growth: *Beware of paying too much for growth*. The fundamentalist wants an accounting that excludes value based on long-run speculative growth. The $12.80 value is value justified by the accounting for three periods ahead, excluding the long run. We know the current book value (for sure) and, if we are reasonably confident about our short-term forecasts, this is an accounting that we can anchor on.

To separate accounting value from speculative value, we might express the valuation model as

$$
\text{Value of equity}_0 = B_0 + \frac{(\text{ROCE}_1 - r) \times B_0}{1 + r} + \frac{(\text{ROCE}_2 - r) \times B_1}{(1 + r)^2}
$$
$$
+ \frac{(\text{ROCE}_3 - r) \times B_2}{(1 + r)^2 \times r} + \text{Value of speculative growth.}
$$

The accounting up to the forecast horizon provides a no-growth valuation, to which the investor can add value in speculative long-term growth (if any). If we feel confident in our short-term forecasts (for three years here), we have moved the accounting anchor from book value alone to accounting for book value and the immediate future. By being careful in not allowing speculation about growth to affect the accounting value, we have honored the fundamentalist principles: *Understand what you know and don't mix what you know with speculation* and *anchor a valuation on what you know rather than speculation.* If we are not confident in forecasts for three years ahead, or even two years ahead, we may account over shorter horizons.[16] We choose the forecast horizon carefully; we must have something we feel we can anchor on with some confidence, for we eschew speculation.

The next chapter applies the anchoring valuation to the task of challenging the market price. At the end of 1999, at the height of the bubble, GE traded at a whopping $52 per share, split adjusted. With only $12.80 of this price accounted for, we have left a lot unexplained. But we have identified the part of the price—$39.20 or 75 percent—about which we are skeptical, the part that the accounting indicates is speculative. Either the accounting for value is missing a lot or market traders are paying too much for growth. The latter is possible—GE has long been nominated as a "growth" company, after all—but 75 percent of the price unaccounted for is a hefty amount. Our accounting for value shows little growth in residual earnings over the years 2000–2004. The subsequent stock price reflected this reality: By 2002, GE traded at $25, more in line with the accounting numbers. By 2008, GE traded below $20, an example of how speculative growth can evaporate. Some of this price decline was due to after-the-fact events, of course, but might a diligent investor have avoided buying GE at $52? It is this speculation about growth that we have to challenge. The next chapter takes up the task, but with the accounting as the tool.

But let us first understand where growth comes from. The no-growth valuation means that residual earnings are deemed to continue at a constant level (with no growth) after the forecast horizon. You observe no growth for GE in exhibit 2.3; residual earnings from 2000–2004 is fairly constant at about $0.860. What does this mean? Well, residual earnings is the product of the rate-of-return on book value, ROCE, and book value, the net assets on the balance sheet at the beginning of the year from which earnings flow. There are two "drivers" of residual earnings, book value and the rate-of-return on book value: Residual earnings$_t = (\text{ROCE}_t - r) \times B_{t-1}$. Moving from 2000 to 2004, GE's ROCE declines but book value increases, and the combination of the decreasing rate-of-return on book value and the increasing book value results in constant, no-growth residual earnings. The declining rate-of-return is quite typical; it is what analysts refer to when they say that profitability tends to decline over time as a firm is challenged by competition. But that is not the whole picture. Value is added from profitability and growth in net assets. So it is quite possible (and even unexceptional) that a firm, like GE here, can maintain residual earnings with declining profitability by adding investment that earns at a rate-of return greater than the required return. With this no-growth benchmark, we understand the necessary condition to add value for growth: The firm must be able to grow residual earnings and that involves either increasing profitability (the rate-of-return) or growing a balance sheet that will add residual earnings despite constant or even declining profitability.

The data show that no-growth residual earnings is typical, thus offering some assurance that the no-growth valuation is something to hold to. Figure 2.1 tracks residual earnings over five years for 10

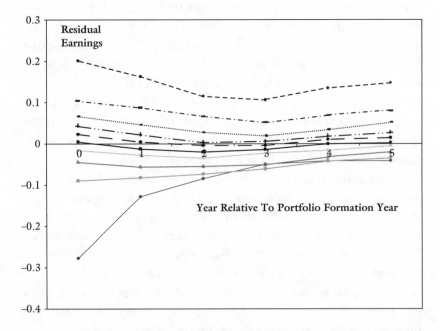

FIGURE 2.1   Path of Residual Earnings Over Five Years, for Ten Portfolios Formed on the Level of Firms' Residual Earnings in the Base Year (Year 0), for Base Years in the Period 1963–1999. Residual Earnings Is Deflated by the Book Value of Common Shareholders' Equity in the Base Year. Source: Doron Nissim and Stephen H. Penman, "Ratio Analysis and Equity Valuation: From Research to Practice," *Review of Accounting Studies* 6 (2001), 140. Copyright and with kind permission of Springer Science and Business Media.

portfolios formed from all U.S. stocks, based on the level of their residual earnings in the base year, year 0.[17] Residual earnings in the base year vary considerably over firms, and extreme residual earnings tend to revert toward the median over the subsequent two years. But after that, the level of residual earnings is a good predictor of where residual earnings will be in the future. In other words, despite the fact that firms differ in the level of their residual earnings, on average there is no growth for all levels. (The question of why firms might have different levels of residual earnings in the long run is answered in Chapter 5). Figure 2.1 supports the notion that the no-growth valuation is a good anchoring valuation; one has to have good reasons for adding value for speculative growth. Growth might well be added for some firms—the numbers here are portfolio averages—but the figure indicates that growth that might be attributed to some firms within each portfolio is canceled by negative growth for others. Negative growth is equally as possible as positive growth. This idea that growth is risky ties us to the no-growth anchor and is a theme that I will pick up on many times as the book progresses.

Anchoring on Earnings: The P/E Ratio

The valuation I have just described starts with book value and then sets about determining the value to add to the book value. Thus the focus is on the P/B ratio. However, analysts tend to talk in terms of price-earnings (P/E) multiples rather than P/B multiples. And they tend to talk in terms of earnings and earnings growth rather than book value and residual earnings. Are they doing a different accounting?

The answer is no. Refer again to the savings account in exhibit 2.1. At the bottom of the exhibit, the value is indicated by its book value of $100 but also by capitalizing the forward earnings by the required rate-of-return of 5 percent:

$$\text{Value} = \frac{\$5}{0.05} = \$100 \text{ (and the forward P/E ratio is 20).}$$

By anchoring on earnings we have the equivalent value to that from anchoring on book value. Can this type of valuation work for GE? GE's forward earnings in exhibit 2.3 are $1.29 per share, so capitalizing forward earnings at the required return of 10 percent yields a value of $12.90. But there is a difference between GE and the saving account: Whereas we know the residual earnings for a savings account are always zero, they can be nonzero for an equity investment. Look at the last line of exhibit 2.3 that gives the year-to-year difference in residual earnings (RE) for GE. Now apply the following model for the three-year forecasting horizon earlier:

$$
\begin{aligned}
\text{Value of equity}_0 &= \frac{\text{Earnings}_1}{r} + \frac{1}{r}\left[\frac{\text{Change in RE}_2}{1+r} + \frac{\text{Change in RE}_3}{(1+r)^2}\right] \\
&= \frac{1.29}{r} + \frac{1}{r}\left[\frac{0.018}{1.10} + \frac{-0.032}{1.10^2}\right] \\
&= \$12.80.
\end{aligned}
$$

We have the same valuation as before but rather than anchoring on book value and adding value for expected residual earnings, we have anchored on earnings and added value for the expected change (or growth) in residual earnings.[18]

"Change in residual earnings" is a concept that is a little difficult to internalize, let alone talk about coherently as an investor. One can be a little clearer by recognizing that

Change in residual earnings = Abnormal earnings growth

Abnormal earnings growth is earnings growth over and above growth at the required rate-of-return:

$$
\begin{aligned}
\text{Abnormal earnings growth} &= [\text{Earnings} + (r \times \text{Prior dividend})] \\
&\quad - [(1+r) \times \text{Prior earnings}].
\end{aligned}
$$

For GE for 2001,

$$
\begin{aligned}
\text{Abnormal earnings growth} &= [\$1.38 + (0.10 \times 0.57)] \\
&\quad - [1.10 \times 1.29] = 0.018.
\end{aligned}
$$

That is, abnormal earnings growth is equal to the earnings for 2001 ($1.38) plus the prior year's dividend of $0.57 reinvested at 10 percent, less a charge for the prior earnings of $1.29 growing at 10 percent. The abnormal earnings growth of $0.018 per share is the change in residual income for 2001 in exhibit 2.3. This measure compares earnings for a year with prior year earnings growing at the required return, so if earnings grow only at the required rate—the normal rate—there is no abnormal earnings growth. However, the earnings are cum-dividend earnings; that is, they include earnings from reinvesting the prior year's dividends. The reinvestment of dividends is not to be overlooked. Shareholders get more earnings by reinvesting dividends (via a dividend reinvestment scheme for example, or in another firm); their earnings come from two sources, earnings in the firm and earnings from reinvested dividends. GE had (slight) abnormal earnings growth in 2001 because cum-dividend earnings were above those that would have been earned if earnings had grown only at the required rate of 10 percent. The savings account, in contrast, has zero abnormal earnings growth; earnings grow, cum-dividend, at the required rate of 5 percent.

It is surely easier to understand earnings growth above a normal rate than to understand "change in residual earnings" (though they are equivalent). We can express the model that forecasts changes in residual earnings as one that anchors on earnings, like the savings account, then adds value for abnormal earnings growth. For a three-year forecasting horizon,

$$\text{Value of equity}_0 = \frac{\text{Earnings}_1}{r} + \frac{1}{r}\left[\frac{\text{AEG}_2}{1+r} + \frac{\text{AEG}_3}{(1+r)^2}\right]$$
$$+\text{Value of speculative growth.}$$

This is sometimes called the AEG (or Abnormal Earnings Growth) model or the Ohlson-Juettner model after its architects.[19] We have adapted it here to separate value that comes from accounting for the short term ($12.90 for GE) and value from speculative growth outside the accounting. The valuation admits growth for the short term but eschews speculation about growth in the long term. The valuation can be restated as follows,

$$\text{Value of equity}_0 = \frac{\text{Dividend}_1}{1+r} + \frac{\text{Dividend}_2}{(1+r)^2} + \frac{\text{EPS}_3}{(1+r)^2 \times r}.$$

For GE,

$$\text{Value of equity}_0 = \frac{0.57}{1.10} + \frac{0.66}{1.10^2} + \frac{1.42}{1.10^2 \times 0.10} = \$12.80.$$

The earnings at the forecast horizon is capitalized at the required rate-of-return, which of course excludes any subsequent growth (like the savings account). So the valuation is equivalent to forecasting that the P/E ratio will be one with no growth, then discounting the price implied to present value along with any intervening dividends.

A P/E without growth is referred to as a "normal" P/E, for it indicates "normal" earnings growth (at the required rate-of-return). For the normal P/E,

$$\text{Price}_0 = \frac{\text{Earnings}_1}{r},$$

the forward $P/E = 1/r$, and the forward earnings yield $E/P = r$. For the saving account the forward $P/E = 1/0.05 = 20$ and the forward E/P is 5 percent. For a required return of 10 percent, more typical for an equity investment, the forward normal (no growth) $P/E = 1/0.10 = 10$ and the corresponding forward earnings yield is 10 percent.

While this valuation adds nothing over the model that begins with book value—it's the same accounting in the two models—the approach uses the familiar language of folks who talk about the P/E ratio; the P/E ratio is based on expected earnings growth. But the valuation has also been stricter in accounting for growth than is usual in analyst circles.

First, I have dispensed with a standard model for the P/E ratio:

$$\text{Value of equity}_0 = \frac{\text{Earnings}_1}{r - g}.$$

This standard model does not work for the savings account. With an earnings growth rate of 5 percent, the denominator is zero (a bit embarrassing!). Equities often have earnings growth rates greater than the required return, yielding a negative denominator. Where there is a mathematical problem there is usually also a conceptual problem, as there is here: One does not buy earnings growth, one buys abnormal earnings growth (AEG). *Beware of paying too much for growth*, and don't pay at all for an earnings growth rate that is less than your required return rate. The standard model will have you paying too much for growth. Both the AEG and the residual earnings model involve accounting that protect you from paying for growth when you should not.

Second, the AEG model says that it is cum-dividend earnings growth that is to be accounted for and valued—earnings with dividends reinvested—not earnings growth. Growth (and value) come not only from earnings within the firm, but also from earnings from reinvesting dividends (back into the same firm or elsewhere). That's a lesson from the savings account; the zero-payout account in exhibit 2.1 has 5 percent earnings growth, but it is worth the same $100 as the full-payout account with zero earnings growth. But actually the two accounts have the same earnings growth; the dividends from the full-payout account can be reinvested in another account earning at 5 percent to recover the same earnings growth as in the zero-payout account. That's dividend irrelevance in action!

Analysts almost always refer to earnings growth rather than cum-dividend earnings growth in talking about P/E ratios. They are missing something. If, in addition, they use the standard P/E model above, they are further compounding errors in accounting for value. If people think this way, one might well ask whether the pricing of earnings in the market is rational: "Does the market misprice growth?" The residual earnings model and the AEG model embed a rational analysis, an appropriate accounting for value.

Accounting for Value

The ideas here correspond with the line that equity investors "buy earnings." That is not a hard line to swallow. We understand that earnings move prices: When a firm's earnings differ from expectation, stock prices change, sometimes dramatically. Indeed, earnings explain most of the movement of stock prices over a number of years.[20] So thinking in terms of accumulated earnings that will be added to book value in the future is equivalent to thinking where the price will be; prices gravitate to earnings. This is of course no news to analysts who sweat on a firm's earnings and provide earnings forecasts to justify their stock recommendations. This chapter has just been a little more circumspect in handling the accounting in order to meet the fundamentalist's requirement of separating what we know from speculation and establishing a starting point on which to anchor a valuation.

Here are the main points to take away from the chapter:

First, understand the implication of the words "accounting for value": Valuation is a matter of accounting for the future so accounting and valuation are very much the same thing.

Second, to actually carry out the accounting for value, first think of where the book value is likely to be in the future, and then what will be the likely earnings on book value. Think of the savings account as a prototype, then move on to the accounting for GE.

Third, in accounting for the future, understand what you are relatively certain about and that which is more speculative, and translate the former into accounting numbers. Ask yourself: Do I have a reasonable handle on sales for the next year or two and the profit margins they will generate? Typically you can account up to two years ahead with some assurance, but then uncertainty overwhelms. Sometimes a forecast for only one year will be secure and (in the extreme) you may only be confident in the numbers you actually see, current earnings and book value. With this parsing of the future, you establish your anchoring no-growth valuation and maintain your cynicism about growth prospects.

Fourth, you should now have a firm appreciation of what a P/B ratio and a P/E ratio are all about.

Finally, understand that our accounting for value is incomplete. I have said nothing about how we might add value for speculative growth to the no-growth value. I have said nothing about another input, the required return. And, importantly, I have not said much about the type of accounting we need. We have a lot more to do.

The line that advises us to "buy earnings" leaves us short. Earnings have to be measured and that raises the issue of how to do the accounting. If accounting and valuation are the same thing, valuation turns on how the accounting is done. Accounting for value invokes the idea that one trades on a book but the trade then depends on how the book is kept. Chapters that follow bear on the question "What do I want the accounting to look like for valuation?"

If accounting numbers are to tell us something about value, they must connect to the firm's business activities that generate value. We have seen in this chapter that free cash flow does not tie to value, so discounted cash flow valuation—essentially cash accounting—is a doubtful accounting for value. Residual earnings valuation seemingly does do. It employs accrual accounting that adds investment to the balance sheet book value, then adds further value if those investments earn superior returns on book value. The savings account cannot earn those superior returns so is worth its book value, but GE can. The valuation thus "thinks" in the way a businessperson thinks: Invest and add value by earning superior returns on your investment. The AEG valuation translates this representation of a business into a form palatable for evaluating the P/E ratio, a form that emphasizes earnings growth but also respects the accounting that protects us from paying too much for growth.

That having been said, accrual accounting covers a multiple of sins. What is good accrual accounting for valuation and what is poor accounting? We have one signpost: The accounting must be something to anchor on so we can challenge the speculation in the market price. We have our work cut out for us. But first, let's go active and see how accounting for value can be deployed to challenge the market price. We do so in the next chapter.

CHAPTER THREE

Challenging Market Prices with Fundamentals (and Deploying Accounting for the Challenge)

THE LAST CHAPTER EXPLAINED that accounting and valuation tie together to such an extent that one can think of valuation as a matter of accounting. But the chapter also showed that accounting for value is typically incomplete, and agreeably so; good accounting minimizes speculation so that one can deploy the accounting to challenge speculation in the market price. This chapter makes the challenge.

The Game of Investing

There are a few points to appreciate before I begin.

DISCARD THE IDEA OF "INTRINSIC VALUE." Even though valuation models specify a number, "value," as the output of the valuation process, it is not helpful to think of a notion of true "intrinsic value." Again deferring to Graham and Dodd,

We are concerned with the intrinsic value of the security and more particularly with the discovery of the discrepancies between intrinsic value and price. We must recognize, however, that intrinsic value is an elusive concept. In general terms it is understood to be that value which is justified by the facts, e.g., the assets, earnings, dividends, definite prospects—as distinct, let us say, from market quotations established by artificial manipulation or distorted by psychological excesses. But it is a great mistake to imagine that intrinsic value is as definite and as determinable as is the market price.

—Benjamin Graham and David L. Dodd,
Security Analysis, 1934, 17.

With intrinsic value being inherently uncertain, the idea of discovering true intrinsic value is misguided.[1] A valuation model should not be employed as a method for determining a value but rather as a way of understanding uncertainty about value. With that understanding, fundamental analysis brings information to the cause of reducing our uncertainty, but not eliminating the uncertainty that inevitably accompanies risky investing.

ACCOUNTING IDENTIFIES WHERE OUR UNCERTAINTY LIES. Provided the accounting involves numbers that we are fairly secure about, it supplies "value justified by the facts," the anchoring value of the previous chapter. Accounting does not render the complete value but does tell us where our uncertainty about the market price lies and where we run the risk of paying too much. The last chapter explained that the uncertainty is about growth. In the case of GE, $12.80 of the $52 market price in early 2000 was accounted for, leaving uncertainty about whether the remaining $39.20—based on speculation about growth—was appropriate.

We could try to come to grips with our own uncertainty, put a value on uncertain growth to add to the accounting value, and ask whether that value matches the market's value. But that is not the way to approach the problem.

INVESTING IS A GAME AGAINST OTHER INVESTORS. Equity investing is not a game against nature, but against other investors. So it serves little purpose to discover the "true" intrinsic value, or the value for speculative growth, as if it existed somewhere out there. Rather, valuation models should be used to understand how an investor thinks differently from other investors in the market. Thus the right question to ask of a model is not what the "right" value is but rather whether the model can help the investor understand the perceptions of other investors embedded in the market price—so those perceptions can be challenged. The investor is "negotiating with Mr. Market" and, in those negotiations, the onus is not on the investor to come up with a forecast or a valuation, but rather to understand the forecast that explains Mr. Market's valuation, in order to accept it or reject his asking price.

With our accounting for value, we are in a position to do just that. We understand the market's valuation of growth, and now it remains to take the accounting further to discover the growth forecast behind that valuation. It is with this growth forecast that any disagreement with Mr. Market is likely to lie.

Challenging Speculation in the Market Price

We could well pursue the GE example, but let's move on to a more current case. At the time of this writing (November 2009), Cisco Systems, the supplier of networking equipment and software for telecommunications was trading at $24 per share, or 3.6 times book value of $6.68 at the end of its July 2009 fiscal year. Analysts were forecasting a consensus estimate of $1.42 EPS for 2010 and $1.61 for 2011.[2] The forward P/E of 16.9 implies some growth expectations, and indeed the growth rate forecasted for 2011 EPS over 2010 is 13.4 percent. The pro forma, like that for GE in the last chapter, is laid out in exhibit 3.1 (Cisco paid no dividends at the time).

With these numbers, I am pushing a couple of things aside for the moment. One might question whether the (U.S. GAAP) earnings in these forecasts are the appropriate accounting for the task, an issue that I will come back to. One might also question whether sell-side analysts' forecasts provide a sound anchor: Analysts can be moved by speculation, offering optimistic forecasts in bull markets and pessimistic forecasts in bear markets. Better to do one's own accounting for the short

EXHIBIT 3.1 Forecasts of Earnings per Share (EPS), Dividends per Share (DPS), and Book Value per Share (BPS) for Cisco Systems Inc., 2010–2011, with Associated Valuation Metrics

	2009A	2010E	2011E
EPS		1.42	1.61
DPS		0.00	0.00
BPS	6.68	8.10	9.71
Book rate-of-return		21.3%	19.9%
Residual earnings (10% charge)		0.752	0.800
Growth in residual earnings			6.38%
Growth in EPS			13.4%

$$\text{Value of equity}_0 = B_0 + \frac{(\text{ROCE}_1 - r) \times B_0}{1+r} + \frac{(\text{ROCE}_2 - r) \times B_1}{(1+r) \times r}$$

$$+ \text{ Value of speculative growth}$$

$$= \$6.68 + \frac{0.752}{1.10} + \frac{0.800}{1.10 \times 0.10} + \text{ Value of speculative growth}$$

$$= \$6.68 + 0.684 + 7.27 + \text{ Value of speculative growth}$$

$$= \$14.63 + \text{ Value of speculative growth}$$

term based on a thorough financial statement analysis of current and past financial statements and what they imply for the near future. We would then be truly anchoring on "what we know."[3] But, again, that would depend on the quality of the accounting in those statements. Indeed, an important criterion for an accounting for value (in later chapters) will be the ability to forecast short-term earnings that we can anchor on.

But let's work with these analyst numbers for illustration. The value implied by these numbers is developed at the bottom on the exhibit, following the accounting for value in the last chapter with the presumption that your required return is 10 percent. With no value for speculative growth, the accounting accounts for $14.63 of the $24 in market value, made up of $6.68 in book value and $0.684 + $7.27 = $7.95 from the short-term forecasts. Thus the amount of the market price unexplained by the accounting is $9.37. That is the value that the market is placing on speculative growth.

Figure 3.1 shows how I have deconstructed the market price into three components: (1) the book value, (2) the value from short-term earnings, and (3) the value the market places on subsequent speculative

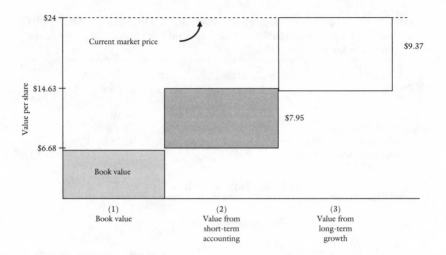

FIGURE 3.1   Building Blocks That Identify the Market's Valuation of Speculative Growth for Cisco Systems, Inc., November 2009.

growth. The accounting has parsed our uncertainty into what we know for sure—book value; what we know with some confidence—value from the short term; and what we are quite uncertain about—value from long-term growth prospects. To use Benjamin Graham's words with some license, the diagram separates "minimum true value" from the additional "speculative component of value." It is the latter where our uncertainty lies. It is the latter where we risk overpaying for growth.

It is the third block in figure 3.1 that I wish to challenge: $9.37 is the price that Mr. Market is asking us to pay for growth. What is the growth forecast implicit in this $9.37 ask? The answer comes quickly by bringing growth back into our valuation:

$$\text{Value of equity}_0 = \$24 = \$6.68 + \frac{0.752}{1.10} + \frac{0.800}{1.10 \times (0.10 - g)}.$$

With value set to Cisco's market price of $24, we can infer the market's long-term growth rate: The growth rate, g, is that growth rate that reconciles the model to the market price. The implied long-term growth rate for Cisco after 2010 is 5.63 percent per year. (The corresponding rate for GE is 8.48 percent.) Rather than applying a model to transform one's own forecast to a value, we have applied the model in reverse engineering mode to extract the market's forecast.[4] This is the way to handle valuation models. By resisting the temptation to plug a speculative growth rate into a model, we have heeded Graham's warning (in the last chapter) about "formulas out of higher mathematics," particularly the growth rate in those formulas. Rather, we have turned the model around as a tool to challenge the market speculation about growth of which he was so skeptical. But let's be clear about what is involved. We are anchoring on the accounting in the book value and short-term forecasts, and only if we are reasonably confident in that accounting can we impute the growth rate that is implied.

The growth rate is the residual earnings growth rate, a little difficult to get our minds around. But we can convert this growth rate to an EPS growth rate by reverse engineering the residual earnings calculation. As Residual earnings$_{t+1}$ = Earnings$_{t+1}$ − (r × Book value$_t$), then Earnings$_{t+1}$ = (Book value$_t$ × r) + Residual earnings$_{t+1}$. Cisco's residual earnings two years ahead (2011) is $0.800 per share, so the residual earnings forecasted for the third-year ahead (2012) at a growth rate of 5.63 percent is $0.845. Thus, with a per-share book value of $9.71 forecasted for the end of 2011, the implicit forecast of EPS for 2012 is 1.816 and the forecasted growth rate over 2011 is 12.8 percent. Extrapolating in the same way to subsequent years, one develops the earnings growth path that the market is forecasting, displayed in figure 3.2.[5]

Inferring growth rates from market prices in this manner was proposed as early as 1938 by John Burr Williams to whom the dividend discount model is often attributed. The "expectations investing" of Rappaport and Mauboussin takes this approach.[6] But the accounting that anchors the endeavor, which provides the base for growth, is important: The reverse engineering to dividend and cash flow growth forecasts is doubtful accounting for value, as the last chapter explained.[7]

The approach to investing here contrasts sharply with the advice to "buy stocks for the long run." Rather than trusting the market to deliver returns in the long run, the investor verifies that the market's forecast for the long run is a reasonable one. The question is turned back on the market: Can the market deliver returns in the long run?

FIGURE 3.2   EPS Growth Path Implied by the Market Price of $24 for Cisco Systems, Inc.

With the growth rates plotted in figure 3.2, the investor has a concrete understanding of the market's speculation about the long term. Taking heed of the warning, *beware of paying too much for growth*, he or she then asks whether to pay for that growth: Is growth likely to be above the projected path—the buy zone, or below the line—the sell zone? Or, to the inquiry of the defensive investor: Does the growth forecast look about right?[8]

In answering either question, the investor will need to do some accounting for growth, and we will do so in the next few chapters. To start, the investor looks at growth up to the forecast horizon as an indication of the firm's ability to deliver subsequent growth. The residual earnings growth rate forecasted for Cisco in 2011 is 6.4 percent, contrasting with the long-term rate of 5.63 percent inferred from the market price. For speculation, he or she may then turn to softer inputs than the accounting. The investor understands, first and foremost, that a good knowledge of the business is a prerequisite for grappling with the issue. He or she understands that exceptionally high growth rates are not likely to eventuate unless the firm has a strong sustainable competitive advantage. He or she understands that technological advantage can be eroded away. The investor is reminded that the implied growth rate of 9.3 percent in the $77 price for Cisco in 2000 looked absurd to anyone who understood business, and proved to be so. He or she dissented from technology analysts at the time who advised "Buy Cisco at any price."

With this understanding, the investor may speculate, but stays within the discipline of the accounting. Any growth forecast, and the added value it implies, must be justified with an accounting for what future book value and return on book value are likely to be. After all, in the long run, the market will price a firm based on its evolving financial statements. The investor recognizes that "sustainable competitive advantage" are only words unless supported by feasible forecasts of sales growth and profit margins. He or she may dig deeper into current and past financial statements to ask whether the implied earnings growth rates he or she is challenging are reasonable given past sales growth rates and profit margins. This discipline is applied in subsequent chapters.

While remaining skeptical of prices, the investor also maintains respect. He or she understands that he or she cannot be the sole possessor of knowledge and is wary of the dangers of self-deception and overconfidence. So the investor allows the market price to challenge him or her: "What do others know that I do not know?" "Is the market speculating about a takeover?" "Am I missing something?" "Or is it the case that I cannot justify the growth expectations in the market price?" The game is against other investors and the consensus view is to be acknowledged and understood. The investor may conclude that "animal spirits" are moving the crowd (and prices), but may also conclude that there are rational explanations for the current price that he or she has not anticipated.

In deploying accounting as the anchor to challenge speculation, one must be realistic about whether the accounting has much to say. For a biotech startup with no product or FDA (U.S. Food and Drug Administration) approval, that is reporting losses and even negative book value, the accounting is not the place to start. That is how it should be; this firm is a pure speculative play and (nonspeculative) accounting should not have much to say. Better to get a degree in biochemistry than to study the financial statements.

I have much to add in the matter of evaluating growth. Indeed the next four chapters will be preoccupied with the question of how much to pay for growth. This chapter is just the set-up.

Benchmarking Growth

Before proceeding, let's establish some benchmarks for evaluating the question of paying for growth.

The No-Growth Benchmark

The fundamentalist who refuses to pay for growth takes a firm stance: Pay only the no-growth price. Pay only for the value justified by the accounting. For Cisco, this is $14.63. This builds in the margin of safety advocated by fundamentalists: "If the shares are trading at less than the no-growth price, I am probably getting a bargain, for in all likelihood there is some growth." But this may just be too conservative. Although this strategy may have delivered some bargains in Benjamin Graham's time, growth delivered considerable value during the last half of the twentieth century; growth characterizes the modern firm. The "growth-stock" movement that took traction during the 1950s departed from Graham on this point. It has been said that Graham would have missed out on the great growth companies of the latter part of the twentieth century, the IBM's of the time. If entrepreneurs adopted Graham's standards of prudence, businesses would never be started. The future must be grappled with. Can we do better?

S&P 500 Growth Benchmark

At the time of our Cisco inquiry, November 2009, the S&P 500 index traded at 1080. This index, covering a good deal of the total market capitalization of traded stocks, is considered to be representative of the market as a whole. Let's calculate the implied growth rate g from a residual earnings model with a forecasting horizon of just one year ahead:

$$\text{Value}_{2009} = B_{2009} + \frac{(\text{ROCE}_{2010} - r) \times B_{2009}}{r - g}.$$

Now for the inputs: The book value for the 500 stocks in the index at the time was 451 (in units of the index) and the average return on common equity, ROCE, over the previous 20 years was about 15 percent. Set the value at the level of the index of 1080 and set $r = 9$ percent, approximately the long U.S. bond rate at the time of 4 percent plus a 5 percent risk premium. Accordingly,

$$1080 = 451 + \frac{(0.15 - 0.09) \times 451}{0.09 - g}.$$

The reverse engineering delivers $g = 4.7$ percent; the market is expecting a 4.7 percent long-term residual earnings growth rate for the market as a whole. That number looks quite familiar; it is close to what we expect for the typical (nominal) gross domestic product (GDP) growth rate.[9] If corporate earnings add value at the same rate as the GDP, this rate looks like a reasonable long-term growth rate for the market as a whole.

Indeed, it is quite impressive how, at various points in time, this reverse-engineering exercise for the index typically produces a growth rate approximating the average GDP growth rate, with some variation. Figure 3.3 plots the price-to-book ratio for the S&P 500 at year end for 1982–2008, along with implied growth rates. The calculation of implied growth rates is the same as above, but now with forward ROCE based on analysts' consensus earnings forecasts for the index at year end. The implied growth rates range from −11.2 percent in 1982 to 8.0 percent in 2001, but the average is 4.2 percent and the median 5.2 percent, much like the typical GDP growth rate.

The average price-to-book (P/B) ratio for the S&P 500 for the period is 2.6, above the longer historical average of just over 2.0. Figure 3.3 indicates that the P/B was particularly high during some of the 1982–2008 period, reaching 5.0 in the bubble years of the late 1990s.

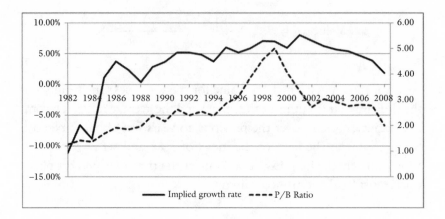

FIGURE 3.3   Price-to-Book (P/B) Ratio and Implied Residual Earnings Growth Rates for the S&P 500, 1982–2008.

The measures are at the end of December of each year. The implied growth rate is indicated on the left axis, and the P/B on the right axis. Implied residual earnings growth rates are calculated by reverse engineering the end-of-year S&P 500 index with a required return of 9 percent and forward return on book value measured with analysts' consensus forward earnings forecasts for the following year. Sources: The S&P 500 index is from the Standard and Poor's website; book value is from the COMPUSTAT data through WRDS; and analysts' forecasts are from IBES, supplied through WRDS.

Correspondingly the implied growth rates were also high. Implied growth rates are an instrument for challenging the market price, as we saw with Cisco. Could it be that when implied growth rates for the S&P 500 are above a normal GDP growth rate, one detects mispricing? Do the implied growth rates predict returns for the index?

Figure 3.4 suggests so. The figure plots the same implied growth rates as in figure 3.3, but now with an overlay of returns for the S&P 500 over the following year. It appears that the implied growth rates predict returns on the index, with higher growth rates predicting lower subsequent returns and vice versa. The correlation is −0.25, and the correlations with returns for two years ahead and three years ahead are −0.26 and −0.33, respectively. These returns can be attributed to the market pricing in too much or too little growth, although they just as well could be due to changing discount rates (that the constant 9 percent rate does not accommodate).[10]

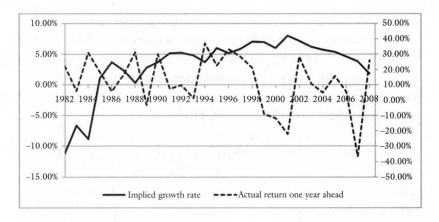

FIGURE 3.4 Implied Growth Rates (left axis) and Subsequent Year-Ahead Returns (right axis) for the S&P 500, 1982–2008.

Take the returns as you may, the analysis suggests that the GDP growth rate provides a useful benchmark. Corporate earnings grow value with the economy, so it makes sense that the investor should recognize such growth in his or her valuations.

Anchoring on Short-Term and Long-Term Growth: The Declining Growth Benchmark

We could specify a (residual earnings) growth rate for Cisco at the GDP growth rate. Applied to the 2011 residual earnings, a 4 percent growth rate (to be conservative) produces a valuation of $19.48 per share.[11] Effectively, we would be saying that Cisco cannot grow residual earnings at more than the GDP rate. However, although it is reasonable to expect the typical firm to look much like the average S&P 500 firm in the (very) long run, it may also be reasonable to expect a firm like Cisco, with its competitive positioning and its history of unusually high growth, to maintain a higher growth rate for some time. Indeed, the accounting for 2011, two years ahead, indicates a residual earnings growth of 6.38 percent rather than 4 percent. Might we not anchor on this accounting?

History affirms that growth rates erode as businesses come under challenge from competitors and technological change. In the words of the statistician, growth mean-reverts to the average growth rate. A simple mean-reversion calculation accommodates this. With residual earnings growth of 6.38 percent forecasted for 2011 and a 4 percent long-term growth rate, we now have two references, a short-term and a long-term rate. Combining the two with weights that sum to 1, forecast the reversion path to the long-term GDP rate:

$$\text{Growth rate for } 2012 = (0.8 \times 6.38\%) + (0.2 \times 4.0\%) = 5.90\%$$

(and so on, recursively for years after 2012). The 2012 growth rate is lower than the 6.38 percent for 2011 because it is on a path to decline to 4 percent in the long run. Applying the weights to subsequent years, the forecasted growth rate for 2013 is 5.53 percent, declining to 4 percent eventually, and 4.4 percent within ten years. So we establish a "fade rate" for growth. This path yields a valuation of $20.33. The path is plotted in figure 3.5 and compared to a path with weights of (0.9, 0.1). The (0.9, 0.1) weighting sees the growth rate nearing 4 percent considerably further in the future, reaching 4.4 percent in twenty years, and yields a valuation of $21.14. As before, these residual earnings growth paths can be converted to EPS growth paths, as in figure 3.2. Although the weights are somewhat arbitrary, they focus our thinking: How long do I expect Cisco to maintain a growth rate superior to the economy as a whole?[12]

One can also turn the exercise around to challenge the market price. Rather than inferring one long-term growth rate from the market price, as before, infer the weights that the market is applying to forecast the decline in growth rates from the short-term rate of 6.38 percent to the long-term anchor of 4 percent. The weights that yield the market price of $24 are (0.98, 0.02), indicating that the market expects reversion of the growth rate to 4 percent far in the distant future, indeed reaching 4.4 percent 100 years hence. The growth path is also plotted in figure 3.5. Is this growth path a reasonable one given one's knowledge of the company?

The analyst may refer to a "competitive advantage period," or "durable competitive advantage" to answer such a question, but these are speculative notions. We must tread carefully. Indeed, a speculation that the GDP growth rate will apply to every firm in the long term is sus-

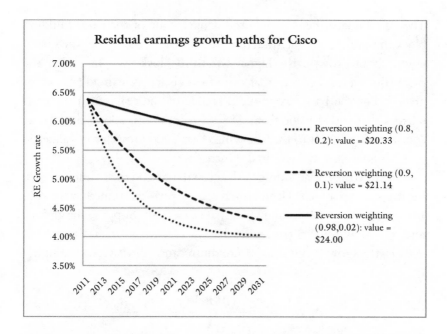

FIGURE 3.5 Residual Earnings Growth Paths for Alternative Weightings of Short-Term and Long-Term Growth Rates and for the Weights Implicit in the Market Price.

The (0.98, 0.02) weights are those implied by the market price of $24.

pect; firms with zero or negative growth rates now or in the near term may never produce such growth.

Nevertheless, don't you feel that this exercise is helping you understand whether the market price of $24 is a reasonable one? You are handling uncertainty.

The Risky Growth Benchmark

Any speculation about growth is risky, so why not simply recognize this in a benchmark valuation?

Consider again, the valuation for Cisco that incorporates growth (with a one-year forecasting horizon):

$$\text{Value}_{2009} = B_{2009} + \frac{(\text{ROCE}_{2010} - r) \times B_{2009}}{r - g}.$$

The denominator here, $r-g$ is the danger zone of the third building block in figure 3.1. For a given required return, r, the higher the speculation about growth, the higher the third block and the higher the price. But we understand that growth is risky; we can add value for growth but the basic economic principle of the risk-return trade-off tells us that added value from growth comes with added risk. These considerations point to the following: Don't add growth to a valuation without adding to the required return.

Now recognize that adding to the growth rate and the required return leaves $r-g$ unchanged. The required return, r, is determined by the risk-free rate, r_f plus a risk premium, r_p; that is, $r=r_f+r_p$. Suppose the growth rate, g, purely reflects risk, such that $g=r_p$, then $r-g=r_f+r_p-r_p=r_f$. That is, the growth and the risk premium cancel exactly. Accordingly,

$$\text{Value}_{2009} = B_{2009} + \frac{(\text{ROCE}_{2010} - r) \times B_{2009}}{r_f}.$$

With the U.S. government long-bond rate of 4.3 percent at the time, the calculated value for Cisco is

$$\$6.68 + \frac{0.752}{0.043} = \$24.17.$$

This number is close to the market price of \$24, so we can now interpret the market as pricing Cisco with the idea that any growth is risky.

This valuation approach is similar to the Fed model, often discussed in the press. The Fed model sees the benchmark E/P ratio for the stock market as equal to the long-term bond rate: $\text{Earnings}_1/P_0=r_f$.[13] So, when stocks are priced with a yield below that for the ten-year U.S. government bond, they are deemed to be overpriced; the market is setting the yield too low.[14] Alan Greenspan is said to have had this model in mind in his "irrational exuberance" speech of the late 1990s. Figure 3.6 shows how well the Fed model works for stocks in aggregate, using analysts' consensus earnings forecasts for the forward E/P ratio; the

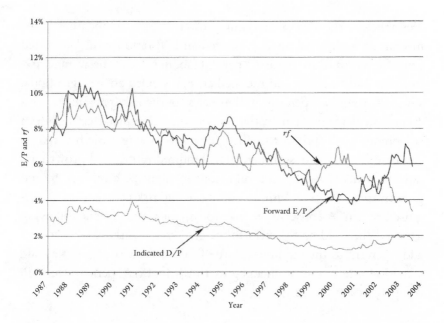

FIGURE 3.6 Forward Earnings Yield (E/P) for Stocks and the Yield on Ten-Year U.S. Government Bonds (r_f), 1987–2004, Along with the Indicated (Forward) Dividend Yield on Stocks (D/P).

The earnings yield is for a portfolio consisting of all U.S.-listed stocks with available analyst consensus forward earnings forecasts and is market value weighted. Source: Jacob Thomas, "Price Equals Forward Earnings Scaled by the Risk-Free Rate: The Implications of this Remarkable Empirical Regularity" (2005), Yale University School of Management, New Haven, CT. With kind permission of Jacob Thomas.

E/P ratio for the market as a whole tracks closely to the ten-year government bond rate, r_f, although not as much after 2000. Though there has been considerable discussion on the validity of the Fed Model, this tracking is quite remarkable (the period after 2000 aside). It seems a strange model given that stocks are risky, the risk-free rate is not appropriate and, further, stocks, unlike bonds, can produce growth. But the implication is that even though these points are true, risk and growth tend to cancel in the valuation. Stocks deliver growth but growth is risky, requiring a higher return.[15]

We must be careful in applying a model that seems to work for the aggregate stock market to individual stocks. Surely firms with a competitive advantage (like Cisco) can add growth over the required return.

Nevertheless, the idea of canceling growth and risk is apparent at the median for individual firms. The median E/P ratio for all U.S.-listed firms from 1963 to 2006 was 6.1 percent, about same as the average risk-free rate. But firms around the median E/P yielded an average annual stock return of 14.8 percent, well in excess of the risk-free rate.[16] If this average stock return is indicative of the required return (that includes a risk premium), it appears that the E/P ratio is pricing growth as risky.

There is a simple lesson here. The required return and growth are not independent inputs to a valuation; it might be a mistake to add growth to a valuation without adding to the risk premium in the required return. A conservative investor might take heed the following advice: When adding 1 percent to the growth rate, ask whether to also add 1 percent to the required return. To do otherwise requires a solid scenario for how a firm can add growth without risk, perhaps through competitive advantage.

Accounting for Value and Accounting for Growth

There is considerable evidence that the market overprices growth, at least some of the time. High P/E stocks—growth stocks—often disappoint, delivering lower returns than low P/E stocks. The high-price multiples of the late 1990s priced growth that was not realized. Indeed, research indicates that over the last fifty years, firms on average did not deliver the long-term cash flows forecast in stock prices.[17] But one must be discriminating. In the 1970s when average P/E ratios were well below 10, the market underpriced growth, at least ex post. In this chapter, I have applied accounting to discern and challenge the market's growth expectations.

Here are the main points to take away from this chapter.

First, don't take a valuation model too literally; instead, see a valuation model as a tool to challenge the stock price. Rather than plugging a growth rate into a model, apply the model to understand the future growth that the market expects. Valuation is not a game against nature, but a game against other investors, and one proceeds by first understanding how other investors think. As an investor, you are not required to establish a valuation, but only to accept or reject the valuation of others.

Second, the accounting for value of the last chapter grounds you for challenging the market price. Start by calculating the value implied by an accounting for value, identify speculative value in the market price, transform that speculative value into an earnings growth path, and then ask whether that growth path is a reasonable one.

Third, understand the basic benchmarks for growth that are applied to test whether growth is reasonable. Test to see whether the implied growth rate for your target firm is in line with these benchmarks. If not, ask why not.

The growth benchmarks give us perspective and an appreciation of what is conservative growth. There is much more to do in evaluating growth, and subsequent chapters take us there.

CHAPTER FOUR

Accounting for Growth from Leverage (and Protection from Paying Too Much for Growth)

CHALLENGING THE MARKET'S GROWTH forecasts, as in the last chapter, requires an understanding of where growth comes from, that is, what drives growth. The standard view is that growth comes from durable competitive advantage, technological innovation, investment opportunities, and, not least, entrepreneurial insight. These are worthy ideas but they are "soft" concepts, very much in the eye of the speculator. They can, of course, be backed up by evidence of growth in the past, but engaging soft ideas is not entirely satisfactory as a check on speculation. This chapter and the next explain how we can be more disciplined, more sure of ourselves, by bringing accounting to bear. It explains that the concrete expression of growth is an accounting issue; to understand the implications of growth for value, one must understand the accounting for growth. An investor who is not attendant to the accounting can read false signals and pay too much for growth.

I examine how accounting informs about growth in two steps. First, this chapter examines growth that comes from leverage, from the financing of the business. Then the next chapter examines growth generated by the business itself. Both chapters do so with the fundamentalist's dictum in mind: *Beware of paying too much for growth.*

Before proceeding, let's first dispel false ideas about growth and bring focus to where it should be; growth that adds value. The term *growth* is widely used but without much clarity. People talk of "growth companies," but what is a growth company? People talk of asset growth or sales growth, but surely asset growth and sales growth are not to be valued if they return losses. One might then latch on to earnings growth, as is common, but, as we will see, that is not entirely satisfactory either. Among investors, "growth" refers to firms with high multiples such as price-to-book. Indeed, some investors distinguish themselves as "growth" investors and "value" investors, where the latter refers to buying firms with low multiples. Surely that does not mean that growth does not yield value or that growth is not an issue in "value" stocks. Clearly there is some sorting out to do. Clarity comes from understanding how one accounts for growth. Can we account for growth in a way that clearly connects to value?

Beware of Growth from Investment

The idea that growth comes from investment opportunities is perhaps the most dangerous. Finance textbooks talk glibly about adding value from "investment opportunities" or "growth opportunities." They talk of value from current investments and added value from growth in future investments. This is tempting language but leaves us with a hazy (and lazy) idea, another invitation to speculate. We can be more concrete by saying that investment adds value because it adds earnings or cash flows. But there is further danger: Investment adds earnings growth (the notorious corporate jet aside), but may not add value. The serial acquirer can produce considerable earnings growth, but are those earnings to be valued?

Take Tyco International with its considerable growth through serial acquisitions in the 1990s. By increasing book value (net assets) from $3.1 billion in 1996 to $31.7 billion in 2001, largely through acquisition, the firm reported earnings per share growth from 8 cents in 1996 to

$7.68 by 2001. The numbers from 1997 onward are in exhibit 4.1. The market, apparently impressed, rewarded the growth with the share price increasing from $53 in 1996 to $236 by the end of 2001. The implied residual earnings growth rate in the $236 market price, calculated with the methods of Chapter 3, was 8.6 percent. Tyco was priced by the market as a growth company. Was this growth to pay for? In 2002, the firm reported a loss of $18.48 per share after large impairment charges to its investments (including significant write-downs on its acquisitions), with additional impairments following in 2003. The share price dropped to $68 by the end of 2002 (and to $40 by 2007). Not a happy experience for investors who attributed value to Tyco's earnings growth.

The rational investor, accounting for value, would not have participated in the Tyco price bubble. That investor recognizes that the accounting for value of Chapter 2 builds in protection from paying too much for growth; residual earnings, not earnings, are the focus, and a firm delivers residual earnings only after covering a charge against the investment (in acquisitions) that produces the earnings. Although Tyco's earnings growth rates were impressive, the residual earnings for the years 1997–2001 are considerably more modest, hardly justifying the high implied growth in 2001. The anchoring, no-growth valuation at the end of 2001 was $85 per share, far below the $236 market price.

The lesson here is important enough to state it as a firm valuation principle:

Valuation Principle 4

Growth that is valued does not come from earnings growth but from residual earnings growth.

The message to the serial acquirer is forceful: The rational investor adds value only if you produce earnings over and above the required return. If you pay fair value for an acquisition, you have your work cut out for you, because an investment at fair value earns only at the required rate of return. The message to the empire builder paying more than fair value: The rational investor expects negative residual earnings

EXHIBIT 4.1 Earnings, Book Values, Residual Earnings, and Stock Price Multiples for Tyco International Ltd., 1997–2005

	1997	1998	1999	2000	2001	2002	2003	2004	2005
Earnings (billions)	$(0.39)	1.17	1.02	2.76*	3.46	(9.18)	0.98	2.88	3.02
Return on common equity (ROCE)	−11.8%	17.5%	9.2%	30.4%	14.2%	−33.1%	3.9%	10.1%	9.6%
EPS	$(0.96)	2.96	2.48	6.54*	7.68	(18.48)	1.96	5.76	6.04
Book value of equity (billions)	$3.43	9.90	12.37	17.03	31.73	24.16	26.48	30.4	32.6
Residual earnings (billions) (10% charge)	$(0.73)	0.50	(0.09)	1.27	1.03	(11.96)	(1.55)	0.04	(0.13)
Stock price per share	$90	151	156	222	236	68	106	143	115
Price/Book (P/B)	4.8	6.2	6.1	5.6	3.4	1.4	2.0	2.3	1.8
Trailing P/E	–	53	74	34	31	–	54	24	19
Net debt (billions)	$2.7	4.5	8.9	10.3	20.4	18.6	17.4	12.8	9.9

*Excluding gains on asset sales; earnings including those gains were $4.52 billion. Numbers in parentheses are negative. Per share numbers are adjusted to 2010 shares for subsequent stock splits.

from your game with other people's money and understands that you may be hiding behind earnings growth as cover.

Growth becomes more enticing when wrapped in a nice-sounding business concept. Remember the "centerless corporation," the "knowledge company," "Internet real estate," and other such slogans of the "new-age" 1990s? This followed the "diversified corporation," the "vertical corporation," and the "horizontal corporation" of an early era (that later were disavowed). These are thought-provoking ideas that every entrepreneur must entertain—management journals and magazines are full of them and consultants push them—but they are untested ideas, and many did not survive the test of time. The appeal of (unspecified) "intangible assets," with its pretext of doing some accounting, is particularly beguiling. The investor must be circumspect.

In 1998, Sanford Weill of Travelers Group developed the idea of a "financial supermarket"; one-stop shopping for banking, investments, and insurance with the merging of Travelers (insurance), Citicorp (banking), and Salomon Smith Barney (brokerage, wealth management, and investment banking) to form Citigroup. A good idea? Exhibit 4.2 reports results for the combined group for selected years from 1996 to 2008. The stock price increased from $15 to almost $56 by 2006, with earnings per share growth from $1.50 to $4.39. Whether the disaster of 2008 can be attributed partly to the merger is an open question, but did the supermarket idea add value? The residual earnings numbers, increasing from $3.7 billion in 1996 to $9.9 billion in 2006 suggest so: Here is residual earnings growth that is to be valued. Was the market adding value for the growth? Yes, the no-growth valuations (of Chapter 2) in the exhibit are considerably less than the share price. Was the market overpricing the growth? The implied growth rates in the market price (calculated as in Chapter 3) are lofty in 2000 and 2004 (for a bank), enough to give the investor looking for a margin of safety considerable concern. (The implied growth rates for 1999, 2001, and 2003 were 6.1 percent, 6.2 percent, and 4.3 percent, respectively.) This was growth at risk and, as it turned out, there was a big shock to Citigroup's growth in the subsequent financial crisis.

Overpaying for growth was a feature of the 1990s. Entrepreneurial ideas are the very essence of value creation, but one must be disciplined in embracing speculative ideas, particularly as management and consultants

EXHIBIT 4.2 Earnings, Book Value, Residual Earnings, Price-to-Book, and Implied Growth Rates for Citigroup Inc. for Selected Years, 1996–2008

	1996	1998	2000	2002	2004	2006	2008
Earnings (billions)	$7.6	7.0	13.5	15.3	17.0	21.5	(27.7)
EPS	$1.50	1.35	2.69	2.99	3.32	4.39	(5.59)
ROCE	19.5%	15.0%	22.3%	18.6%	16.6%	18.6%	-30.1%
Book value of equity (billions)	$40.5	48.8	64.5	85.3	108.2	119.8	71.0
Residual earnings (billions) (10% charge)	$3.7	2.3	7.5	7.1	6.7	9.9	-36.9
Stock price	$15.13	24.85	51.06	35.19	48.18	55.70	6.71
Price/Book (P/B)	1.3	1.7	4.0	2.1	2.3	2.3	0.5
No-growth valuation	$22.9	21.29	27.68	30.31	33.78	44.63	—
Implied growth rate in price*	—	3.4%	6.1%	2.7%	5.3%	3.5%	—

*Implied residual earnings growth rate, as calculated in Chapter 3. The 1996 numbers are for Travelers Group prior to the acquisition of Citicorp.

tend to overmarket them. Business concepts, often couched in enticing language, helped promote the Internet and telecom bubble of the 1990s. Enron was wrapped in talk of a new energy corporation, enhanced as it turned out by suspect accounting. Business concepts need to be challenged with an appropriate accounting, an accounting that protects the investor from paying too much for speculative growth: What will be the likely book value in five years, and what is the likely return on the book value?

Beware of Earnings Growth and Profitability Generated by Leverage

Investors understand that leverage adds risk; when things go wrong, leverage adds to the pain (as the recent financial crisis clearly made plain). The point is evident in exhibit 4.1, where you can see from the net debt numbers that Tyco was operating with considerable leverage. When the shock hit in 2002, the loss of $18.48 per share was magnified by leverage. But there is a more subtle danger when it comes to valuation. Leverage increases ROCE, earnings per share, earnings growth, and indeed residual earnings, but it is very doubtful that it adds value: *Beware of earnings created by leverage.*

Let's turn to a simple example to explain. Exhibit 4.3 runs through the accounting before and after a stock repurchase financed by borrowing. To keep it simple, the firm is very much like the zero-payout savings account in Chapter 2 where I first demonstrated accounting for value, except that the book rate-of-return is higher than the required return (now 10 percent, which befits an equity investment). The first panel depicts the firm with no borrowing. With no payout, earnings are reinvested in assets, producing book value growth and earnings growth (like Tyco) at 10 percent per year. But the associated residual earnings calculation—constant over years—tells us that this is not growth to pay for. With ROCE expected to be above the required return, residual earnings is positive each year ($2), and the (no-growth) valuation at the end of 2010 is $100, with a P/B of 1.25 and a (no-growth) forward P/E of 10. With no debt on the balance sheet, the firm is an all-equity firm, with the equity value of $100 made up of 10 shares at $10 each.

Accounting Before a Stock Repurchase

	2010A	2011E	2012E	2013E	2014E
Income Statement					
Earnings		10	11	12.1	13.31
EPS (on 10 shares)		$1	1.1	1.21	1.33
EPS growth rate			10%	10%	10%
Balance Sheet					
Assets = Equity	$80	90	101	113.1	126.41
Book rate-of-return (ROCE)		12.5%	12.2%	11.9%	11.8%
Residual earnings		$2	2	2	2

Value of the equity $= \$80 + \dfrac{\$2}{0.10} = \$10.$

Value per share (on 10 shares) $10

Price/Book (P/B)   1.25
Forward P/E ($100/$10)   10

Accounting After a Stock Repurchase

	2010A	2011E	2012E	2013E	2014E
Income Statement					
Operating income		10.00	11.00	12.10	13.31
Interest expense (at 5%)		2.50	2.50	2.50	2.50
Earnings		7.50	8.50	9.60	10.81
EPS (on 5 shares)		1.50	1.70	1.92	2.16
EPS growth rate			13.3%	12.9%	12.6%
Balance Sheet					
Operating assets	$80	90.00	101.00	113.10	126.41
Debt (5%)	$50	50.00	50.00	50.00	50.00
Equity	$30	40.00	51.00	63.10	76.41
	$80	90.00	101.00	113.10	126.41
Rate-of-return for operations		12.5%	12.2%	11.9%	11.8%
Rate-of-return on equity (ROCE)		25.0%	21.2%	18.8%	17.1%
Residual operating income		$2.00	2.00	2.00	2.00
Equity residual earnings:					
$7.50 - (0.15 \times 30)$		$3.00			

Value of equity $= \$30 + \dfrac{3}{0.15} = \$50$

Value of the equity = Value of the operations − Value of debt

Value of the operations $= \$80 + \dfrac{2}{0.10} = \$100$

Value of debt   (50)
Value of equity $50
Value per share (on 5 shares)   **$10**

Price/Book (P/B)   1.67
Forward P/E ($50/$7.50)   6.67

The firm now decides to repurchase half of the outstanding shares and to finance the required $50 with debt at a borrowing rate of 5 percent. The balance sheet after the transaction (in the second panel of the exhibit) thus reports $30 in equity and $50 in debt. In the parlance of finance, there has been a change in capital structure and an increase in leverage. The transaction does not, of course, affect the operating business, so operating income from the business—sometimes called enterprise income—and operating assets in the business—sometimes called enterprise assets—are unaffected. But now the income statement subtracts interest on the debt to arrive at earnings (for the common shareholder). Earnings are accordingly lower than with the all-equity firm, but with only five shares outstanding, EPS has increased (from $1 to $1.50 in the forward year; 2011, for example). But focus also on the earnings growth (increasing from 10 percent to over 12 percent per year); leverage increases earnings growth. Moreover, while the profitability of the business (the book rate-of-return for operations) remains the same, the rate-of-return on common equity (ROCE) increases to 25 percent in the forward year (from 12.5 percent) and continues at a high level.[1] With a higher ROCE and lower book value, residual earnings also increase, from the $2 in the all-equity firm in the forward year to $3 in the levered firm; leverage not only increases earnings growth and ROCE, but also increases residual earnings.[2]

These effects are in no way confined to a specific example. They are universal and deterministic because they are simply due to how accounting works. Two fixed accounting relations describe the growth effects and profitability effects, so we have accounting principles to add to those of Chapter 2, illustrated with the numbers in exhibit 4.3 for 2012.

Accounting Principle 3a

Leverage increases earnings growth.

Growth rate for earnings to common$_t$ = Growth rate for operating income$_t$ + [Earnings leverage$_{t-1}$ × (Growth rate for operating income$_t$ − Growth rate for interest expense$_t$)]

For 2012: Earnings leverage, $2011 = \dfrac{\text{Interest expense}}{\text{Earnings}}$

$= \dfrac{2.50}{7.50} = 0.333$, so

Growth rate for earnings to common
$$= 10\% + [0.333 \times (10\% - 0\%)] = 13.33\%$$

Accounting Principle 3b

Leverage increases profitability (the return on common equity).

ROCE = Rate-of-return on operations + [Balance sheet leverage × (Rate-of-return on operations – Borrowing cost)]

For 2012: Balance sheet leverage, end of 2011 =

$\dfrac{\text{Financing debt}}{\text{Common equity}} = \dfrac{50}{40} = 1.25$, so

$$\text{ROCE} = 12.2\% + [1.25 \times (12.2\% - 5\%)] = 21.2\%$$

The effect of leverage in the income statement, measured by earnings leverage = interest expense/earnings, determines the increase in the earnings growth rate from leverage. Balance sheet leverage (financing debt/equity book value) determines the increase in the rate-of-return to equity. (Balance sheet leverage is also referred to as "book leverage.") Leverage increases earnings growth only if leverage is "favorable," that is, enterprise earnings growth exceeds the growth in interest expense. Similarly, leverage increases ROCE and residual earnings only if the leverage is favorable, with the rate-of-return for operations greater than the borrowing cost. (Interest expense and borrowing costs are after-tax, that is, effective interest costs.) Otherwise these relations go the other way, demonstrating the effect of unfavorable leverage.

Now to the ultimate issue, the valuation effects. With higher earnings growth, higher ROCE, and higher residual earnings, one might be tempted to attribute a higher valuation. But, again, *beware of paying too much for growth* (and profitability) from leverage. Anchor to the financing irrelevance principle of modern finance (see Chapter 1): *Borrowing does not add value.* In the example, this principle simply says that, if the firm borrows at a fair market value and repurchases stock at fair market value, it cannot add value to its stock price. Financing transactions at fair market prices are zero-net-present-value transactions; a firm adds value in its business from trading with customers, not from buying and selling bonds and shares at fair market value. The reason is that leverage does indeed add expected earnings growth and ROCE, but also adds risk (Tyco shareholders will testify that leverage can be unfavorable, as will those of Lehman Brothers and Bear Stearns.) Although higher profitability (ROCE) and earnings growth add to price, risk discounts price and the two cancel to leave price unchanged; the higher ROCE in the example is offset by a higher required return for equity of 15 percent.[3] As a matter of anchoring a valuation, this is a principle to hold to, though exceptions can be explored.[4]

Accordingly, the value of the equity in the example is $50 (after the repurchase of half the shares) but, with only five shares now outstanding, the value is the same $10 per share as the all-equity firm. One can see the canceling of growth and risk in the price in the operation of the formula that accounts for value. Before the leverage change,

$$\text{Value of equity} = \$80 + \frac{2}{0.10}$$
$$= \$100, \text{ or } \$10 \text{ per share on 10 shares.}$$

After the leverage change:

$$\text{Value of equity} = \$30 + \frac{3}{0.15}$$
$$= \$50, \text{ or } \$10 \text{ per share on 5 shares.}$$

(as in the exhibit). While there is a numerator effect—residual earnings increasing from $2 to $3—there is also a canceling-denominator effect for added risk—the required return increasing from 10 to 15 percent—such as to leave the value per share unchanged.[5]

The fundamentalist understands the effects of leverage, and then turns to the market to ask: Does the market penetrate the source of value in this way? Does the market understand the effect of leverage or does the market naïvely price on the basis of EPS, ROCE, and earnings growth? When analysts increase their EPS forecasts in response to an increase in leverage, does the market naïvely increase the price? One takes for granted that leverage is risky and so requires a high return but, surprisingly, empirical research has failed to show that leverage actually adds to returns in the stock market, a glaring empirical result given the principle is so fundamental in the theory of finance.[6]

There is also a lesson here for corporate boards that tie executive compensation to return on equity or EPS growth. With such a compensation plan, you can expect an increase in borrowing (and perhaps a stock repurchase) that adds to management bonuses but puts more risk on the shareholder without adding to shareholder value. Compensation should be tied to unlevered metrics, those that focus on earnings from the business and the value it adds.

The effects of leverage on the P/B and P/E ratios are also given in exhibit 4.3; P/B increases from 1.25 for the all-equity firm to 1.67 but the forward P/E decreases from 10 to 6.67. The all-equity P/B is of course also the P/B for business operations (without the effect of leverage), often referred to as the enterprise P/B = enterprise value/enterprise book value = $100/$80 = 1.25 (it is sometimes also referred to as the unlevered P/B). Correspondingly, the all-equity P/E is the enterprise P/E, sometimes referred to as the unlevered P/E = enterprise value/forward operating income = $100/$10 = 10. Both the enterprise P/B and the enterprise P/E remain unchanged after the change in leverage in the example; as always, only the levered multiples change. The relationship between the (levered) equity multiples and enterprise multiples is fixed and deterministic.

Valuation Principle 5a

Leverage reduces the P/E ratio from the enterprise P/E if the enterprise P/E is less than 1/Borrowing cost.

Equity P/E = Enterprise P/E + [Earnings leverage × (Enterprise P/E − 1/Borrowing cost)]
= 10 + [0.333 × (10 − 1/0.05)] = 6.67

(Continued)

(Leverage increases the equity P/E if enterprise P/E is greater than 1/Borrowing cost)

Valuation Principle 5b

Leverage increases the P/B ratio over the enterprise price-to-book if the enterprise price-to-book is greater than 1.0.

Equity P/B = Enterprise P/B + [Balance sheet leverage ×
(Enterprise P/B − 1)]
= 1.25 + [1.667 × (1.25 − 1)] = 1.67

(Leverage decreases the P/B ratio for an enterprise price-to-book less than 1.0)

An enterprise P/E less than 1/Borrowing cost implies an enterprise earnings yield (E/P) greater than the borrowing cost. So, in the example, the equity P/E is less than the enterprise P/E because the enterprise E/P of 10 percent is greater than the borrowing cost of 5 percent.[7] So for the equity P/E to increase over the enterprise P/E, the enterprise E/P would have to be quite low (or equivalently, the enterprise P/E would have to be quite high, over 20 in the example here).

With both P/B and P/E changing with leverage but price remaining unchanged, there are many traps for young players here. A stock screener who buys firms with low P/E ratios, thinking they are cheap, could be loading up on leverage risk, for leverage typically reduces P/E. A common belief (among asset pricing modelers, for example) holds that leverage increases book-to-price (justifying higher book-to-price as an indicator of risk in an asset pricing model). This is misconceived because book-to-price increases with leverage only if the enterprise book-to-price is greater than 1.0 (enterprise P/B is less than 1.0), which is typically not so. The investor can mishandle growth; leverage increases earnings growth and one typically thinks of earnings growth as increasing the P/E, so the naïve might price the share higher. But typically earnings growth induced by leverage decreases the P/E. The reason is that the leverage also increases the risk and the required return, which reduces the P/E, and this effect overwhelms the effect on earnings and earnings growth. The rational investor does not price the growth generated by leverage. The investor who prices earnings with a fixed P/E irrespective of leverage is in danger of bubble pricing. As it turns out, firms often lever more in bubbles, feeding the effect. The accounting must be done to avoid these traps.

Accounting for Leverage

The valuations above that yielded the same $10 share value were accomplished with an adjustment in the denominator for a higher required return. This is accounting for value of a sort, but it is hardly accounting. However, accounting can be brought to the task: Unlever the accounting numbers and develop the valuation from these unlevered numbers. In so doing, one protects from paying for profitability and growth generated by leverage.

Unlevering the accounting involves separating those accounting numbers that have to do with the business operations from those that have to do with financing activities. No alternative accounting measurement is involved, only a reshuffle of the numbers in the financial statements. To demonstrate, let's start with the balance sheet under GAAP and IFRS and identify assets and liabilities associated with the business enterprise and those associated with the financing of the business:

The Standard Balance Sheet	
Assets	**Liabilities and Equity**
Financial assets	Financial liabilities
Operating assets	Operating liabilities
	Shareholders' equity
Total assets	Total liabilities and equity

Operating assets are those employed in the business, like receivables, inventory, and plant. Operating liabilities are liabilities incurred in the course of business, like accounts payable, deferred revenues, and accrued expenses. Financial liabilities are the debt from raising cash to finance the business, like bonds payable and bank loans, whereas financial assets are (interest-bearing) debt in which the firm invests to hold "excess cash" not required for business operations (like cash equivalents and short-term debt investments). In fancier terms, operating assets and liabilities arise from trading in product and input markets (with customers and suppliers), whereas financial assets and liabilities arise from trading in debt markets to raise cash for the business and to store cash from the business. The distinction makes a clear break between assets and liabilities that add value for shareholders versus the (zero-net-present-value) assets and liabilities associated with financing activities that do not.

By netting assets and liabilities in these two categories against each other, common shareholders' equity is represented by net operating assets and net debt, as below. The numbers are for the exhibit 4.3 example and for General Mills, the large manufacturer and marketer of processed foods (Pillsbury, Progresso, Green Giant, Old El Paso, Häagen-Dazs, and Uncle Toby's being among its brands).

	The Unlevered Balance Sheet	
	The Example (2010)	General Mills (2008, in millions)
Net operating assets (Operating assets – Operating liabilities)	$80	12,847
Net debt (Financial liabilities – Financial assets)	50	6,389
Common shareholders' equity	$30	6,458

Net operating assets are sometimes referred to as net enterprise assets, invested capital, or enterprise book value. The standard GAAP and IFRS balance sheet, with its distinction between current and long-term assets and liabilities, is set up for credit analysis such that the balance sheet aggregates operating and financing items within current and long-term categories. This is apples to oranges as far as the equity analyst is concerned. The reformulated balance sheet here sets up the accounting numbers for valuation.[8]

Correspondingly, an unlevered income statement distinguishes enterprise income (from the business) from the net financing expenses associated with the financing activities:

The Unlevered Income Statement		
	The Example (2011)	General Mills (2009, in millions)
Operating income (after tax)	$10.00	1,544
Net financing expense (after tax)	$2.50	240
Earnings to common	$7.50	1,304

Net financing expense is the interest expense on the financial liabilities minus any interest income on financial assets (it could be called net interest expense but also includes preferred dividends, for these are financing expenses as far as the common shareholder is concerned). Both components of the income statement are after-tax.[9]

The reformulated statements yield the return on net operating assets, RNOA (otherwise called the enterprise rate-of-return) and the net borrowing cost, along with the balance sheet leverage.[10] For General Mills for 2009,

Return on net operating assets
$$(\text{RNOA}) = \$1,544/\$12,847 = 12.02\%$$
$$\text{Net borrowing cost} = \$240/\$6,389 = 3.76\%$$
$$\text{Balance sheet leverage} = \$6,389/\$6,458 = 0.989$$

The three measures determine ROCE, by *Accounting Principle 3b*. For General Mills, the ROCE of 20.2% for 2009 is

$$\text{ROCE} = 12.02\% + [0.989 \times (12.02\% - 3.76\%)] = 20.2\%.$$

An ROCE of 20.2 percent looks quite good. But one pulls back when it is appreciated that the return in the business is considerably less at 12.02 percent. The 8 percent difference is simply a premium for risk, and one that we should not pay for.[11]

With an eye on a valuation that protects us from paying for profitability generated by leverage, the unlevering also delivers a residual earnings number for operations that removes the effect of leverage on equity residual earnings:

$$
\begin{aligned}
\text{Residual operating income}_t &= \text{Operating income}_t \\
&\quad - (r \times \text{Net operating assets}_{t-1}) \\
&= (\text{RNOA}_t - r) \times \text{Net operating assets}_{t-1}
\end{aligned}
$$

(where r is the required return for operations, or the WACC, in business school jargon). In the example in exhibit 4.3, residual operating income is $2, in contrast to the residual earnings for equity of $3. For General Mills,

$$
\begin{aligned}
\text{Residual operating income}_{2009} &= \$1{,}544 - (0.075 \times \$12{,}847) \\
&= (0.1202 - 0.075) \times \$12{,}847 \\
&= \$580.5 \text{ million.}
\end{aligned}
$$

With the risk-free rate low at the time (less than 4 percent) and the low operating risk of this firm, a required return for operations of 7.5 percent has been applied.

With this unlevering, one can proceed directly to the equity valuation with the appreciation that Value of equity = Value of the operations – Value of net debt. For a two-year forecasting horizon, the value of the operations (enterprise value) is given by

$$
\begin{aligned}
\text{Value of operations}_0 &= \text{Net operating assets}_0 \\
&\quad + \frac{\text{Residual operating income}_1}{1 + r} \\
&\quad + \frac{\text{Residual operating income}_2}{(1 + r) \times r} \\
&\quad + \text{Value of speculative growth}
\end{aligned}
$$

Equity value = Value of operations – Value of net debt.

The value of the operations is simply what one would pay to buy the business without taking on its debt, and the value of the equity is the price of buying it with the debt. The book value of net debt is typically close to its value, but can be marked to market with market values usually reported in the debt footnote. This unlevered valuation was applied as an alternative valuation in exhibit 4.3. Applying it to General Mills, with just a one-year forecasting horizon and a forecast that residual operating income for 2010 will be the same $580.5 million as in 2009, the no-growth anchoring equity value is

$$\text{Value of equity}_{2009} = \$11,550 + \frac{580.5}{0.075} - 6,376 = \$12,914 \text{ million}$$

or $39.37 per share on 328 million outstanding shares. (The net operating assets of $11,550 million and net debt of $6,376 million are those on the balance sheet at the end of fiscal-year 2009.) By accounting for value appropriately we have protected ourselves from paying too much for the increased earnings per share, earnings growth, profitability, and residual earnings generated by leverage. We have not been fooled by the high 20.2 percent return on common equity. But note the accounting employed; we have unlevered the income statement and balance sheet to disentangle the leverage effects.

General Mills's stock traded at $50 in early fiscal 2010, so this no-growth valuation imputes $10.63 to the value of speculative growth in the market price. The implied residual earning growth rate to be challenged (as in Chapter 3) is 2.3 percent. But, importantly, this is now the residual operating income growth rate, the growth in the business. That makes enormous sense as we do not want to challenge levered growth, for growth added by leverage is not valued. Accounting for value challenges the growth rate for the business, not levered numbers.

The drivers of (levered) residual earnings, laid out in Chapter 2, are ROCE and the book value of common equity. Correspondingly, the drivers of (unlevered) residual operating income are the rate-of-return on net operating assets, RNOA, and the book value of net operating assets. A firm grows residual operating income by increasing RNOA or

Figure 4.1a: Evolution of Residual Operating Income Over Time

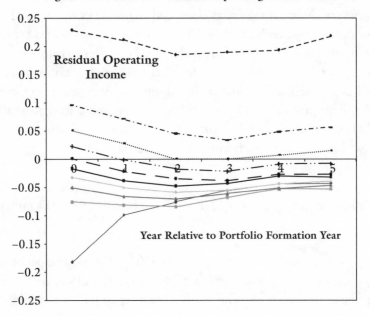

Figure 4.1b: Evolution of Rate-of-Return on Net Operating Assets (RNOA) Over Time

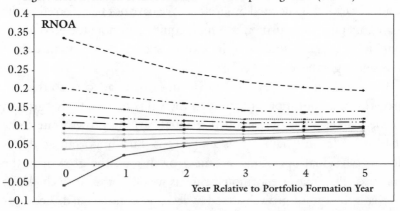

FIGURE 4.1   Path of (a) Residual Operating Income and (b) Rate-of-Return in Business Operations (RNOA) for Ten Portfolios Formed on the Level of Each Measure in the Base Year (Year 0), for Base Years in the Period 1963–1999.

Residual operating income in figure 4.1a is deflated by the net operating assets in the base year. Source: Doron Nissim and Stephen H. Penman, "Ratio Analysis and Equity Valuation: From Research to Practice," *Review of Accounting Studies* 6 (2001), 140–141. Copyright and with kind permission of Springer Science and Business Media.

by growing investments in net operating assets. Figure 4.1a shows how residual operating income typically evolves over time for different levels of residual operating income in base years. It is simply the unlevered equivalent of figure 2.1 in Chapter 2 (and is constructed in the same way). As for unlevered residual earnings in figure 2.1, residual operating income typically reverts toward the median in the first three years, but subsequently no-growth is typical (though, as before, there is a slight upward tilt to the whole graph, indicative of the growth that was suggested for the S&P 500 in the last chapter).

Figure 4.1b depicts the typical evolution of RNOA. This "fade diagram" shows the same mean reversion for the RNOA; as most analysts recognize, profitability fades toward the average (of about 10 percent here) over a "competitive advantage period" as competition sets in, though firms in the higher RNOA groups are able to sustain high (though decreasing) RNOA on average. The relative constancy of residual income in figure 4.1a in association with changing RNOA is due to the second driver; although a firm's RNOA may decline, it maintains residual income because of growth in book value.

Stock Repurchases and Growth

The growth and profitability effects are evident with any increase in leverage, but the example in exhibit 4.3 explicitly introduced leverage with a stock repurchase to make another point. When announcing share repurchases, firms often state that they do so to increase EPS. A survey indicates that 76 percent of surveyed CFOs say that increasing EPS was an important factor in share repurchase decisions.[12] Indeed the claim is legitimate; the example demonstrates that stock repurchases increase EPS. But there is slight-of-hand in the claim; the example also demonstrates that the increase in EPS does not add value to the price—it's just an accounting effect. The economics also so declare that one cannot add value by buying stock at fair market value. Don't add value because EPS has increased from a stock repurchase. Add to EPS, but decrease the P/E to keep price the same. To do so, unlever the accounting and the valuation.

Is the market fooled by increases in EPS from stock repurchases? If so, management might well entertain the practice, but they will be contributing to a price bubble that, with the added leverage involved to finance the stock repurchase, may prove dangerous to shareholders.[13] Indeed, firms that levered stock repurchases with borrowing in the 1990s and early 2000s ran into "balance sheet problems" in the subsequent financial crisis as leverage became unfavorable and debt became hard to refinance.

Share repurchases at fair market value do not add value, but repurchases at fair value below market value do. Indeed, the same survey that reported that 76 percent of respondents made stock repurchases to increase EPS also reported that 86 percent of CFOs say they repurchase when they consider their stock to be good value. They compare price with value. In 2010, Microsoft Corporation borrowed (for the first time), reportedly to finance stock repurchases. With stock prices low at the time and the cost of borrowing at records lows, this seemed like a pure arbitrage play: Sell debt, buy (own) stock. The market seemed to think so: The stock price rose by 5.3 percent on the announcement.

Accounting for Growth from Leverage

Most investors know that leverage is dangerous, for it turns on you when things go sour. But fewer appreciate that there are dangers when it comes to valuation. Here are the main takeaways from this chapter.

First, although investors are often advised to "buy earnings" and earnings growth, do not buy earnings that simply come from investment growth. Buy residual earnings and residual earnings growth, for these add value.

Second, in focusing on residual earnings, be wary of leverage. Leverage increases EPS, earnings growth, and ROCE, and it also increases residual earnings. One needs a very good story to buy earnings generated by leverage, for leverage typically adds risk but does not add value.

Third, to protect yourself from paying for leverage, unlever the accounting numbers. Employ an accounting for value based on income and net assets that pertain to the business operations rather than levered earnings and book values.

Finally, beware of levered P/B and P/E multiples. Leverage typically increases the P/B and decreases the P/E, but does not change price. Work with unlevered (enterprise) P/B and P/E ratios.

Concern with growth does not end here. This chapter has separated growth from the business from growth from leverage, but that brings the focus to evaluating growth from the business. That is growth to be valued indeed, but there one can still overpay for growth. For this discussion, we turn to the next chapter.

CHAPTER FIVE

Accounting for Growth in the Business (and More Protection from Paying Too Much for Growth)

HAVING ADOPTED UNLEVERED ACCOUNTING, the investor can focus where it matters—on the business where the firm adds value. Businesses promise growth and the market prices growth, but the investor is wary. He or she seeks an accounting for growth that, like accounting for leverage, provides protection from paying too much for growth.

The previous chapter helps, for it identifies residual earnings growth rather than earnings growth as the measure of value added. One is thus protected from buying earnings growth that does not add value. That chapter also shifts the focus to residual income from business operations rather than levered residual earnings. However, residual operating income is an accounting measure, so it depends on how the accounting is done. Different accounting methods generate different income, and indeed different residual income, but accounting should not affect a valuation. *Beware of earnings generated by accounting.* But fear not because appropriate accounting for value provides protection.

Beware of Profitability Generated by Accounting

The point can be appreciated fairly quickly with a simple example. Suppose you purchase some inventory at the end of 2010. Your accountant records the inventory investment on your year-end balance sheet at its cost of $100. You expect to sell the inventory for $110 in 2011 and then close down the enterprise. You take on no leverage. Your hurdle rate for investment is 10 percent. This is a simple business, much like your one-time lemonade stand. The accounting for the business and its value is below.

Accounting Treatment I

	2010	2011
Revenue		$110
Cost of goods sold		<u>100</u>
Operating income	$0	<u>10</u>
Book value of net operating assets	$100	0
RNOA = $10/$100		10%
Residual operating income = $10 − (0.10 × 100)		0
Value of the operations = Book value = **$100**		
Price-to-book (P/B) 1.0		
Forward P/E ($100/$10) 10		

The inventory on the balance sheet becomes the cost of goods sold when sold in 2011, yielding operating income (and earnings) of $10 when expensed against the $110 revenue from the sale. Thus the profitability of the investment—your RNOA for this business—is expected to be 10 percent. Your required return is 10 percent, so you forecast zero residual operating income and, with no residual income to add to book value, you value the enterprise at book value, $100, and at a P/B of 1.0 and a forward P/E of 10. With no leverage, $100 is also the value of your equity.

Now suppose that your accountant decides to write down the inventory to $80 on the 2010 balance sheet. The accounting and valuation for the business now run as follows:

Accounting Treatment II

	2010	2011
Revenue		$110
Cost of goods sold		80
Operating income	$(20)	$30
Book value of net operating assets	$80	0
RNOA = $30/$80		37.5%
Residual earnings = $30 − (0.10 × 80)		$22

$$\text{Value of the Operations} = \$80 + \frac{\$22}{1.10} = \$100$$

Price-to-book (P/B) ($100/$80)   1.25
Forward P/E ($100/$30)   3.33

The write-down incurs a charge of $20 to earnings in 2010 but, with lower cost of goods sold in 2011, produces higher earnings from the revenue. The accountant has effectively shifted earnings from year 2010 to 2011. The expected book rate-of-return, RNOA, is now $30/$80 = 37.5 percent. The accountant has also added to residual income, now $22 = $30 − (0.10 × $80) rather than zero. That is growth, but is it growth you would pay for? Clearly it is not; accounting methods cannot affect the value we get from a business. The stock market might be fooled (perhaps by multiplying the $30 in earnings by the same P/E multiplier of 10), but not so the disciplined analyst. Our accounting for value still yields a value of $100; we have been protected from paying too much for growth.

GAAP and IFRS accounting allow inventory write-downs only under restricted conditions.[1] The example, however, is illustrative of the effect of a number of accounting practices. View the $100 investment as $80 invested in inventory and $20 in advertising, the latter an investment to entice customers that GAAP requires to be expensed immediately. See the $20 as an investment in marketing research or product research that must be expensed, or as other start-up costs that also must be expensed immediately. GAAP requires firms to write down

("impair") plant under certain conditions, reducing future depreciation and thus increasing future profitability, all else being equal. Accelerated depreciation will yield the same effects, as will excessive reserv-
ing. Indeed the effects can flow from the revenue side. When launching
iPhone in 2007, Apple promised customers free subsequent software
upgrades at little additional cost to Apple. "In accordance with GAAP,"
the firm deferred substantial revenue from the sale of iPhones to the
future rather than booking it immediately. Deferred ("unearned") revenues on the balance sheet increased from $1.425 billion in 2006 to
$15.015 billion in 2009 as sales of the iPhone grew. Analysts worth their
salt knew these deferred revenues would run through to the income
statement in the future, increasing profitability significantly and adding to earnings growth. The firm was shifting earnings to the future
(in accordance with GAAP).

Businesses are going concerns, but the accounting effects in the one-
period firm also turn up with going concerns. Indeed the effects persist, so additional issues arise. Look at the accounting for the going
concern in exhibit 5.1. The firm is set up to look like the one-period
business rolled over many times. In the first panel (Accounting Treatment I), the firm begins with an investment of $100 in 2010, books the
investment to the balance sheet, and then earns at 10 percent on that
investment in 2011. But it continues with $100 of new investment each
year thereafter with the same accounting reporting earnings at 10 percent on the investment. With full payout of earnings as dividends,
book value remains the same each year; there is no growth in earnings
or book value. With a required return of 10 percent and residual income of zero, the firm is worth its book value. The P/B is 1.0 and the
forward P/E is 10. The business is unlevered (to remove the issues of
the last chapter), so the numbers are both for the operations and the
equity, and the value of the operations equals the value of the equity.

The second panel in exhibit 5.1 applies the alternative treatment (Accounting Treatment II): Twenty percent of the investment is expensed
immediately each year, reducing the book value of net operating assets
on the balance sheet. You could see this as a write-down of inventory
each year but, closer to practice, see the $100 investment each year as an
investment of $80 in inventory and $20 in advertising to sell the inventory in the following year.[2] This is U.S. GAAP and IFRS accounting at

EXHIBIT 5.1 Accounting for Value Under Different Accounting Treatments for Investments: The No-Growth Case.

Accounting Treatment I: Booking Investment to the Balance Sheet

	2010	2011	2012	2013	2014
Income Statement					
Revenue		$110	110	110	110
Cost of goods sold		$100	100	100	100
Operating income		$10	10	10	10
Balance Sheet					
Net operating assets = Equity	$100	100	100	100	100
Investment	$100	100	100	100	100
Dividends		$10	10	10	10
RNOA		10%	10%	10%	10%
Operating profit margin		9.1%	9.1%	9.1%	9.1%
Residual operating income = $10 − (0.10 × 100)		0	0	0	0

Value of the operations = Book value = **$100**
Price/book (P/B)   1.0
Forward P/E   10

Accounting Treatment II: Expensing 20% of Investment Immediately

	2010	2011	2012	2013	2014
Income Statement					
Revenue		$110	110	110	110
Cost of goods sold		$ 80	80	80	80
Advertising		20	20	20	20
Operating income	$(20)	10	10	10	10
Balance Sheet					
Net operating assets = Equity	$80	80	80	80	80
Investment	$100	100	100	100	100
Dividends		$10	10	10	10
RNOA		12.5%	12.5%	12.5%	12.5%
Operating profit margin		9.1%	9.1%	9.1%	9.1%
Residual operating income = $10 − (0.10 × 80)		$2	2	2	2

Value of the operations = $80 + $\dfrac{\$2}{0.10}$ = $100

Price/Book (P/B)   1.25
Forward P/E   10

work where advertising expenditures must be expensed when incurred, even though the revenue from the advertising has not been earned. In accounting parlance, it involves "mismatching" of revenues with the expenses incurred to generate them.

Note the accounting effects. Book value is permanently $80 rather than $100, due to the expensing of what otherwise would have been an advertising asset (a brand asset). Earnings are unchanged from Accounting Treatment I: Earnings in 2011 would have been $30, as in the one-period business, but now the $20 of advertising incurred in 2011 is expensed in that year to restore expenses to what they would have been with the appropriate matching. The lower book value increases the book rate-of-return, RNOA, to 12.5 percent (the same income on lower net operating assets). Due to the higher book rate-of-return, residual income is no longer zero. The P/B ratio has increased to 1.25, but the P/E ratio is unchanged. Finally, despite the different accounting treatments, the accounting for value yields the same value of $100.

These examples make four points.

First, while earnings at $10 are unaffected (in this no-growth case), Accounting Treatment II adds residual earnings that do not represent added value. Firms can produce earnings and residual earnings with inventory write-downs, as in the one-period example, or with impairments and restructuring charges to any asset (that reduce further depreciation and other expenses). They will generate residual earnings under the GAAP and IFRS requirement to expense R&D investments and brand-building advertising expenditures. Just as in the one-period example, Cisco Systems took a $2.2 billion charge to its inventory in 2001 after the collapse of the telecom bubble left it facing a secondhand market with excess inventory; the result was higher profit margins in subsequent periods than would otherwise be reported. Tyco increased the reported earnings from its mergers by taking merger charges that would otherwise increase expenses later. Firms can produce higher expected revenues with "deferred revenue" recognition (deferring revenue to the future), as with Apple. Firms can accrue higher expenses, reducing current income but increasing future income. These practices are sometimes referred to as cookie jar accounting—creating a cookie jar that can be dipped into in the future. Firms reported considerable earnings growth in the 1990s, which investors took to be value-adding growth. But some of that growth came from the large restructuring charges of the early 1990s and later dipping into cookie jars. Earnings growth, so constructed, produces earnings momentum that in turn can lead to price momentum; that is, a recipe for a bubble.[3]

The second point warns about using book rates-of-return (return on common equity or return on net operating assets) as an indication of business profitability. Before the inventory write-down, the one-period business was expected to earn a 10 percent return, but 37.5 percent after the write-down. For the going concern, RNOA increased from 10 to 12.5 percent with the different accounting treatment. Yet it is the same business with the same value of $100. Clearly, the difference in the book rates-of-return is an artifact of the accounting employed rather than enhanced business profitability. This is the case when firms expense R&D and brand-building expenditures, carry inventory at LIFO (last in, first out), accelerate depreciation (with short estimated asset lives), or keep intangible assets off the balance sheet. Indeed, this will always be the case when accountants keep book values low on the balance sheet for any reason; a lower book value results in a higher book rate-of-return (all else constant). This point is so important as to warrant a statement as *Accounting Principle 4*:

Accounting Principle 4

Book rate-of-return is an accounting measure determined by how one accounts for book value. It is not necessarily a measure of real business profitability. Accounting that keeps book values lower generates higher book rates-of-return and higher residual earnings.

R&D firms and brand-name firms are good examples of where assets are kept low on the balance sheet; GAAP (and IFRS to a lesser degree) demand that investments in R&D and brand-building must be expensed to the income statement immediately rather than placed on the balance sheet. Thus the Coca-Cola Company reported an RNOA of 26 percent in 2007, and Pfizer, the pharmie, 21 percent, well in excess of the 10-percent return we expect as normal for businesses. Cisco Systems had an RNOA of 40.1 percent in 2009. Do these firms have abnormally high returns on their business investments? Is Coca-Cola really more profitable than Pfizer? Well, maybe or maybe not, but these accounting rates-of-return cannot be taken as evidence. They simply represent that earnings from these investments are flowing through their income statements, but the assets that generate the income are missing from their balance sheets, due to the accounting that typically excludes most intangible assets from the balance sheet.

Under GAAP and IFRS, intangible assets (like a patent or copyright) are booked to the balance sheet if purchased, as are "identifiable intangible assets" and "goodwill" purchased in an acquisition. This almost always lowers reported profitability, making the acquisition appear unprofitable when in fact it may be otherwise. With $35 billion added to its balance sheet as goodwill on its acquisition of Gillette in 2006, Procter & Gamble's RNOA decreased from 28.8 to 12.7 percent. This is not necessarily indicative of the effect of the merger on shareholder value but rather due to intangible assets being brought onto the balance sheet.

Economists often talk of the "economic rate-of-return" as the real profitability of investment. The notion yields useful insights in theory but when it comes down to putting a finger on it, there is no such thing. It is never observed. To put it differently, it can only be observed by doing some accounting; it is a product of the accounting employed to measure it. Consultants market various measures of economic profit (sometimes under names like "economic value added," "shareholder value added," or just "economic profit"), but when all is said and done these are just accounting measures, a different measurement method from GAAP.[4] Beware of appeals to "economic profit"; it cannot be observed, it is not concrete, it is in the eye of the speculator.

With economic profitability in mind, analysts often talk of rates-of-return reverting to "normal" rates-of-return, meaning the required return for the risk born. They talk of a "competitive advantage period" over which the rate-of-return is expected to fade to a normal rate after the effects of competition set in; economics tells us that firms just earn a normal return under competition. For valuation, they advise us to forecast to a forecast horizon where the rate-of-return is expected to be normal, that is, equal to the cost-of-capital (say, 10 percent). This is a misconception. Although one might think of unobservable economic rates-of-return to be normal in the long run, not so observable book rates-of-return. The book rate-of-return for our going concern under Accounting Treatment II is 12.5 percent, indefinitely. Figure 4.1b in the previous chapter shows that, although RNOA typically reverts towards a central level (of about 10 percent), there are permanent differences across firms in the long run: A firm with a high RNOA now is likely to have a relatively high RNOA in the future. This may be due to "durable competitive advantage" but the accounting is also at work. Catastrophe aside, we don't expect the rate-of-return for Coca-Cola, Merck, or Pfizer ever to be 10 percent (or whatever their required return is); even though they might have normal economic profitability, their accounting rates-of-return will always be higher because of the accounting for book value.

If one must rely on an observable but possibly suspect accounting measure, where does this leave us? The third point is the good news. Accounting for value finesses the problem of not being able to observe real economic profitability. A built-in feature protects us from attributing value to profitability that is merely by construction of the accounting. By following the accounting for value of Chapter 2, the value of both the one-period business and the going concern above is $100, invariant to the accounting treatment. This is because of the way accounting works: One cannot increase future earnings without decreasing current book values. Thus, even though Accounting Treatment II increases future residual earnings, the calculated value is unaffected because the lower book value is also carried along in the valuation to offset the higher earnings. Although the value of the going concern under Accounting Treatment I is equal to a book value of $100, the value under Accounting Treatment II is also $100 because the higher residual earnings of $2 is matched with a lower book value of $80:

$$\text{Value of operations}_{2010} = \text{Book value of net operating assets}_{2010}$$
$$+ \frac{\text{Residual operating income}_{2011}}{r}$$
$$= \$80 + \frac{2}{0.10} = \$100.$$

The lower book value offsets the higher residual earnings generated by the accounting exactly, to conserve the value calculated under the alternative accounting treatment. This is very nice! So much so that we must formally state a valuation principle to add to those earlier:

Valuation Principle 6

Accounting for value produces valuations that correct for the accounting employed; as earnings can be generated by accounting methods only by reducing book value, the appropriate valuation is preserved by employing book value and earnings together.

We see this principle operating in Procter & Gamble's acquisition of Gillette. Though the acquisition reduced the RNOA from 28.8 to 12.7 percent, it also added $35 billion to the balance sheet. The two offset in valuation, to cancel each other. So any increase in valuation from the merger would have to come from real effects on the RNOA—marketing efficiencies, cost reduction and other "synergies"—rather than the accounting effects of the merger. Rather than frustrating the valuation, the accounting is working to capture any value added. But note: Never buy a firm because it has a high book rate-of-return.

The fourth point sends a warning about handling multipliers. In the one-period example, the earnings shift left value unchanged, but increased the P/B ratio from 1.0 to 1.25. (Well, of course; if the return on book value increases from 10 to 37.5 percent because book value is lower, the book value must be priced higher!) The forward P/E decreased to $100/$30 = $3.33 from the P/E of 10 before the earnings shift. That is how it should be; that is, a good deal of the $30 is earnings we are not willing to pay for—$20 of it is solely an accounting effect—so it should get a lower multiplier. Those who value firms with standard multipliers without regard to the accounting (as analysts are wont to do) run the danger of applying the P/E of 10 (or the usual P/E for the firm or the industry, they might say) to the $30 of earnings, producing a value of $300. That's a bubble price based on bubble earnings from the accountant. The appropriate accounting for value provides the protection. (I will show in later chapters how appropriate accounting cuts across bubble accounting, which can be very deceptive.) In the going concern, P/B also increased from 1.0 to 1.25, but the P/E remained at 10. But this is a case with no growth in investment, and growth in investment introduces additional issues to which I turn in the next section.

The practice of keeping book values low in the balance sheet is referred to as conservative accounting, and *Accounting Principle 4* is a statement of its effects. The U.S. GAAP and IFRS requirements to expense advertising is conservative accounting (which keeps the brand asset off the balance sheet). But it is just one example. R&D investments are also expensed as incurred (though less under IFRS), omitting a technology asset from the balance sheet. Conservative accounting can also be applied by reporting assets that are in fact booked to the balance sheet at low carrying values. Firms can carry net property, plant, and equipment at low amounts by expensing with accelerated depreciation (with short estimated asset lives). Other cases involve the expensing of start-up costs, LIFO accounting for inventories, excessive reserves for credit losses, excessive allowances for warranties, and of course, the restructuring charges and asset impairments that yield more future earnings. The same effects can arise from the deferral of revenue to the future (that books higher liabilities on the balance sheet). In some cases conservative accounting is a requirement of GAAP (as with advertising and R&D expensing). In other cases, it is a matter of accounting policy choice, perhaps imposed by conservative auditors wary of lawsuits. Whatever the reason, conservative accounting keeps book values low in the balance sheet and defers earnings to the future, producing higher book rates-of-return, higher residual earnings, and higher P/B ratios.[5]

Figure 4.1a of the last chapter shows that firms tend to have different levels of residual income permanently. We now understand why. This is not necessarily because they have different real profitability. Maybe so, but firms have different accounting for the balance sheet—different degrees of conservative accounting—yielding different RNOA and book value, the two drivers of residual operating income. But we also understand that valuation is not affected by these differences in the accounting.

Beware of Growth Generated by Accounting

In the example in exhibit 5.1, investment is at a constant level each year, and so are earnings and book value. Accordingly, residual income, though higher under the conservative accounting treatment, is also constant. But typically firms grow investments and that has an additional effect: Even though growing investment may not add value, the accounting produces residual earnings growth.

Exhibit 5.2 examines the same going concern with the same two alternative accounting treatments, but now with growing investment. The initial investment is again $100, with 80 percent in inventory and 20 percent in advertising. Both investments grow at 5 percent per year, producing sales growth also of 5 percent.

With Accounting Treatment I, both investments are booked to the balance sheet ("capitalized," as accountants say) and then expensed against sales in the following year (the inventory becomes cost of goods sold and the advertising investment is "amortized" to the income statement). You can see that the investment growth adds to earnings but does not add value; the book rate-of-return is 10 percent per year and residual earnings are zero. Accordingly, despite the growth, no value is added and the firm is worth its book value of $100. This is the protection from paying too much for investment growth that we saw with Tyco in the last chapter.[6]

With Accounting Treatment II, the conservative accounting treatment, the growing investments are accounted for under an accounting policy of expensing 20 percent of investment (advertising) each year. With growing advertising expensed as incurred, higher expenses are recorded against those sales, so earnings are depressed below those under Accounting Treatment I (and indeed below the earnings for the same accounting treatment with no growth in exhibit 5.1). The profit margin, which we might be tempted to think of as a "real" markup, drops from 9.1 percent in Accounting Treatment I to 8.2 percent, simply because of the accounting. With a lower book value, the conservative accounting reports a book rate-of-return higher than 10 percent, but now 11.25 percent rather than the 12.5 percent with no growth in exhibit 5.1 (because the advertising growth depresses the numerator, the earnings). But here is the important point, the punch line: For the same business we now

EXHIBIT 5.2 Accounting for Value Under Different Accounting Treatments for Investments: The Growth Case.

Accounting Treatment I: Booking Investment to the Balance Sheet

	2010	2011	2012	2013	2014
Income Statement					
Revenue		$110.00	$115.50	$121.28	$127.34
Cost of goods sold		$80.00	$ 84.00	88.20	92.61
Advertising		$20.00	21.00	22.05	23.15
Operating income		$10.00	10.50	11.03	11.58
Balance Sheet					
Net operating assets = Equity	$100	105.00	110.25	115.76	121.55
Investment	$100	105.00	110.25	115.76	121.55
Dividends		$5.00	5.25	5.52	5.79
RNOA		10%	10%	10%	10%
Operating profit margin		9.1%	9.1%	9.1%	9.1%
Residual operating income = $10 − (0.10 × 100)		0	0	0	0

Value of the operations = Book value = $100
Price/book (P/B)   1.0
Forward P/E   10

Accounting Treatment II: Expensing 20% of Investment Immediately

	2010	2011	2012	2013	2014
Income Statement					
Revenue		$110.00	$115.50	$121.28	$127.34
Cost of goods sold		$80.00	84.00	88.20	92.61
Advertising	$(20)	21.00	22.05	23.15	24.31
Operating income	$(20)	9.00	9.45	9.92	10.42
Balance Sheet					
Net operating assets = Equity	$80	84.00	88.20	92.61	97.24
Investment	$100	105.00	110.25	115.76	121.55
Dividends		$5.00	5.25	5.52	5.79
RNOA		11.25%	11.25%	11.25%	11.25%
Operating profit margin		8.2%	8.2%	8.2%	8.2%
Residual operating income (10% charge)		1.00	1.05	1.1025	1.1576
Residual income growth rate			5%	5%	5%

Value of the operations $= \$80 + \dfrac{\$1}{0.10 - 0.05} = \mathbf{\$100}$

Price/book (P/B)   1.25
Forward P/E   11.11

have residual income growth of 5 percent per year. This is solely a result of the conservative accounting when investments are growing; investment growth and conservative accounting interact to produce residual earnings growth. The point is stated as another accounting principle:

Accounting Principle 5

Conservative accounting with investment growth induces growth in residual income.

However, again, growth induced by the accounting is not to be paid for: The value is still $100 and accounting for value protects us from paying for it. Simply adjust the capitalization rate of 10 percent for the induced growth:

$$\text{Value of operations}_{2010} = \text{Net operating assets}_{2010}$$
$$+ \frac{\text{Residual operating income}_{2011}}{r - g}$$
$$= \$80 + \frac{1}{0.10 - 0.05} = \$100.$$

The P/B ratio has, once again, increased from 1.0 to 1.25 with the conservative accounting treatment, but now the forward P/E has also increased, from 10 to 11.11. This is, of course, correct: Forward operating income is depressed by the investment growth so, for the same value of $100, the P/E multiple must be higher. Or put differently, P/E reflects residual earnings growth (see Chapter 2) and residual earnings growth has increased.

Hidden Reserves and Liquidation of Hidden Reserves

Conservative accounting reduces income and pushes it to the future, thus adding growth. The effect creates a hidden profit reserve that runs back into income later. But it can also work the other way; just as increasing investment reduces income and profit margins, reducing investment increases income and profit margins. In other words, increasing investment creates hidden reserves, and reducing investments liquidates those reserves. This is clear in the case of R&D; that is, increasing R&D expenditure reduces current income and reducing R&D spending increases income. If R&D investment were booked to the balance sheet, that would not happen. The same applies with advertising. Indeed, the same applies with any form of conservative accounting. In one case, the effect is explicitly tracked: A firm using LIFO—conservative accounting for inventories—must report (in footnotes) the amount of its "LIFO reserve" (the amount of unrecognized profit built up by applying LIFO) and any change in the LIFO reserve.

The change in the LIFO reserve is the amount by which income has been reduced by increasing inventory purchases or has been increased by reducing purchases. The disclosure provides a warning to the analyst: A firm can increase income and margins by reducing its investment in inventories. It's called LIFO dipping—dipping into the LIFO reserve. The effect is perverse, because lower inventories mean lower future income, yet current income is higher, a poor forecast of the future. But the same applies for all aspects of conservative accounting, though unfortunately the effects are not explicitly disclosed. In extrapolating from current income and margins, the analyst must be careful. This is a quality-of-earnings issue: one can get a misread of future profitability by observing current profitability.

Figure 5.1 illustrates this concept. Year 0 is the year when a change in the hidden reserve from conservative accounting for inventory, R&D, and brand building (advertising) is observed. A Q-score—a quality-of-earnings score—is calculated for each firm based on the change in the reserve. A high Q-score indicates operating income (and RNOA) depressed by increasing investment, and a low Q-score indicates income (and RNOA) inflated by dipping into reserves by slowing investment. The figure plots RNOA for five years before and after year 0. For the five years before year 0, RNOA for the high Q group declines as investment depresses income, but subsequently levels off. But RNOA for the low Q group, equal to that for high Q in year 0, subsequently declines significantly: The RNOA spread between the two groups one year ahead is 1.5 percent, quite significant to a residual operating income calculation, and the difference persists up to five years.

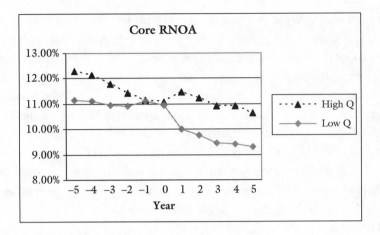

FIGURE 5.1   Path of Return on Net Operating Assets (RNOA) for High and Low Q-Scores, for U.S. Listed Firms, 1975–1997.

The Q-score is a measure of how operating income is affected by changing investment with conservative accounting for inventories, R&D, and advertising. A high Q-score indicates a relatively large income-decreasing effect and a low Q-score indicates a relatively high income-increasing effect. The high Q-score group consists of firms with the top third of scores in each year, and the low Q-score group the firms with the lowest third of scores. Source: Stephen H. Penman and Xiao-Jun Zhang, "Accounting Conservatism, the Quality of Earnings, and Stock Returns," *The Accounting Review* 77 (2002), 249. Copyright and with permission of the American Accounting Association.

The RNOA of low Q firms, bolstered temporarily by dipping into their profit reserve, could not be sustained.

The analyst might keep these patterns in mind when forecasting future operating residual earnings. Proceeding with valuation in the prescribed way will then protect him or her. (The analyst might make some calls on accounting standard setters to help out here, as I will do in Chapter 9.) One might be tempted to throw up one's hands and say, "Accounting is too complicated, too many traps; I'm going back to cash accounting and discounted cash flow valuation!" That would be a mistake, for it only compounds the problem. Free cash flow in those valuations is cash flow minus investment, so the same problem arises, but in the extreme. A firm reduces free cash flow in making an investment and increases it by reducing investment. That is perverse, for investment begets higher future cash flows.

Starbucks Corporation: A Promise of Growth

I have illustrated the accounting and valuation effects with a modified version of the savings account that introduced accounting for value in Chapter 2. This allows us to see the effects clearly. But is this how it works in the real world? The answer is yes; the effects are deterministic, fixed effects by construction of the accounting. That is to say, the effects are a certainty among the uncertainties we must handle in valuation. Nevertheless, you might be frustrated by constructed examples, so let's illustrate with an actual company.

Starbucks has built a far-flung franchise that has made it almost a household word. Growth under a franchise is the type of growth that fundamental value investors will buy, for they see the franchise, with its brand recognition, protecting the growth. The franchise indeed has delivered growth, as the revenue, income, and (most importantly) the residual operating income numbers in exhibit 5.3 indicate. The firm's stock price increased from $2.64 in 1995 to a high of $38 in 2006, settling at $22 by the end of 2009, a handsome return (the firm also paid dividends).

So much for after-the-fact success, but would a fundamentalist have bought Starbucks in 1995 on a promise of growth? He or she would have qualms. Starbucks was trading at an enterprise P/B of 4.4, with an enterprise P/E of 63; rather pricey. By 1999 (at the end of the period in the first panel in exhibit 5.3), those multiples were still high at 5.3 and 51, respectively. The investor was offered many promises of franchise value at the time, with IPOs coming to market asking similar in-the-sky multiples. (Remember Krispy Kreme Doughnuts, Planet Hollywood, priceline.com, and other hot stocks that did not fulfill their promise?) This was a time when speculation about growth was rampant. Would the accounting have helped sort things out?

If the investor were evaluating Starbucks' stock in 1999, the accounting (in the first panel in exhibit 5.3) would give pause. He or she would observe tremendous sales and asset growth from 1995–1999 and indeed significant operating income growth. But, the number that really matters, residual operating income, is not impressive; the average residual income over the five years (with a 10 percent charge for the required return) was about zero, with little growth (though somewhat higher in

EXHIBIT 5.3   Analysis of the Profitability and Pricing of Starbucks Corporation for Two Periods, 1995–1999 and 2005–2009.

(Dollar amount in millions, except per-share numbers)

Early Stage, 1995–1999

	1995	1996	1997	1998	1999
Revenue	$465	696	967	1,308	1,608
Operating income	$24	31	53	65	98
Net operating assets	$343	413	578	726	934
Net operating asset growth	79.0%	20.5%	40.0%	25.6%	28.7%
Operating profit margin	5.2%	4.5%	5.5%	5.0%	6.1%
Asset turnover	1.7	1.8	2.0	2.0	1.9
RNOA	9.1%	8.2%	10.7%	10.0%	11.8%
Residual operating income	$(2.3)	(6.7)	3.7	0.0	15.4
Free cash flow	$(127)	(39)	(112)	(73)	(84)
Stock price	$2.64	4.28	4.36	5.77	6.64
Enterprise P/B	4.4	6.4	4.9	5.7	5.3
Enterprise trailing P/E	63	85	53	64	51

Mature Stage, 2005–2009

	2005	2006	2007	2008	2009
Revenue	$6,369	7,787	9,412	10,383	9,775
Operating income	$468	581	673	511	602
Net operating assets	$2,081	2,532	3,180	3,483	2,973
Net operating asset growth	12.8%	21.7%	25.3%	9.5%	–14.6%
Operating profit margin	7.6%	7.5%	7.2%	4.9%	6.2%
Asset turnover	3.2	3.4	3.3	3.1	3.0
RNOA	24.8%	25.2%	23.6%	15.3%	18.6%
Residual operating income	$289.7	350.4	387.4	177.9	279.2
Free cash flow	$250	230	142	149	981
Stock price	$30.5	35.3	23.4	8.9	21.9
Enterprise P/B	11.2	10.5	5.4	1.9	5.4
Enterprise P/E	46	46	26	20	24

Operating income, profit margin, and RNOA are after-tax and exclude gains on asset sales and other one-time items. Asset turnover is revenue/net operating assets. Both RNOA and asset turnover are based on average balances of net operating assets over the year. Residual operating income applies a charge of 10 percent for the required return. Stock prices are on a 2009 post-split basis. Numbers in parentheses are negative.

1999). That means the no-growth valuation is equal to book value, $1.54 per share, in contrast to market price of $6.64 in 1999, and the no-growth P/B is 1.0 rather than the market's 5.3. The accounting explains why: Despite the high sales growth, Starbucks' profit margins were low—on the order of 5 percent in the exhibit. Further, it required considerable, increasing investment in net operating assets to support the sales growth. The combination of the resultant asset turnover (sales relative to net operating assets) of about 2.0 with the 5 percent margins produced an RNOA of only 10 percent, on average; the same as the 10 percent charge for the required return. (By the Dupont decomposition, RNOA = Profit margin × Asset turnover.) Starbucks was not adding value from growing sales; by *Valuation Principle 2* in Chapter 2, one should price a firm above book value only if one expects the rate of return to be greater than the required return. The implied growth forecast in Mr. Market's asking price of $6.64 in 1999 (calculated as in Chapter 3) was 9.8 percent. Against the accounting benchmarks, this looks excessive.

The accounting points to where the investor looks to challenge the market's growth rate; this firm must not only maintain sales growth but must also increase the amount of sales it generates from its assets. In the parlance of retailing, same-store sales must increase significantly. And/or, Starbucks must increase its profit margins from those sales. If we had forecast in 1999 that sales growth would continue up to 2002 at the 1999 rate of 22.9 percent, the profit margin would increase to 8 percent and the asset turnover to 2.5; the no-growth valuation (applying the accounting for value in Chapter 2) would have been $2.78. If we added a 4 percent GDP growth rate for the years after 2002, the valuation would have been $3.68. With this sort of scenario testing, we are really negotiating with Mr. Market!

But there is one further aspect of the accounting to check. During 1995–1999, Starbucks looks very much like the growth case under Accounting Treatment I in exhibit 5.2. But could it be the firm with Accounting Treatment II? That firm is one with growing investment (like Starbucks) but one subject to conservative accounting. The accounting depresses operating income and RNOA, but the depressed earnings mean more growth in the future. Starbucks' accounting is indeed conservative. It expenses advertising immediately, indeed all of its investment is in brand building. It expenses training of its growing number of employees (its investment in its human capital) immediately. It expenses all costs in developing its important supply chain with coffee growers around the world. And it expenses store-opening costs, an investment to produce future sales. With such a high-investment growth rate, the effects on income are likely to be significant.

Unfortunately, GAAP does not give us the detail to sort out the effect. But the investor is aware that some growth is to be expected (and indeed materialized in the 2005–2009 period as investment growth slowed). Accordingly, as in Accounting Treatment II in exhibit 5.2, the no-growth valuation should be modified for the anticipated growth due to the accounting. The valuation in exhibit 5.2 added a growth rate to the no-growth valuation to accommodate growth induced by the accounting. But, being the real world, this is implemented for Starbucks, not by assuming some constant growth rate but by forecasting residual income over an anticipated path that recognizes that investment growth rates will slow, producing higher profit margins and higher residual operating income. (Starbucks cannot maintain the high growth rates of the 1990s—How many Starbucks' stores do we need?) As investment slows, profit margins increase because those charges against income from conservative accounting, like store-opening costs, are reduced. Indeed that was the outcome in 2005–2009.

At this point, you might be a bit frustrated with the accounting (and I will have some complaints about GAAP accounting, and some remedies, in Chapter 9). You might be tempted to say, "Let me just deal with the cash flows rather than accrual accounting." Well, this is no remedy. The free cash flows for 1995–1999 in exhibit 5.3 are negative, hardly something to base a valuation on. We know the reason from Chapter 2: Cash accounting expenses all investments immediately, so free cash flow is low for a growing business. This is conservative accounting, but far too conservative.

Let's look at the years, a decade later, when Starbucks was more mature, and the investment growth slowed. The numbers for 2005–2009 show that buying growth, which looked so risky in 1999, paid off (unlike growth for Krispy Kreme and Planet Hollywood). Residual operating income, now about $300 million on average, came from considerable sales growth, but also with higher profit margins and asset turnovers. Would you pay the asking price of $21.9 in 2009? You would once again be facing high enterprise multiples; a P/B of 5.4 and a P/E of 24. We understand that, with conservative accounting, a firm can have a high P/B even though it does not have growth prospects, but the high P/E indicates growth expectations. The no-growth valuation in 2009 is $7.56 and the market's implied growth rate is 7.9 percent. Residual operating income growth is the key and, deferring to the accounting, you observe little residual income growth from 2005 to 2009. Indeed, residual income took a shock in 2008, not only because of the recession, but because Starbucks actually withdrew from some markets (Australia, for example). So now you observe that residual income is indeed at risk. You also observe a declining sales growth rate and declining growth in net operating assets. With these accounting benchmarks, you once again begin your negotiation with Mr. Market. You do so with an understanding of where your uncertainty lies: in the future sales growth rate, profit margin, and asset turnover. These three accounting features connect to the business and they connect the business to residual operating income that measures value added. The next chapter will help you analyze your uncertainty and the possible growth paths. It will also tell you your likely return to buying growth.

One last point before finishing my conversation over coffee. Starbucks' free cash flow from 2005 to 2009 is now positive. But that is with declining investment growth. Indeed, the large FCF of $981 million in 2009 is due to a large reduction in net operating assets. If you were not convinced in Chapter 2 that FCF is not a valuation attribute, I hope you are now.

Accounting for Growth and Value

There is much to mull over in this chapter. Book rates-of-return, earnings growth, P/E ratios, and P/B multipliers must be carefully evaluated in drawing the appropriate implications for value. Many of their properties are induced by the accounting. Indeed, residual earnings, the measure for adding value to book value, is an accounting measure that varies with the accounting employed. However, the accounting for value of Chapter 2 survives in the face of the evident traps. One can proceed with the valuation because it has built-in protection from paying too much for earnings and earnings growth.

Here are the main points in the chapter to keep in mind.

First, accounting profitability is not necessarily real profitability, but also a reflection of how the accounting is done. Don't interpret an R&D firm, like a pharmaceutical, as necessarily adding a lot of value because it has a high book rate-of-return.

Second, growth is also an accounting measure but it depends on how the accounting is done. Growth generated by the accounting does not add value.

Third, despite the accounting effects on profitability and growth, the investor is protected from paying too much for profitability and growth by sticking to the accounting for value of Chapter 2, but now with a modification of the no-growth valuation to accommodate expected growth due to the accounting.

Fourth, the accounting that produces the effects in the first two points is called conservative accounting. Conservative accounting keeps book values low, resulting in higher profitability. However, with growth in investment, conservative accounting results in lower profitability (as with Starbucks in 1995–1999), but yields higher residual income growth.

Accounting, Growth, and Risk

Fundamentalists see growth as risky. But when growth is generated by the accounting (as in exhibit 5.2, Accounting Treatment II), one might be tempted to say: It's just accounting, it's not real growth, and it's not risky! But two fascinating questions lurk in the background: What if the accounting were applied in response to risk? and What if conservative accounting were applied when firms are particularly risky? This is not hard to imagine when firms are making risky investments in R&D with uncertain outcomes. That's a reason to be conservative, as the fundamentalist well appreciates: Don't put speculative R&D on the balance sheet! Conservative accounting might be just what the fundamentalist wants for firms like Starbucks, Krispy Kreme, or Planet Hollywood, opening outlets rapidly in the hope that customers might come. As conservative accounting produces growth, accounting-induced growth would be seen as an indication of risk. So we are right back where we started; the fundamentalist sees growth as risky, including growth induced by the accounting. Accordingly, we might pay less for the firm or, to put it another way, our required return would be higher. The idea that accounting, growth, and risk are connected is the kernel to the discussion in the next two chapters.

CHAPTER SIX

Accounting for Risk and Return (and a Remedy for Ignorance About the Cost-of-Capital)

THE VALUATIONS TO THIS point have one startling omission. They have been devoted to the question of how to account for payoffs, the numerator in a valuation model, but have been silent about how to measure the required return, the denominator that discounts the expected payoffs for risk. This chapter comes to grips with the problem and, in so doing, also handles the issue of paying for risky growth, left dangling at the end of the last chapter.

First a reminder: A valuation model is a way to think about valuation, not necessarily a direct prescription for how to do it. Our valuations have heeded Benjamin Graham's warning—*beware of valuation models*—and particularly his warning about plugging growth rates into these models. Indeed, our accounting for value is designed to finesse this problem. But we can just as well say: Beware of plugging in an assumed discount rate, the so-called cost-of-capital or required return. Valuations are quite sensitive to the discount rate; one can do a lot of work in accounting for value, only to have it destroyed by a guess at the discount rate. The thinking behind these models is correct—expected payoffs must be discounted for risk and the time value of money—but the models cannot work in practice if we do not know the discount rate. We must finesse this problem as well.

The State of the Art: A Lament for Capital Asset Pricing

Well, you ask, "Does not the CAPM give us a cost-of-capital? That's what they teach in business school!" Let's be frank: After fifty years of research, with Nobel Prizes won, we do not know how to measure the cost-of-capital. The investigation has been the province of "asset pricing" that has produced not only the CAPM but successor multifactor models such as the popular Fama and French model. The research has enhanced our understanding of risk and the pricing of risk tremendously, worthy indeed of Nobel Prizes, and admirably has always had a product focus. The models were greeted with considerable excitement, holding promise not only for estimating the cost-of-capital, but also providing risk-adjusted benchmarks to evaluate investment performance. But the products just did not work out. Alas, more models that provide insight but which are not to be taken literally.

As I lamented in Chapter 1, the CAPM and like models require inputs of covariances, betas, and expected market risk premiums, all of them expectations (in the mind of the beholder) rather than concrete observables. These features are then deemed to vary randomly; correlations change, betas change, the market risk premium changes, all unpredictably, to overwhelm the investor trying to find an anchor. To alleviate the problem, the theory advises us to use a "conditional CAPM" that initializes on the state we are in, but identification of the state is elusive, so it further confounds. The fundamentalist turns aside; lacking any concreteness, these measures are wide open to speculation. One can use any discount rate over a wide range and claim it is sanctified by an asset pricing model. Plugging a CAPM estimate of the cost-of-capital into a valuation formula is simply adding speculation to the valuation. The fundamentalist will not participate: *Separate what you know from speculation.* As buy-side investors, we must be honest about our ignorance of the cost-of-capital. Those on the sell side, pushing stocks, might play with mirrors to justify the price of a stock offering, but not us.

In theory, asset pricing has it right; one's required return depends on risk and one's price for taking on risk. In the CAPM, beta is the risk and the "market risk premium" is the price of risk (and the multiplication of the two, added to the risk-free Treasury rate, supposedly yields the required return). Nice insight, but not practical. The risk premium in particular is hard to estimate—the inside secret among asset pricing theorists is that no one knows what the number is—but that is not the root of the problem. One's price of risk is a very personal thing, it depends on one's tolerance for risk, so objective measurement of a risk premium is misdirected. Surveys report a large variation in people's estimate of the risk premium.[1] Not as wide as the taste spectrum perhaps, but you get the point.

Let's recognize this upfront rather than pushing things into never-never land. Your disposition to risk may be quite different from mine. In the depths of the financial crisis in the fall of 2008 when asset prices dropped precipitously, it was said that the fall in prices was partly due to a large revision in the risk premium as investors faced an uncertain world. But individuals' feelings about risk, and the risk premium they require as the price for risk, might differ significantly. If I am heavily leveraged, my house price is falling, and I am in danger of losing my job in the crisis, my risk premium goes up. I dump risky stocks, an act that, when coordinated with others in a similar predicament, forces prices down. (Indeed, the drop of stock prices at the time was attributed to people unlevering and running to the safety of cash.) You, on the other hand, have no debt, have sold your house, already have a lot of your investments in cash—as a fundamentalist, you saw it coming—and have security of employment. Your risk premium is low relative to others, so you see stocks as a bargain. This is your time.[2] Your disposition to risk and my disposition to risk, and our required return, are personal matters.[3]

Rather than maintaining a pretense of objectivity by measuring risk premiums that are, after all, in the mind of the beholder, we will treat the problem for what it is, one that requires your (subjective) input as to your tolerance for risk. You will need some appreciation of the risk involved in a particular investment—so you require some accounting for risk—but only you can decide the risk you will accept. Only you can price risk. You will take personal responsibility for taking on risk, rather than delegating the task to a machine model that pretends to deliver your required return. But you will do so with consideration of the accounting that informs about risk.

Finessing the Cost-of-Capital

The fundamentalist departs from modern finance in one further respect. Asset pricing theory sees the market price as efficient, pricing stocks appropriately to yield the required return. The fundamentalist has doubts; after all, the required return is an elusive notion. His or her concept of risk is different. Although the fundamentalist is concerned that an investment may turn out differently than expected, his or her primary concern is *the risk of paying too much.* Anchored on the no-growth value indicated by the accounting, the concern is with paying too much for growth. Accordingly, the fundamentalist approaches the market, not with a precise cost-of-capital in mind to challenge the price, but with the question: What is my expected return to buying at the current market price? If that return is low, the stock is probably overpriced; if that return is high, it might be cheap.

The answer to this question falls out immediately from our accounting for value. Let's work with a valuation model with just a one-year forecasting horizon, unlevered to escape the misleading effects of leverage on growth uncovered in Chapter 4. Rather than looking at the valuation model with the pretense of determining value on the left-hand side, express the model as the market asking price (on the left-hand side) with inputs (on the right-hand side) that challenge that price:

$$\text{Market price for operations}_0\,(P^{\text{NOA}}) = \text{NOA}_0 + \frac{(\text{RNOA}_1 - r) \times \text{NOA}_0}{r - g}.$$

The market price for operations (the enterprise price, P^{NOA}) is, of course, the market price of the equity plus the net debt. In this form, r is not the required return, but an instrument for challenging the price;

r is the expected return from buying the stock at the current market price given a growth forecast, *g*, the anchoring book value of net operating assets (NOA), and the forward return on that book value, $RNOA_1$. This is what we are looking for: Is that return high or low? So, reverse engineer the model to solve for *r*:

$$r = \left[\frac{NOA}{P^{NOA}} \times RNOA_1\right] + \left[\left(1 - \frac{NOA}{P^{NOA}}\right) \times g\right].$$

$\frac{NOA}{P^{NOA}}$ is the book value of net operating assets relative to the market price of operations, the enterprise book-to-price ratio of last chapter.[4] The expression simply says that the expected return from buying the business at its current market price (without taking on the debt) is a weighted-average of the profitability, $RNOA_1$, and expected growth, *g*, with the weights given by the enterprise book-to-price ratio. Call it the weighted-average return formula. We are buying short-term RNOA and subsequent growth, and it is a question of whether the market, in assigning a book-to-price multiple, is weighting the two appropriately.

Let's return to Cisco Systems whose price we challenged in Chapter 3. We made the challenge there by anchoring on two years of forecasts, but will work here with a one-year forecast. (This is just to keep it simple. The analysis can be adapted to any forecasting horizon; the analyst should always push the horizon to a point where he or she feels that forecasts are hard enough to rely on.[5]) Cisco traded in early fiscal-year 2010 at $24 per share, or a total (equity) market capitalization of $138.8 billion. With negative net debt of $24.7 billion, the market value of operations is $114.1 billion (yes, Cisco has more financial assets (cash) than financing debt, a net creditor rather than a debtor). With a book value of net operating assets (enterprise book value) of $13.9 billion, Cisco has an enterprise book-to-price ratio of 0.122 (or an enterprise P/B of 8.2). With a forecast of 57.1 percent for RNOA in fiscal year 2010 (the forward year),[6] and a forecast of residual income growth at the GDP growth rate of 4 percent, the weighted-average return formula yields the expected return:

$$r = [0.122 \times 57.1\%] + [0.878 \times 4\%]$$
$$= 6.97\% + 3.51\%$$
$$= 10.48\%.$$

Thus we expect an annual return of 10.48 percent from buying Cisco at $24 with a 4 percent growth rate.

You can see that we are adopting the approach that we take when we estimate the required return for a bond from its expected yield. Indeed, as $\dfrac{\text{NOA}}{P^{\text{NOA}}} \times \text{RNOA} = \dfrac{\text{Operating income}_1}{P^{\text{NOA}}}$, the weighted-average return can be expressed as

$$r = \frac{\text{Operating income}_1}{P^{\text{NOA}}} + \left[\left(1 - \frac{\text{NOA}}{P^{\text{NOA}}} \right) \times g \right].$$

The first term, $\dfrac{\text{Operating income}_1}{P^{\text{NOA}}}$ is the forward (enterprise) earnings yield, and that is the expected return if this were a bond. But stocks can yield growth, and thus the addition of the second (growth) term: The weighted-average return formula is just the expected return formula for a bond (that does not yield growth) adapted for a stock (that can yield growth). The 10.48 percent expected return for Cisco comes in part from the 6.97 percent return we would earn with an RNOA of 57.1 percent with no growth (like a bond). But added growth of 4 percent yields an additional return of 3.51 percent.

Whether a 10.48 percent return is a good return (for you) depends on your pricing of the risk in the growth. That involves two things: first, your understanding of the risk involved (with help from an accounting for risk in the next section), and second, your tolerance for risk. The latter only you can supply. Over to you: What's your hurdle rate?[7]

Does this work for the market as a whole? You'll remember that we calculated implied growth rates for the S&P 500 for a given required return in Chapter 3 (figure 3.3). Figure 6.1 now plots the implied expected return on the index with an assumed GDP growth rate of 4 percent. The average expected return over the years 1982–2008 is 8.8

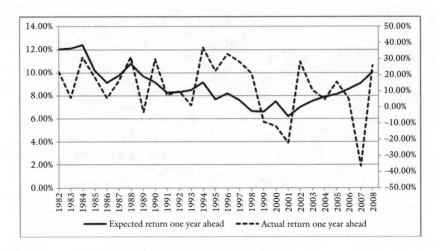

FIGURE 6.1   Expected Year-Ahead Returns and Actual Year-Ahead Returns for the S&P 500, for 1982–2008.

Expected returns are inferred from the level of the index at the end of December of each year using book value at that date and analysts' consensus forward earnings forecasts for the following year, along with a GDP growth rate of 4 percent. The expected return is indicated on the left axis, and the actual return on the right axis. Sources: The S&P 500 index and dividends for the index are from the Standard and Poors' website; book value is from the COMPUSTAT data through WRDS; and analysts' forecasts are from IBES, supplied through WRDS.

percent. (These are levered returns as the index prices levered firms.) Whether the expected return indicates the required return for risk born or is due to mispricing is an open question. An 8.8 percent return looks a bit low for equities, but the period did include the bubble years: Were the low expected returns in those years a warning of the actual poor returns that were to follow? Note that the implied expected returns predict the actual year-ahead returns in the figure; the correlation is 0.29.

Ah, but we have speculated about growth; we have built in speculation of 4 percent into the calculation! We may be more comfortable about this GDP-like rate for the market as a whole, but not for Cisco. Well, once again, a formula functions to lead our thinking, and this it indeed does. As a conservative investor concerned about paying too much for growth, you might conclude that you will never speculate growth over 4 percent. The weighted-average return formula says that, if you can see no more than 4 percent growth is possible for Cisco, then you can expect a return of 10.48 percent at most. But it can take you further. The formula gives the expected return for different growth forecasts: Each percentage point of added growth adds 0.878 percent to your expected return. So here is your growth-return profile for Cisco:

Growth–Return Profile for Cisco Systems

Growth	Return
−3%	4.34%
−2%	5.21%
−1%	6.09%
0%	6.97%
1%	7.85%
2%	8.73%
3%	9.60%
4%	10.48%
5%	11.36%
6%	12.24%
7%	13.12%

The return of 6.97 percent for zero growth has a special meaning. It is the return to the no-growth valuation anchored on the accounting for value. You may be skeptical about growth, for growth is risky, so will not pay for it. To be conservative—to maintain a margin of safety, as Benjamin Graham would advise—you might dismiss growth; if so, you expect a 6.97 percent return by buying at $24. But the profile also gives the payoff for added growth.[8] So you understand the upside; you may only earn a 6.97 percent return but, if growth of 4 percent materializes, you expect to earn 10.48 percent, and if things were to go very well with 7 percent growth, you expect 13.12 percent. And you understand the downside; if there is negative growth of 3 percent per year, you expect only 4.34 percent in return. Not only do you understand that growth is risky, you have a quantification of the risk-return tradeoff.

Whether this tradeoff is acceptable is a personal question as it depends on your risk tolerance: How much upside do you need for taking on downside risk? But you need benchmarks. One might be the firm's (unsecured) bond yield or the yield on bonds with similar risk. If the yield for the (no-growth) bond is 7 percent, you must get at least this for the equity where you take on risky growth. (The no-growth return for Cisco of 6.97 percent compares with a yield of 5.5 percent on ten-year AA corporate bonds at the time.)

Alternatively, a given profile can be compared with that of another firm in which you might invest. Indeed, a portfolio manager picking stocks might sort firms based on their growth-return profiles. Cisco's growth-return profile is displayed in figure 6.2 along with those of General Electric and Starbucks. GE is the firm that introduced our accounting for value in Chapter 2, trading at $52 with an enterprise book-to-price of 0.192 (an enterprise P/B of 5.21). Starbucks was featured at the end of the last chapter with a share price in 2009 of $21.9 and an enterprise book-to-price of 0.184 (an enterprise P/B of 5.4). We

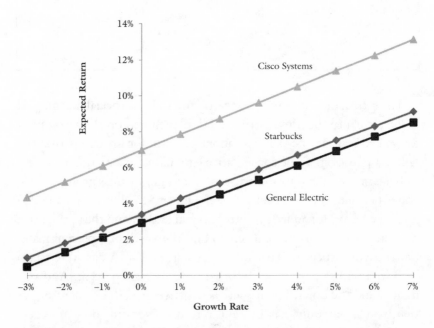

FIGURE 6.2   Growth-Return Profiles for Cisco Systems, Starbucks, and General Electric.

were left with the outstanding question of how much to pay for Starbucks' growth.

With a forward RNOA of 15.0 percent, the expected return with no-
growth for GE (from the weighted-average return formula) is 2.9 percent. GE's growth-return profile in figure 6.2 is derived from this starting point, with 0.808 added in return for each percentage increase in
the growth rate. The no-growth valuation in Chapter 2 suggested that
the market was overpricing GE's growth prospects at the time, and this
growth-return profile indeed suggests so; even if one concedes 7 percent growth, the expected return is only 8.6 percent. The downside is
0.5 percent with negative growth of 3 percent. With an RNOA of 18.6
percent, Starbucks' expected return with no-growth is 3.4 percent and,
with a slope to the growth-return profile of 0.816 for each percentage
increase in growth rate, one earns 9.1 percent with a 7 percent growth
rate and 1.0 percent for growth of minus 3 percent. If your required
return for Starbucks were 9 percent and you would only get a 9.1 percent return for an unlikely 7 percent growth, so you might see Starbucks as not a good deal. Particularly as there is also a downside. If you
saw Cisco, GE, and Starbucks as having similar business risk, you
probably would prefer the Cisco investment.

This is how to handle a valuation model. The approach not only finesses our ignorance of the cost-of-capital, but helps us profile payoffs
to growth, the aspect of valuation that we are most unsure about.

Growth rates in the profile are residual income growth rates, but these
can be reversed engineered into earnings growth rates, as in Chapter 3.
(Figure 3.2 plots the market's forecast of Cisco's earnings growth; the
path would now be for operating income rather than net [levered] earnings.) But there is a problem: Reverse engineering residual income (and
its growth) requires a required return to be specified.[9] The problem can
be finessed. The no-growth anchoring valuation compares to a bond
(that also has no growth). Take the firm's unsecured borrowing rate for
this purpose. One could add a couple of percentage points to the borrowing rate to recognize that forward earnings may be more at risk than
a bond return. This, admittedly, is somewhat arbitrary, but as growth
rates are based on changes, they are not too sensitive to the rate used.

Another approach is more attractive: Group firms by risk class and
benchmark growth-return profiles against those of firms within the

same risk class. With risk deemed to be constant within a risk class, one does not need the required return at all; it falls out as a constant for the group. This requires the determination of a risk class, which brings us to accounting for risk.

Accounting for Risk

Investors see risk as the possibility of an unfavorable outcome; one can be worse off. Being risk averse, as most of us are, they require compensation for this downside risk with a good chance of receiving favorable outcomes; one can also do very well. Fundamental investors approach risk defensively, with an eye to minimizing downside risk. Defensive investors first ask the question "What can I lose?" Only then does the active investor ask "What can I gain?" Such a disposition protects against hasty speculation about the upside without an appreciation of the downside. How can accounting analysis help?

The Modernist Approach to Risk

First, I entertain the solutions supplied by modern finance. Modern finance formalizes the notion of risk as a set of good and bad return outcomes in two ways, but neither is quite satisfactory.

One approach appropriates a formal return distribution from statistics that specifies both the set of possible outcomes and the probability of those outcomes. The normal distribution is the overwhelming favorite. Risk is then characterized by features of the assumed distribution. Those features might be the mean and the variance (as with the normal distribution) or, in the case of the CAPM, the covariance or beta that recognizes that returns are correlated across stocks (they are jointly normally distributed, to use the statistics term). The introduction of formal statistics leads to a "precise" number for the required return. Modernism in action. But, as I have argued, that number is deceptively precise.

The normal distribution is convenient—all aspects of the investor's gamble are summarized by just the mean and the variance—but history tells us that the normal distribution just does not hold up to the data. Actual return distributions are considerably more "fat-tailed" than the normal distribution; witness the 25 percent drop in the stock market in 1930, followed by a 43 percent drop in 1931, a 35 percent drop in 1937, 26 percent in 1974, and the 26 percent drop on one day in 1987. In the recent collapse in the financial crisis of 2008, the market dropped 38.5 percent for the year. These are returns for the market as a whole; those for individual stocks can be far more extreme (where, of course, −100 percent returns are possible). Risk is in the tail, once called the "peso effect," now popularized as "black-swan" outcomes. It is here that we are really concerned about getting hit. Though modern finance has long recognized that return distributions are fat-tailed, it has had little to say about our risk in the tails.[10] Fortunately, fat-tails are also in the data for positive outcomes: The market yielded a (positive) return of 54 percent in 1933, 48 percent in 1935, 53 percent in 1954, 43 percent in 1958, 38 percent in 1995, and 34 percent in 1997. After dropping 38.5 percent in 2008, the market returned 25.9 percent in 2009. Returns for individual stocks have been considerably more extreme, with returns of over 1,000 percent observed.[11] Investing is not a gamble with the normal distribution but a matter of trading off downside risk for upside potential with the appreciation that risk and reward are more extreme than the normal distribution indicates. Our growth-return profile provides a depiction.

The second standard approach throws away the notion of an assumed return distribution and goes straight to the data: What does the history of returns tell me about the distribution of return outcomes and their likelihood? Financial engineering often embraces this approach, as do asset pricing models that impute risk factors and the premiums associated with them from correlations in the data. The approach presumes that things will be the same in the future as in the past. Importantly, it presumes that the extreme events that we are likely to be subject to are evident in the past so we can understand their frequency and consequences. However, the world is hardly stationary and rare events are rarely observed. The financial crisis, with its unanticipated (and unmodeled) consequences, called these techniques into question with AIG, the insurance firm that sold "insurance" of risky debt with credit default swaps as the reluctant poster boy.

Both methods are the modernist's admirable attempts to quantify risk, one by assuming statistical parameters and the other by inferring "objective probabilities" from the history. In the words of Frank

Knight, they deal with "risk" (randomness that can be quantified) rather than "uncertainty" (randomness that lacks definition).[12] "Uncertainty" recognizes that outcomes do not necessarily conform to the form of prescribed statistical models and, as every prospectus states, the past is not necessarily a guide to the future. The world moves in unpredictable ways that cannot be reduced to a few parameters. To the extent that investors are unsure of the set of possible outcomes or the probabilities to ascribe to those outcomes, they face uncertainty, and, they require help in handling uncertainty.

These two approaches have something else in common: Risk measures are based on prices. Beta, for example, is typically estimated from past prices, as are risk premiums. This, of course, makes some sense, for the investor's return is determined by price outcomes, and one would certainly not want to put aside the history of price outcomes. But observed prices provide limited information on which to make a risk assessment, and the fundamentalist is concerned: *Ignore information at your peril.* He or she sees risk as primarily something internal to the firm, the risk in producing products and finding customers to buy them, not something external in the share market—just as the business manager does. The fundamentalist observes prices in order to learn what others think rather than to determine his or her own thinking. He or she is concerned that share prices may be inefficient, disturbed by the whims of traders (indeed, he or she may see the opportunity this presents as a positive). The fundamentalist sees prices as too volatile, moving more than is justified by fundamentals. He or she holds investments with future book value in mind—future book value is at risk—so is not overly concerned with the volatility of prices on the road to getting there. Most of all, the fundamentalist craves concreteness: What on earth is a "two–standard-deviation event?" What actually is behind a price drop? The investor would like to get closer to the fundamentals. The investor requires some accounting for risk.[13]

Accounting Modeling of Risk

Accounting for risk models uncertainty as a set of accounting outcomes rather than price outcomes; uncertainty is described by the set of possible financial statements the firm could end up reporting under different scenarios. The investor's eye is on the long-run price, of course, but future book values and return on book values in the financial statements connect to prices via our accounting for value. Future financial statements, when released, determine future prices and thus the return from investments. And forecasted financial statements indicate growth under alternative scenarios that, in turn, map to the expected returns in the growth-return profile.

I alluded to the process when introducing scenarios to challenge the high implied growth rates for Starbucks at the end of the last chapter. Full operationalization involves setting up pro forma income statements and balance sheets under different scenarios that indicate sales, profit margins, and asset turnovers, the drivers of residual income growth for Starbucks, under each scenario. One scenario for Starbucks in 1999 could have been the actual path the firm took with the 2005–2009 numbers. That path would be modeled against other scenarios to get a feel of its relative likelihood. Can Starbucks maintain or increase sales growth and at the same time turn that sales growth into growth in residual income? One answers this question with the understanding that not only must profit margins increase, but so must asset turnovers—more sales without a lot more of investment, that is, more same-store sales.

This modeling is a simple technical task to anyone who can work a spreadsheet, so I won't hold us up with the tedium of a full demonstration.[14] But suppose you hold to the CAPM thinking where economy-wide movements are the source of risk. You see two outcomes, boom and recession. Then your task is to model the financial statements—sales, operating income, operating assets, operating liabilities, leverage, and so on—under those two scenarios and to translate book value and earnings outcomes to a value in each scenario. Widening the set of outcomes—alternative levels of GDP rather than just boom or bust—expands the task, as does the admission of other exposures: competition risk, risk of changes in consumers' tastes, the risk of technological change, and so on. For Starbucks, these conditions would indicate different sales growth paths, different profit margins, and different asset turnovers, and thus different future financial statements. Uncertainty is inherent in laying out possible scenarios and in forecasting the outcomes in those scenarios. But past business experience guides (and surely adds more than a variance or covariance measure). You'll find that the accounting outcomes collide to yield the extreme, perfect-storm (tail) outcomes about which you are most afraid: Sales declines will combine with fixed costs and an inflexible asset base to deliver severe outcomes, and leverage will add to the disaster. Accordingly, tail outcomes are less mysterious; they can be modeled and their genesis understood. With accounting outcomes forecasted, the value implied by an outcome is determined from forecasted book values and earnings on those book values. Accordingly, the final product is a profile of values under different scenarios. Value at risk, but with an entirely different meaning.[15]

The analysis is done with the assurance that the accounting system captures everything that is relevant to the value of the firm, comprehensively, countering the danger of evaluating risk in decentralized "silos." The most common risk metric for financial firms, VaR (Value at Risk), is deficient in this respect: It reports a firm's exposure by estimating the chance of incurring a loss in one day in excess of a certain amount, but it does not model a firm's reaction to that loss or those of its trading partners or customers, nor how these reactions flow through to the financial statements. If the risk of credit default swaps written by AIG had been modeled in terms of consequences for the firm as a whole rather than the underlying instruments alone, the firm might have been more cautious.[16] Every banker worth his or her salt knows that it is the bank's balance sheet that is at risk, so risk management involves evaluating the effect of scenarios on the balance sheet and the income statement with which it articulates. To anticipate a financial crisis (or any outcome for an economy), it helps to have a macro accounting model of financial flows (of credit, interest, and income) and stocks (of debt and wealth) that separates the financial sector from the real economy.[17] In a similar vein, an accounting model of flows (income statement) and stocks (balance sheet) for a firm that separates the business from its financing helps to anticipate business outcomes.

The lattice of scenarios paths could become quite expansive, so your response might be to run to a computer. That may help, but the important thing is to think contingently down alternative possible paths. The ability to weigh alternatives strategically defines intelligence generally, but is certainly the mark of an intelligent investor. In negotiating with Mr. Market on price (and his implied growth rates), your advantage lies in understanding the business as a set of alternative paths that the business can take. That surely beats assuming a normal distribution. Indeed, resorting to assumptions about a distribution is mentally lazy, hardly a substitute to confronting the information. Remember, the onus is not on the investor to complete a full mapping of probability weighted scenarios, but to develop some thinking to challenge the growth expectations in the market price, to understand whether the price is out of bounds.

This approach permits more information to enter the risk assessment than prices alone. But it also requires the investor to engage and render some judgment. To this point in the book, we have distanced ourselves from judgment, relying rather on objective accounting to ground us. But that being done, the investor must then take some personal responsibility. The analysis does not supply the set of scenarios under which the accounting is to be modeled. This is your responsibility, based on business experience. Stated more positively, you can bring your knowledge of the business to the task. The flexibility is there to model scenarios, including those "tail" outcomes that may hit you but that are not in the history. The analysis will not supply the probabilities of each outcome either. But, really, the notion of an objective probability, embedded in many risk models, is a pretense. Rather than being strapped in by a "distributional assumption," the investor supplies his or her own probabilities—subjective probabilities—gained from experience with the world, and then weighs the odds.[18]

Although the analysis does not supply probabilities, it does help to work through scenarios and enlightens as to the consequences of different scenarios. The modeling of alternative paths often produces insights into opportunities or dangers. It facilitates thinking "outside the box." It enlightens as to the "real options" available to the business. Indeed, the analysis helps to elicit our subjective probabilities, prompting us and helping us with our cognitive limitations and our limited mental accounting. Appreciating that a bad state can occur revises one's probabilities of a good state, for probabilities must total to one. Applied dynamically, one foresees outcomes and revises probabilities as firms move along a given path in time. Further, the analysis can be turned on oneself, to understand one's lack of understanding; it enlightens the investor about what he or she does not know. He or she can thus judge, defensively, which stocks to stay away from—stocks where others are likely to have more knowledge—versus stocks where he or she might take an active position.

The quant models of modern finance just don't get the job done. Those models substitute mathematics and statistics for a human sense of possibilities. The seeming objectivity would, on the surface of it, appear to be a plus, but reducing uncertainty to a few parameters identified with an assumed statistical distribution cannot hope to embed the breadth of knowledge gained by experience, nor the understanding of subtleties that the socialization of human beings produces. With their too-easy quantification, these models can provide a false sense of security. The risk to BP of a possible oil well blowout in the Gulf of Mexico is not captured by a beta measure. According to the fundamentalist creed, *one does not buy a stock, one buys a business,* and *when buying a business, know the business.* For this, the accounting model replaces the statistical model of modern finance.

There is a fine line between informed judgment and speculation, so one must be disciplined. Indeed, behavioral economists blame seemingly irrational prices on the limitations and failures of human judgment. Clearly, the investor must guard against self-deception, overconfidence, and all those other all-too-human failings, testing scenarios against the facts. The accounting for value that we have done to this point grounds us. If one forecasts that future accounting numbers will be different from the past, one must have very good reasons. But further, the accounting framework within which we forecast also restrains us. First, the value implied by a scenario must be justified by an accounting for future book value and return on book value; one is constrained to scenarios with plausible financial statement outcomes. Second, the chart of accounts defines the elements that must be forecasted to model the balance sheet and income statement, so ensures that we forecast book value and return on book value comprehensively; nothing is left out or added redundantly. (Those accounts might be aggregated into the drivers of residual income, like sales, profit margins, and asset turnovers for Starbucks.) Third, these elements are governed by fixed relationships that tie them together, outside of which one cannot stray. Earnings forecasts must be justified by sales and expense forecasts; earnings must reconcile to the change in assets and liabilities in the balance sheet; and both must reconcile to cash flows, simply by accounting identities. Residual operating income for Starbucks is explained by sales, profit margins, and asset turnovers, and nothing else. Forecasts that violate these relations are inadmissible. That's a check on speculation.

Not only does the accounting check the tendency to speculate, but it also serves to check more formal forecasting schemes. Statistical forecasting models, estimated from data, often produce forecasts outside the accounting bounds, particularly when model parameters estimated in sample are applied in real time out of sample.[19] In short, viewing uncertainty through an accounting lens reduces "model risk."

But, to be sure, the result is a sharpened appreciation of uncertainty, not its elimination.

Accounting for Value

After refining accounting for value in the last two chapters, this chapter has picked up the focus of Chapter 3, going active again by applying the accounting to challenge the market price. In so doing, we have finessed the troublesome aspect of valuation of not knowing the cost-of-capital. You will have noticed that we have distanced ourselves from many of the techniques of modern finance, simply because they push the analysis of uncertainty through too tight a straight jacket, producing risk measures that are seemingly precise but are actual quite speculative. To be sure, we are left with uncertainty, but accounting for risk ameliorates.

Here are some practical points to take away from this chapter.

First, be honest about what you know and what you don't know and, in the fundamentalist tradition, separate what you know from what you don't know. We do not know the cost-of-capital, despite the tempting availability of asset pricing models. Plugging in a discount rate from the CAPM into a valuation formula adds speculation to the valuation. Don't play with mirrors.

Second, appreciate that risk tolerance, and the price you are willing to pay for risk, is a personal attribute. The active investor understands when his or her appetite to risk differs from others, and sees that difference as providing opportunities.

Third, rather than seeing valuation as a matter of determining the cost-of-capital, turn the exercise around and work in reverse-engineering mode to estimate the expected return from buying at the current market price. The weighted-average-return formula is your tool. This engages you in a negotiation with Mr. Market.

Fourth, (again) understand that Mr. Market may be asking you to pay for growth, so support your negotiations with growth-return profile: At his quoted price, what is the expected return for different growth rates?

Fifth, understand that risk cannot be adequately quantified with the metrics of modern finance. Uncertainty needs to be understood with the methods of accounting for risk. That accounting allows you to introduce your knowledge of the business to reduce your uncertainty, but also to understand where your uncertainties lie.

Finally, maintain the attitude that you are not calculating "intrinsic value" but rather challenging the market price. The onus is not on you to model uncertainty completely, but only to take it as far as needs be to accept or dismiss the market price. The chapter supplies additional tools for doing so.

CHAPTER SEVEN

Pricing Growth (and a Revision to Value Versus Growth Investing)

THE FUNDAMENTALIST UNDERSTANDS that growth is risky. But that is not the view of modern finance, nor indeed among many investment professionals. "Growth" is viewed as yielding lower average returns than "value." The investor may attribute this to market inefficiency; growth stocks tend to be overpriced. But, for those embracing market efficiency, the lower return must mean that growth is low risk. Extensive academic research has been devoted to explaining the "value-growth spread" as reward for risk.

Fundamentalists are perplexed. They might attribute these returns to market mispricing, but to see them as returns for risk, with growth being less risky, throws them for a loop. Their disposition is to view growth with considerable reservation. They understand that growth is the risky part of a valuation and would think that efficient markets would price it as such.

Indeed, fundamentalists see the idea that growth is low risk as inconsistent with the basic risk-return tradeoff so fundamental in economics.

One buys (future) earnings and sees those earnings at risk: How can one buy more earnings (growth) without added risk? How can a firm produce more earnings without taking on more risk? The fundamentalist knows (from the accounting for leverage in Chapter 4) that leverage adds earnings growth, but modern finance (and common sense) recognizes that leverage also adds risk. Growth and risk go together. The idea that growth is less risky indeed conflicts with his or her reading of modern finance; the theory identifies a high-risk investment as one that delivers a bad return in bad times. It provides little as a hedge against a hit to consumption, and the fundamentalist knows that growth gets hit in bad times. That's why the prices of consumer staple stocks with moderate growth but steady product demand in both good and bad times—like General Mills, Procter & Gamble, and Kimberley Clark—held up in the 2000 crash and the financial crisis of 2007–2008, whereas the startups and young firms whose prices were based on growth prospects took a beating. As prospects for growth subsequently increased, the prices of the young growth firms increased significantly. Growth represents downside risk rewarded with upside potential.

There is some sorting out to do if one wants to reconcile modern finance to the fundamentalist view. Accounting for value ties it together, and in such a way as to lead the investor to view "growth" and "value" in quite a different way.

Growth Versus Value

In the standard "growth" versus "value" dichotomy, a growth stock is seen as one with high multiples of earnings and book value, and a value stock one with low multiples. High multiples ("growth") yield lower returns on average than low multiples ("value"). The quant investor, the stock screener, interprets these returns as those to a contrarian strategy; when the market enthusiastically overprices a stock with a high multiple, sell, and when the market pessimistically underprices with low multiples, buy.

The strategy has been applied many times and indeed exhibit 7.1 shows that these strategies hold up in the data. The exhibit compares

EXHIBIT 7.1   Annual Returns to Portfolios Formed on the Basis of Earnings-to-Price (E/P) and Book-to-Price (B/P), 1963–2006.

Firms are ranked on each multiple each year and formed onto five portfolios from the ranking. Returns for the five portfolios are then observed for the following year. Returns in the exhibit are averages from replicating this strategy each year, 1963–2006.

Ranking Firms on E/P			Ranking Firms on B/P		
E/P Portfolio	E/P	Annual Return	B/P Portfolio	B/P	Annual Return
5 (high)	14.1%	23.5%	5 (high)	1.64	25.0%
4	9.3%	18.2%	4	0.93	19.1%
3	6.7%	14.9%	3	0.68	15.8%
2	3.2%	12.4%	2	0.46	12.9%
1 (low)	–18.4%	13.9%	1 (low)	0.22	9.7%

SOURCE: As reported in Stephen H. Penman and Francesco Reggiani, "Returns to Buying Earnings and Book Values: Accounting for Risk and Growth," manuscript, Columbia University and Bocconi University (2008) at http://ssrn.com/abstract=1536618.

returns on portfolios formed on the basis of different levels of E/P and B/P (equivalent to levels of their reciprocals, the multiples P/E and P/B). Both multiples clearly rank return outcomes, with the return spread between high and low multiples being quite considerable.[1]

The contrarian sees the rewards to the strategy as due to market mispricing, whereas the efficient-market believer sees the returns as reward for different risk associated with high and low multiples. The fundamentalist is also somewhat uncomfortable with the contrarian strategy because it is based on just a couple of bits of information, earnings, and book values. *Ignore information at your peril;* this is hardly a full accounting for value. Here the fundamentalist and the adherent to market efficiency agree: The strategy could be loading up on risk of which you are unaware. *Ignore information about risk at your peril.* Indeed, this simple strategy has been known to backfire, and not too infrequently.

E/P and Risk

It does not require much stretch of the imagination to see E/P as indicating risk. After all, earnings-to-price is the earnings yield and we expect the yield on an asset, like a bond yield, to reflect its risk.[2] We understand from the accounting for leverage in Chapter 4 that leverage increases the E/P ratio because it increases risk *(Valuation Principle 5a);* so might the risk in the operations imply a higher E/P. Investors buy earnings but earnings should be discounted for risk such that E/P is higher, the higher the discount in the price for risk. An investor buying high E/P (low P/E) stocks might indeed be buying a risk exposure.

The picture is a little more complicated, for the investor buys not only one year of earnings but also earnings growth, and the E/P reflects expected growth. If growth is risky, the price might be further discounted. I will try to sort this out, but first let's look at how the B/P ratio might be related to risk and return.

B/P and Risk

In the early 1990s, it hit home among academics that book-to-price predicts stock returns. Although known among contrarian traders (and indeed the fundamentalists of old), the formal documentation emphasized that, of all measures that predict returns in the data (including beta), B/P performs the best.[3] The cry, "Beta is dead" went out, with B/P now offered as the premier variable to explain returns. The demise of beta (and the CAPM) is much debated, but B/P has been brought very much to the fore in asset pricing.

The observation that B/P predicts returns is sometimes referred to an "anomaly," alongside other unexplained empirical relationships (like small firms yielding higher returns than large firms). Academics tend to cling to market efficiency as an imperative, so the observation that B/P predicts returns is interpreted as pricing for risk; the returns to buying high B/P stocks ("value") must be return for risk born, and the lower return to low B/P stocks ("growth") must mean lower risk. Accordingly, they have developed asset pricing models that incorporate book-to-price to replace the CAPM. The premier model is the Fama and French three-factor model that has gained wide recognition in practice.[4] The model retains the market factor, as in the CAPM—investors are exposed to the risk for the overall market—but also a size factor and a book-to-price factor; a firm's size (measured by market capitalization) and its B/P ratio indicate additional risk exposures that require a higher return.

These factors, it should be stressed, are added only because it has been observed empirically that firm size and B/P predict returns; the model comes simply by gazing at historical returns like those in exhibit 7.1. There is little theory to explain it, so the model really does not put much on the table. Based solely on empirical observation, the attribution of risk to B/P is simply by fiat, that is, someone just said it. In one respect, B/P asset pricing models are doubtful. When book-to-price is unlevered, as in Chapter 4, enterprise book-to-price predicts returns, but leverage adds negatively to returns in these models. That is a clear violation of the principles of modern finance that maintain that risky leverage must be rewarded with a higher expected return.[5] Nevertheless, the model and its variants have taken a prominent position in asset pricing. Every research paper and investment strategy that predicts returns is subject to the inquisition "Ah, but have you controlled for the Fama-and-French factors?"

Words, Words, Words

With no satisfactory explanation for the higher empirical returns to B/P, conjectures abound; book-to-price indicates distress risk, the risk of assets in place, Tobin's *q*, the risk in growth options, and liquidity risk, to name a few. These attributions amount to wordsmithing, to mere labeling. "Words! Words! Words! I'm so sick of words! Is that all you blighters can do?" asks Elisa Doolittle of the males around her in *My Fair Lady*. The list of labels plonked on B/P is staggering and propels the confusion. The designations, "value" versus "growth" are among the labels that give the adopter a false security that an important idea has been embraced. A labeling game does not advance the field; indeed, it distracts, just as astrology distracts from astronomy. Putting labels on things is pseudoscience. Real science involves rigorous analysis that develops predictions and then takes the predictions to the data for validation. (The CAPM was so developed and so tested.)

As behooves those accounting for value, let's get concrete. In doing so, we might be able to actually sort out whether B/P indicates risk and return.[6] Let's call book-to-price for what it is: Given price, B/P is an accounting phenomenon, it depends on how the accounting for book value is done. Thus, if B/P indicates risk and return, it is likely to have something to do with the accounting. The point can be seen quite vividly in the case of a money market fund and a risky hedge fund. Both have B/P = 1; investors move in and out of both funds at book value ("net asset value"), taking book value as the price at which to trade. But, despite the same B/P, the two funds have very different risk. The reason is that both employ a particular accounting—mark-to-market accounting or fair value accounting—that results in B/P = 1; that accounting takes away the ability for B/P to indicate the differential risk. That opens up the question of whether the accounting that produces a B/P that is different from one in some way indicates risk. If so, it must be embedded in the way the accountant accounts for book value, and that accounting would explain (concretely) why B/P is related to returns.

E/P, B/P, and Accounting for Growth

To gain some insight as to how both E/P and B/P might connect to risk and return, consider the weighted-average return formula of the last chapter. This formula combines earnings-to-price, book-to-price, and growth, and together they deliver an expected return. On an unlevered basis, the expected return (for the operations) is

$$
r = \left[\frac{\text{NOA}}{P^{\text{NOA}}} \times \text{RNOA}_1 \right] + \left[\left(1 - \frac{\text{NOA}}{P^{\text{NOA}}} \right) \times g \right]
$$

$$
= \left[\frac{\text{Operating income}_1}{P^{\text{NOA}}} \right] + \left[\left(1 - \frac{\text{NOA}}{P^{\text{NOA}}} \right) \times g \right].
$$

To remind you, $\dfrac{\text{NOA}}{P^{\text{NOA}}}$ is the enterprise book-to-price (for the business operations) and $\dfrac{\text{Operating income}_1}{P^{\text{NOA}}}$

is the forward enterprise E/P ratio. The corresponding formula for the (levered) equity return is

$$r = \left[\frac{B}{P} \times ROCE_1 \right] + \left[\left(1 - \frac{B}{P} \right) \times g \right]$$

$$= \left[\frac{Earnings_1}{P} \right] + \left[\left(1 - \frac{B}{P} \right) \times g \right].$$

The fundamentalist takes these tools into his or her arsenal to challenge the market price. But suppose for a moment that the market is efficiently pricing risk as asset pricing models would have us believe; in that case, the expected return is the required return.[7] The weighted-average return formula then indicates the role of B/P in pricing risk. Book-to-price is not a risk attribute itself; rather, short-term ROCE and subsequent growth are at risk and B/P prices the two expectations with weights (that sum to 1.0) to yield a required return commensurate with the risk in the two payoffs. How does this work?

You might expect that we have the answer to our puzzle already, for Chapter 5 demonstrated how E/P and B/P change under various accounting treatments that also change growth. To walk through it once again, we begin with the case where P/B = 1 and then proceed to the demonstration of how E/P, B/P, and growth change with the accounting employed. The demonstration in Chapter 5 was for a firm with zero leverage, so the corresponding levered and unlevered numbers are the same. We will work with levered numbers here, with the understanding that the same effects apply for the operations (without leverage). In the demonstration, the required return for risk was specified as 10 percent, so we can work back from the accounting to that required return. Be assured that the relationships we are about to observe are accounting relationships. They have to hold—there is no playing with mirrors—they are something to anchor on. Here's a summary of what happens:

- *The Case of P/B = 1* (Exhibit 5.1, Accounting Treatment I). By applying a weight of 1.0 to the ROCE and zero weight to growth in the weighted-average return formula,

$$r = \frac{B}{P} \times \text{ROCE}_1 = 1.0 \times 10\% = 10\%.$$

As

$$\frac{B}{P} \times \text{ROCE}_1 = \frac{\text{Earnings}_1}{P},$$

this return also equals the forward enterprise E/P ratio. Here P/B does not indicate the required return—as with the money market fund and the hedge fund—but the earnings yield does.

- *The No-Growth Case* (Exhibit 5.1, Accounting Treatment II). When earnings are deferred to the next period with no subsequent growth, P/B increases from 1.0 to 1.25 (B/P decreases to 0.8) and the forward ROCE increases, from 10 to 12.5 percent. In this no-growth case, the weighted-average return equation says

$$r = \frac{B}{P} \times \text{ROCE}_1 = 0.8 \times 12.5 = 10\%,$$

which is also the forward earnings yield. The B/P ratio plays the role of correcting the (now inflated) book rate-of-return of 12.5 percent to yield the required return of 10 percent (equal to the earnings yield). However, B/P does not indicate the required return, but the earnings yield does.

- *The Growth Case* (Exhibit 5.2, Accounting Treatment II). Earnings growth does not change the P/B from 1.25, but the accounting that induces growth reduces the forward earnings yield (now 9 percent) so that it no longer indicates the required return of 10 percent. With the depressed earnings, forward ROCE is now 11.25 percent, down from 12.5 percent with no growth. The depressed earnings induces subsequent residual earnings growth of 5 percent. The weighted-average return formula (with a B/P of 0.8) recovers the 10 percent required return from the accounting:

$$r = \left[\frac{B}{P} \times ROCE_1 \right] + \left[\left(1 - \frac{B}{P} \right) \times g \right]$$
$$= [0.8 \times 11.25\%] + [0.2 \times 5\%] = 10\%.$$

The valuation in Chapter 5 that accommodates the growth induced by the accounting was

$$Value_{2010} = B_{2010} + \frac{Residual\ earnings_{2011}}{r - g}$$

$$= \$80 + \frac{1}{0.10 - 0.05} = \$100.$$

This value is the same $100 as that for the no-growth case and indeed the case of P/B = 1. As demonstrated in Chapter 5, adding growth to the denominator corrects for what is seemingly a pure accounting effect, the growth induced by the accounting. It's just accounting junk, so adjust for it! This is where we stood at the end of Chapter 5, except that we now have shown how the same required return is reversed engineered despite the different accounting. Essentially the formula serves to cancel out the accounting to get to the expected return explicit in the market price.

But now entertain a provocative idea: The accounting applied may have something to do with risk! Maybe the firm with the expensed advertising is not the same as the firm that invested in inventory rather than a mix of inventory and advertising; if the firm needs advertising to sell its inventory, maybe there is lower probability that the inventory will sell. The same might be said of a firm where the expensing is for R&D, because R&D investment to design a product is more risky than having a product in hand. If these types of firms are riskier, you require a return of more than 10 percent. Suppose, because of this risk, your hurdle rate goes to 10.5 percent. Then,

$$Value_{2010} = \$80 + \frac{0.60}{0.105 - 0.05} = \$90.91.$$

(It is easy to confirm, by working the numbers in exhibit 5.2, that the forward residual income is 0.6 if the required return is 10.5 percent and that the growth remains at 5 percent.) With the lower value, B/P is higher at 0.88 and that higher B/P applies weights that imply a higher required return:

$$r = \left[\frac{\text{NOA}_0}{P^{\text{NOA}}} \times \text{RNOA}_1\right] + \left[\left(1 - \frac{\text{NOA}}{P^{\text{NOA}}}\right) \times g\right]$$

$$= [0.88 \times 11.25\%] + [0.12 \times 5\%] = 10.5\%.$$

This is the clue as to why a higher B/P indicates a higher required return: The accounting that yields a higher B/P gave us growth and growth is risky.

In Chapter 5 we referred to the accounting that expenses investment by its standard name: conservative accounting. What if conservative accounting is applied in response to risk? The name, used for generations, suggests so. Indeed, there is an important feature of conservative accounting that reinforces the idea. Call it *Accounting Principle 6* and add it to the earlier principles.

Accounting Principle 6

Under uncertainty, (conservative) accounting defers the recognition of earnings to the future until the uncertainty has been resolved, and the deferral of earnings results in earnings growth.

This principle is not a minor one. It is central to the accounting system. Accounting, as practiced for centuries, does not recognize earnings until there has been significant resolution of uncertainty. That usually requires a firm to have found a customer with a legal, enforceable claim (a receivable) against the customer or indeed with cash in hand. This accounting of course suits the fundamentalist who does not want the accounts to anticipate future customers, for such anticipation is speculation, and speculation is risky. Conservative accounting treats it as such; growth and risk go together in the accounting.

The operation of *Accounting Principle 6* can be seen by contrasting the accounting for the risk-free savings account in Chapter 2 with the accounting for a risky business in Chapter 5. For the savings account, there is no earnings deferral, and the required return equals the forward earnings yield and the forward rate-of-return on book value. Thus P/B = 1. In contrast, the business enterprise defers earnings recognition and adds growth. The deferral is usually implemented by historical cost accounting that records assets at cost rather than at their value, and waits for a customer to turn up before adding value to book value. So, historical cost accounting typically produces a P/B greater than 1.0. But additional accounting methods are applied when there is more risk, producing more deferral and thus growth. The accounting treatment in exhibit 5.2 expenses advertising expenditures; the accounting explicitly sees investments in advertising as risky, because it may not deliver customers. But it may just as well be risky R&D expenditures, for R&D is risky.[8] It could be expensed startup costs. It could be investment in training, market research, or in any intangible to generate future earnings at the expense of short-term earnings, as is also the case with deferred revenues where the accountant awaits the resolution of uncertainty.[9]

Indeed, we saw the accounting operating with Starbucks at the end of Chapter 5. In 1999, Starbucks' price-to-book of 5.3 built in significant growth expectations, yet the RNOA was only 10 percent, equal to the required return assumed. We asked: How can a firm earning just the required return be worth 5.3 times book value? *Valuation Principle 2* says that, if one forecasts that the rate-of-return on book value will be equal to the required rate-of-return, the asset must only be worth its book value. Starbucks in 1995–1999 looked very much like the savings account. But we recognized that Starbucks' conservative accounting—expensing investment in store openings, advertising and promotion, employee training, and supply chain development—depressed the RNOA and added to expected growth, just like the RNOA in our growth example was reduced from 12.5 to 11.25 percent by conservative accounting. That suits the prudent, conservative investor; putting these investments on the balance sheet would be speculative: Will they pay off? That was an important question for the investor at the time, for it was not at all clear whether Starbucks would deliver the speculative value of growth in the market price. Mr. Market, with his high asking price, apparently thought so, but the fundamental investor is more cautious. By depressing RNOA and deferring earnings to the future, conservative accounting adds to growth, to put the investor on notice that the growth is both speculative and risky. He or she can then go about evaluating the likelihood that growth will be delivered. As it turned out, growth materialized for Starbucks, though not at the level of Mr. Market's forecast. Other growth prospects such as Krispy Kreme, Planet Hollywood, priceline.com and the many start-ups of that time did not pan out.

The reader of modern finance might well ask: Is the risk that the accounting responds to the type of risk I care about? Modern finance does not price risk that can be diversified away; "systematic risk" rather than "idiosyncratic risk" is what's important. That could be so, but we now recognize that diversification does not work well when things are really bad. The fundamentalist is not usually "well diversified" in any case, preferring to deal with the risk in the few companies he or she knows rather than buying a market portfolio he or she does not know. And the accounting is not necessarily inconsistent with the pricing of systematic risk: Accounting defers earnings until the firm has a low-beta asset (cash or a receivable from the customer), an asset that looks very much like the risk-free savings account or a bond. Prior to that point, the risk and the beta are higher, and growth does get hit in bad times. Curiously a behavioral element is involved. Conservative accounting has been practiced for a long time, so is well ingrained. Its origins, however, are obscure. Historically it appears to be an instinctive, behavioral reaction to uncertainty rather than a regulation; only in 1933, after the speculation of the 1920s and its disastrous aftermath, did the Securities and Exchange Commission (SEC) adopt conservatism as a principle for regulation. Could that behavioral response be a natural human reaction to the type of risk that counts?

The analysis of leverage in Chapter 4 reinforces the point that growth adds risk. Under *Accounting Principle 3a*, leverage increases earnings growth but, by the principles of modern finance, also increases risk. The net effect is to leave value unchanged, as exhibit 4.3 demonstrates. Effectively the added growth and risk cancel each other, and leave value unchanged. This just reflects the risk-return trade-off of standard economics, that is, a firm can add more earnings with leverage, but only by taking on more risk. One might well imagine that the same could apply to the business activities.

Before turning to examining the returns to E/P and B/P, let's summarize the accounting effects on these multiples. First, with no growth, B/P is reduced by deferring earnings to the future, but there is no effect on E/P (remaining at 10 percent in the demonstration). With growth, B/P is unchanged but E/P is reduced (to 9 percent) as earnings in the numerator are depressed. Note now that these accounting effects contrast to the case where growth does not just reflect risk, but actually adds value; if growth adds to price it also reduces E/P, but now B/P is also lower. It is this contrasting effect on B/P of the case where growth adds risk (but does not add to price) and the case where growth adds to price that cues our analysis of returns. Note also that, for given earnings and price, a higher book value means a lower book rate-of-return, and that is exactly what we saw in the growth scenario earlier—an ROCE of 11.25 percent rather than 12.5 percent. And that is exactly what we saw with Starbucks in 1995–1999 at the end of the last chapter where we questioned why a firm with such high anticipated growth could have such a low book rate-of-return: Starbucks was offering growth, but risky growth.

Returns to "Value" and "Growth" Investing

Now to the issue of whether the returns to E/P and B/P in exhibit 7.1 are returns for bearing risk. With respect to E/P, the no-growth accounting case shows that indeed $E/P = r$ (in an efficient market) so that ranking firms on the earnings yield, as in exhibit 7.1, is the same as ranking them on risk and the required return. Stock screeners beware! But in this no-growth case, like the P/B = 1 case, there is no role for B/P to indicate the required return; indeed, for a given E/P, B/P can be any value but not indicate returns. The no-growth case is a special case. Growth depresses E/P (it increases the P/E) so E/P alone cannot indicate returns. In the case where growth goes into price—the growth indicates added value—E/P is depressed because the higher price (in the denominator) values the future growth. In the case where growth is risky, E/P is also depressed; price is not affected but the accounting that produces the growth depresses forward earnings (in the numerator), down to 9 percent in our demonstration. Is there any role for B/P to sort this out? The answer is yes, because B/P is higher when growth does not add to price.

Exhibit 7.2 conducts similar trading strategies to the screens in exhibit 7.1, but now with a two-way screen. Firms are first ranked in each year, 1963–2006, on their E/P ratios and then, within each E/P portfolio, on their B/P ratios, to yield 25 portfolios with different combined levels of E/P and B/P. The E/P and B/P ratios are levered ratios so they pick up both enterprise risk and leverage risk.

This two-way screen has been trolled many times by quant investors and indeed there is a spread of returns across E/P and B/P portfolios. Those quant investors may see these returns as returns to identifying market mispricing, and indeed they may well be. A fundamental investor might lean that way. But the quant stock screener and the fundamentalist might well recognize that, in the no-growth case, the ranking on E/P across rows in the exhibit is a ranking on risk and the required return. Further, moving down columns in the exhibit, returns increase when B/P is higher for a given E/P. A given E/P could be due to growth that is priced (yielding a lower E/P) but also growth where the conser-

EXHIBIT 7.2   Annual Returns on Portfolios Formed on the Basis of Earnings-to-Price (E/P) and Book-to-Price (B/P), 1963–2006.

Firms are ranked on E/P each year and formed onto five portfolios from the ranking. Firms are then ranked within each of these E/P portfolios on their B/P ratios to form five B/P portfolios within each E/P portfolio. Returns for the resulting 25 portfolios are then observed for the following year. Returns in the exhibit are averages from replicating this strategy each year, 1963–2006.

		E/P Portfolio				
		1(low)	2	3	4	5(high)
	1	4.3%	10.9%	14.2%	17.1%	19.7%
	2	8.8%	9.1%	13.0%	16.0%	22.1%
B/P Portfolio	3	14.4%	8.5%	12.1%	17.0%	21.6%
	4	15.5%	13.4%	14.7%	18.0%	24.3%
	5	26.4%	20.1%	20.2%	22.6%	30.0%

SOURCE: Stephen H. Penman and Francesco Reggiani, "Returns to Buying Earnings and Book Values: Accounting for Risk and Growth," manuscript, Columbia University and Bocconi University (2008), at http://ssrn.com/abstract=1536618.

vative accounting reduces the earnings but not the price (also yielding a lower E/P). B/P discriminates on these two scenarios because a low B/P is indicative of growth being valued in price but a high B/P is indicative of risky growth that does not go into price.

To complete this picture, let's return to the fundamentals. Panel A of exhibit 7.3 reports the actual average earnings growth rates two years ahead for the 25 portfolios in exhibit 7.2. You see that growth is negatively related to E/P (across rows), conforming to our understanding that higher P/E indicates higher subsequent earnings growth. But the growth rates are also increasing in B/P for a given E/P (down columns); the combination of E/P and B/P indicates expected earnings growth. (A similar pattern is observed for growth rates three years ahead.) The returns in exhibit 7.2 are related to these growth rates in accordance with the idea that the market sees growth as risky. And the

EXHIBIT 7.3 Average Earnings Growth Rates and Their Standard Deviation for Portfolios Formed on the Basis of Earnings-to-Price (E/P) and Book-to-Price (B/P), 1963–2004.

Growth rates are growth in earnings per share (before extraordinary and special items) two years ahead (that is, one year after the forward year). To handle negative denominators, growth rates are measured as $(EPS_t - EPS_{t-1})/(|EPS_t| + |EPS_{t-1}|) \times 2$.

Panel A: Average Earnings Growth Rates

		E/P Portfolio				
		1 (low)	2	3	4	5(high)
	1 (low)	15.2%	−4.8%	−4.6%	−5.9%	−11.5%
	2	19.6%	−1.6%	−3.2%	−1.6%	−5.6%
B/P	3	25.8%	3.3%	−3.6%	−0.1%	−5.9%
Portfolio	4	30.1%	5.8%	0.6%	0.6%	−3.1%
	5 (high)	38.0%	18.7%	10.7%	3.6%	−2.0%

Panel B: Standard Deviation of Earnings Growth Rates

		E/P Portfolio				
		1 (low)	2	3	4	5(high)
	1 (low)	18.9%	16.1%	10.4%	13.2%	15.2%
	2	19.7%	18.5%	11.3%	11.3%	13.3%
B/P	3	21.0%	19.4%	12.0%	11.4%	14.7%
Portfolio	4	26.2%	21.7%	13.3%	10.2%	14.3%
	5 (high)	28.1%	25.7%	19.8%	17.5%	19.3%

SOURCE: Stephen H. Penman and Francesco Reggiani, "Returns to Buying Earnings and Book Values: Accounting for Risk and Growth," manuscript, Columbia University and Bocconi University (2008), at http://ssrn.com/abstract=1536618.

average growth is indeed risky: Panel B of exhibit 7.3 reports the standard deviation of growth rates for the 25 E/P-B/P portfolios, and one can see that portfolios with higher growth rates also have a high variance in growth rates.

The accounting analysis provides a risk-based explanation for why B/P is related to returns. Earnings are at risk and B/P is correlated with E/P—the correlation is 0.31 on average and 0.48 for firms with positive earnings—so that is one reason why B/P predicts returns, just as E/P does. But growth is also risky and B/P additionally picks up on that risky growth. The returns in exhibit 7.2 support this explanation (though they may be returns to market mispricing as well).[10] Fama and French may have gotten it right, if for the wrong reason.

One of the names plonked on B/P by the labelers is "growth," with a lower B/P indicating more growth. We have now seen that, in the no-growth case, B/P can be any number but cannot indicate growth. A firm can have a very high P/B yet have no growth; a pharmaceutical firm can have a high P/B (because it expenses R&D), but little (or even negative) earnings growth. A "value" stock with a low P/B can have relative high earnings growth. In short, a high P/B is not necessarily a growth stock. P/B can only indicate growth in conjunction with E/P, and then a higher B/P indicates more growth, rather than a lower B/P. The labels "growth" versus "value" need to be revised to align with how one accounts for value.

Accounting for Value

What does all of this mean for the investor? The following are the takeaways from the chapter.

First, for the investor who screens stocks on just a few multiples, beware. By ignoring information—failing to complete an accounting for value—you might find yourself trading with those using more information than you. And you may be loading up on risk. Ranking on levered P/E certainly picks up leverage risk: As leverage typically reduces P/E, buying low-P/E stocks buys leverage risk. Always unlever the accounting. Then understand that buying unlevered P/E also involves risk; a low unlevered (enterprise) P/E may be due to the market pricing risky earnings lower. If a P/E coincides with a relatively low P/B, you may be taking on risky growth. This points you back to earlier chapters; be diligent about evaluating risky growth. Maybe the returns in exhibit 7.2 are due, in part, to market mispricing that the active investor seeks to exploit. But tread carefully, for those returns may also, in part, be due to risk.

Second, drop out of the labeling game. Mere labeling is bad science, but it also leads to bad investing. Beware of "growth" attributions. A high P/B is not necessarily growth; you will find that a no-growth valuation can yield a high P/B, as with the brand company or pharmaceutical with little growth prospects. Forget the labels applied to P/E and P/B. Rather, work through the accounting for value. Understand the growth expectation and ask whether you wish to buy: Is it growth to pay for or is it risky growth? The tools in the preceding chapter will help you. If you deem growth to be risky, require a higher hurdle rate in evaluating growth-return profiles.

Third, dismiss the claim in the standard value versus growth dichotomy that growth is low risk. Rather, stick to the fundamentalist view that growth is risky.

The last point bears on formal valuation. Valuation models typically add growth as an adjustment to the required return in the $r - g$ calculation in the denominator. Merrily adding growth (with a higher g) for a given required return yields a higher value. The investor should ask whether, in adding g, one should also add to r. This is the rough-cut protection we built in Chapter 3 where we also appreciated that the S&P 500 portfolio is roughly priced as if growth and risk cancel. This is another reason to heed Benjamin Graham's advice about plugging growth rates into a formula; you might end up paying too much for growth.

See it this way: A U.S. government bond yields no growth and no risk and, accordingly, the required return is the risk-free rate. In moving to risky equities, you are buying growth, and growth is risky. Accordingly, you require a risk premium over the risk-free rate, and the higher the growth, the higher the required risk premium. Indeed, we saw in Chapter 3 that the Fed model implies that growth and the risk premium cancel, and this appears to hold up (though only approximately) in the aggregate stock market data.

But growth can also add value. As modern finance teaches, positive net-present value investments add expected growth, and the additional growth (over that for the risk involved) goes into price; it adds value. One might think of Cisco's expected earnings growth (in the preceding chapter) as risky, but surely some of it adds value, increasing the P/B ratio. So, with the tools in the preceding chapters, the onus is on the investor to assess how much he or she is willing to pay for growth.

It is time to gather the *Accounting Principles* and *Valuation Principles* of the book into one basket. Here is the list thus far:

Accounting Principles

1. Future book value = Current book value + Future Earnings – Future Dividends.
2. Accrual accounting brings the future forward in time, anticipating future cash flows.
3. a. Leverage increases earnings growth.
   b. Leverage increases profitability (the return on common equity).
4. Book rate-of-return is an accounting measure determined by how one accounts for book value. It is not necessarily a measure of real business profitability. Accounting that keeps book values lower generates higher book rates-of-return and higher residual earnings.
5. Conservative accounting with investment growth induces growth in residual income.
6. Under uncertainty, (conservative) accounting defers the recognition of earnings to the future until the uncertainty has been resolved, and the deferral of earnings results in earnings growth.

Valuation Principles

1. To get a handle on value, think first of what the book value is likely to be in the future.

---

2. If one forecasts that the rate-of-return on book value will be equal to the required rate-of-return, the asset must be worth its book value.

3. To get a handle on value, think first of what the book value is likely to be in the future and, second, what the rate-of-return on that book value is likely to be.

4. Growth that is valued does not come from earnings growth but from residual earnings growth.

5. a. Leverage reduces the P/E ratio from the enterprise P/E if the enterprise P/E is less than 1/Borrowing cost.

   b. Leverage increases the P/B ratio over the enterprise price-to-book if the enterprise price-to-book is greater than 1.0.

6. Accounting for value produces valuations that correct for the accounting employed; as earnings can be generated by accounting methods only by reducing book value, the appropriate valuation is preserved by employing book value and earnings together.

For the investor, there is one last (but not least) aspect of accounting for value to focus on, and that is the accounting itself. What does good accounting look like—accounting that provides the anchor for challenging prices? This and previous chapters have emphasized that the investor wants accounting to be conservative. Unfortunately, this is not the drift of modern GAAP and IFRS accounting. Chapters 8 and 9 tackle the issue.

CHAPTER EIGHT

Fair Value Accounting and Accounting for Value

THIS BOOK BUILDS ON the idea that valuation, at the heart of it, is a matter of accounting. However, I have not yet dealt with the form of the appropriate accounting. Examples to this point have employed GAAP accounting, but GAAP has been extensively criticized in many quarters, not least by equity analysts. Is GAAP appropriate accounting for value? Is GAAP accounting something to anchor on? If not, what is the alternative? This and the next chapter deal with these questions.

These questions are timely, for both the Financial Accounting Standards Board (FASB) and International Accounting Standards Board (IASB) are currently developing a new "Conceptual Framework" to lay a foundation for accounting in the future.[1] They are faced with a stark choice, to proceed with recent moves toward fair value accounting or hold fast to the traditional methods of historical cost accounting:

A fundamental conceptual issue [facing accounting standard setters] is the extent to which the standards should move away from traditional cost based accounting to marking assets and liabilities to market, euphemistically referred to as "fair value" accounting. There is without doubt considerable momentum to move toward fair value methodologies, but there are also significant questions about the practical and useful application of that approach to certain industries and firms.

—Paul A. Volcker, Chairman of the Trustees, International
Accounting Standards Committee Foundation in a
statement before the Capital Markets, Insurance
and Government Sponsored Enterprises Subcommittee
of the U.S. House of Representatives,
Washington, DC, June 7, 2001

The choice is pivotal, for a move the wrong way could weaken the ability of accounting to serve as the anchor that the investor needs. That would not only be a loss for the investor, increasing rather than reducing uncertainty, but could also result in less efficient capital markets.

Traditional historical cost accounting carries assets and liabilities on the balance sheet at their cost. Critics see this as a gross deficiency; historical costs (they say) are old prices, often with little connection to the current value of the assets and liabilities. Fair value accounting remedies by reporting the balance sheet at current values that investors need. As a sound bite, this is enticing. "Fair value" sounds right; value, after all, is what we are after. "Historical cost" sounds out of date. Historical cost accounting (it is said) is "accounting for the industrial age," unsuitable for the "information age," and unsuitable for valuation. Fair value accounting has become the vanguard of current-day accounting policy. Is it good accounting for value?

Sound bites are for politicians rather than investors. This chapter shows that the critique of historical cost accounting rests on a gross misconception of how accounting works for valuation. And it shows that, in most cases, fair values are not something to anchor on, despite the appealing language.[2]

Historical Cost Accounting and Fair Value Accounting

Firms invest in assets like plant, inventories, and mortgages in order to employ them in their business to add value. Historical cost is the amount paid for these investments. Clearly, historical cost balance sheets ignore the potential value that can be added by the business, and accordingly, price-to-book ratios are typically greater than one. But historical cost accounting does not ignore value added. It updates the balance sheet for value added when the firm trades with customers. Revenues (sales) from customers are recognized in the income statement, along with the expenses—value given up in earning those revenues—subtracted to yield a net measure of value added; that is, earnings. Those earnings are then added (in the accountant's closing entry) to the book value of shareholders' equity from which dividends can then be paid. *Accounting Principle 1* in Chapter 2 outlines the scheme. Inventory is a good example: Record inventory on the balance sheet at its cost, and then add value to the balance sheet when the inventory is sold (with a [hopefully] higher accounts receivable number replacing the inventory cost). But do not add value to the inventory cost until a customer has been nabbed; do not fair value inventory by recording it at what it could be worth *if* a customer could be found. That would be speculation.

Historical cost accounting follows the business process: Invest in the business (and record the investments on the balance sheet at cost), add value to those investments by selling products and services to customers (and record the amount added in the income statement), and then pay dividends out of those earnings. One important feature dominates: Don't add value in the accounts until you get a customer who will pay you. That suits the fundamentalist well: Don't book expected sales; don't speculate about what the firm might be able to do in the future; *tell me what you know, leave the speculation to me*. That is accounting I can anchor on; I can speculate about future revenues and earnings but, to be anchored, I need the accounting to show me that the firm can attract paying customers and can earn a profit from doing so. Indeed, that anchor will help me challenge speculation; a forecast of future sales and earnings is more difficult to justify if the firm cannot find customers now or is making little progress in doing so. That accounting served us well in the 1990's Internet bubble. While the market, with its valuations of "new economy" stocks in the sky, speculated outlandishly about future sales and earnings, the losses reported by those firms was a check and, indeed, forecasted their ultimate demise. The principle is ingrained in society; we put executives in jail if they book revenue when they do not have a customer. "An outrage!" we say.

Fair value accounting proponents look at the historical-cost balance sheet and call it a disgrace: "How can a firm report assets that are not indicative of their 'true' value?" "Reporting assets at their historical cost is like driving down the road looking in the rear-vision mirror!" The shareholder needs to know what the assets and liabilities are really worth. With fair values, investors would only have to look at the balance sheet to read "value"—an immediate anchor. The accounting would be much more timely; rather than waiting for the firm to add value by conducting business, the accounting would indicate value immediately. Clearly, these ideas differ from those imbedded in historical cost accounting.

To date, fair value accounting under GAAP and IFRS is limited to financial instruments, with financial institutions particularly affected, though firms have a "fair value option" to apply fair values to a wider set of assets and liabilities. Should fair value accounting be expanded, or is it enough already? Should there be less fair value accounting, even for the financial assets like mortgages? For the analyst, the issue is a pragmatic one: Does fair value accounting help or hinder valuation?"

Fair Value Accounting as an Anchor

You can see fairly quickly that the fundamentalist may have trouble with fair value accounting. Value is in the mind of the beholder, the speculator. This is not something to anchor on. Whose "fair" value?

The FASB has a reply: Fair value is the market 'exit' price, the amount that the firm can sell the asset for at market or would have to pay to be relieved of a liability.[3] The fair value of inventory is what it can be sold for, and the fair value of a mortgage loan is the amount a bank could sell the loan for in a market that trades mortgages. A market price is said to be objective. But the seeming objectivity is not the objectivity that fundamentalists seek, for they are skeptical about prices. They understand that market prices are what speculators think about value, not necessarily value justified by the facts. Prices can deviate from fundamentals. Indeed, markets can produce price bubbles.

We have clearly reengaged the efficient markets discussion that separates fundamentalists from modern finance. Fair value accounting finds its justification in efficient market theory; price summarizes all available information, so price supplies the accounting for value. The fundamentalist sees price as different from value, so demands an autonomous accounting, independent of price, which provides information about value to challenge price. Indeed, such accounting promotes efficient prices.

The fair value gains and losses in exhibit 8.1, reported in the financial statements of Cisco Systems, Intel, and Microsoft, highlight the problem.

During the technology bubble, these firms held significant investments in technology companies and marked them to market, as required by GAAP. These were not trading portfolios, but largely holdings as part of an operational strategy for acquiring, developing, and marketing technology. You can see significant unrealized gains on these investments as the firms booked bubble gains from the investments.[4] A fundamental analyst who compared prices to fundamentals would have seen that these gains were fictitious, "water in the balance sheet," as Benjamin Graham would say. As in the 1920s (when accountants were accused of putting water in the balance sheet with asset revaluations), the asset values vaporized as the technology bubble burst, as the subsequent reported losses (of billions of dollars) in fiscal-years 2000 and 2001 indicate. In all cases, the losses wiped out the gains in the preceding years.

EXHIBIT 8.1 Fair Value Gains and Losses on Investments Reported by Intel, Microsoft, and Cisco Systems, Fiscal-Years 1998–2002 (in millions of dollars).

	1998	1999	2000	2001	2002
Cisco Systems	28	234	3,240	(3,812)	224
Intel	545	3,188	(3,596)	(163)	(19)
Microsoft	627	1,052	(283)	(1,460)	5

NOTE: As the three firms had different fiscal years, the drop in the prices of their technology holdings (at about the same time) affected them in different fiscal years.

Putting prices in the financial statements defies a fundamentalist principle: *When calculating value to challenge price, beware of putting price in the calculation.* The practice induces circularity where the accounting that is supposed to challenge prices incorporates the prices to be challenged. The anchor drifts. Such accounting can even promote bubbles; that is, investors infer higher prices from higher reported earnings and book values, but those higher earnings and book values are due to higher prices.[5] Prices thus feed on themselves, with accounting as the instrument. Such feedback loops may be quite dangerous, leading to crashes and adding to systemic risk.[6] Rather than supplying information that cuts across bubble prices, accounting becomes an instrument in promoting bubbles and associated momentum investing. Warren Buffett said that the 1990s Internet bubble was a chain letter, and the investment bankers were the postmen. Fair value accounting is in danger of taking on that role.[7]

History repeats: With a real estate bubble in the mid-2000s, the market value of mortgages and the securities that packaged them increased. Mark-to-market accounting brought these speculative gains into the accounts, increasing bank's capital ratios, encouraging more dubious lending to record even more fair value gains. Such a bubble must burst, with prices now cascading downward, as the sorry aftermath tells.

A crash is no time to read "fair" value from market prices for, just as momentum pricing develops in a speculative bubble, cascading prices can lead to depressed prices as investors flee (A negative bubble? A black hole?). With the market for mortgage-backed securities no longer functioning in the financial crisis, banks had only fire-sale prices from illiquid markets as reference. Not something to anchor on. In 2008, Vikram Pandit, the CEO hired to pull Citigroup out of the mire, complained before the U.S. Congress that his bank was required to fair value mortgages at prices below what they considered them to be worth.[8] This raises the specter of banks recognizing losses on initiation of loans that are considered to be good business, discouraging lending and exacerbating the credit crunch. Whereas in a rising mortgage market, banks may record "first-day" gains on initiation of loans (before any loan servicing), in a down market they may recognize "first-day" losses. Again, such accounting has feedback effects. In boom times, banks have incentives to make bad loans, supplying the increasing securitization pyramid and recording securitization gains in the process. They develop large marketing and sales forces to promote refinancing. In a bust, they have reduced incentive to make good loans and to work through loan problems with their customers, leading to further cascades in value.[9] Collateral demands against immediate prices rather than the long-run value of lending activity lead to further distress. In both boom and bust, the measure of value changes value, the Heisenberg principle (of a sort): The measurement of position necessarily disturbs momentum, and vice versa.

The mortgage crisis sorely tested the fair value accounting assumption of efficient markets. How can the price of a securitized mortgage obligation, trading far from the originator, reflect the information that a bank on the ground has about its customers, their credit quality, and the ability of customers to work through their credit problems? It is on the ground that accountants and auditors do their field work, to get to the facts on which value is based. And that value is in a bank's success in long-term lending, in managing credit risk through boom and bust. By substituting prices for historical cost information about that value, information that serves as a check on speculation is lost; prices evolve without an anchoring accounting for value in mortgages, so they take on a life of their own, detached from fundamentals. Market prices are determined by liquidity, and the demand for liquidity is driven by banks seeking the liquidity that responds to their asset writedowns. Yet liquidity is in short supply in a crash, resulting in large liquidity discounts in prices.[10] Fundamentalists are concerned about underlying fundamentals, not short-term liquidity. They are investors in the long-run value in mortgage lending, not day traders; *price is what you pay, value is what you get.*

Unfortunately it gets worse. Recording fair values at market prices is called "mark-to-market" accounting or so-called Level 1 fair value accounting in accountant-speak. But GAAP insists that fair value accounting be applied when there is no market price. Level 2 fair value accounting uses "other market inputs" to infer a price when there is no active market, like the price of comparable assets. Level 3 fair value accounting is applied when there is no market data at all; management must estimate, hypothetically, what an asset would be worth if there were a market. Now we are in never-never land. The fundamentalist knows the hazards of estimating value, with all the uncertainties involved. Fair values are based on the "present value of cash flows," which not only includes speculation about future cash flows, but also the expectations necessary to estimate a discount rate in the denominator. The fundamentalist understands that discount rates from asset pricing models are a false reality. The fundamentalist understands that "marking to model" is a cover for introducing speculative expectations.

Add the tendency of managements to use accounting to paint the picture they want, and the fundamentalist is increasingly nervous. They think that accounting should not only be independent of prices, but also independent of managers. Accounting should be invariant to ourselves, to guard against our tendency to speculate, but more importantly, it must be invariant to our agents to whom we trust our money. Fundamentalists are concerned that the FASB and IASB in their Conceptual Framework have (controversially) decided to downgrade "stewardship" as a leading reporting objective. Logical, perhaps, if management expectations are now to be the basis of accounting, but the steward's masters, the shareholders, are not well served. Imagine reporting earnings that are just the change in expectations; earnings have to be earned! Won't management set fair values as a reverse engineering of their desired compensation? If we desire accounting to be as independent of human foibles as possible, this is not what we want. One is (guardedly) interested in what managements think about value, so management forecasts are welcome (outside of the accounts). But to put a self-interested forecast into the financial statements is to defile what the fundamentalist sees accounting as all about, a travesty.

With respect to mortgage loans, a similar problem arises with "amortized historical cost," for that accounting requires estimates of credit losses. Indeed, mark-to-market accounting (with actual prices) is often proposed as a remedy. Accounting methods should be compared against alternatives, and the next chapter provides one for mortgage accounting that satisfies the fundamental investor, one that minimizes estimates, and one that is far from appealing to speculative prices for information.

Again history instructs: Although other accounting issues were also involved, Enron, at its core, was a fair value accounting scam. With permission from the SEC to employ fair value accounting for long-term energy contracts, Enron booked fictitious profits based on a business idea rather than its execution, building a house of cards that ultimately collapsed. The opening scene of *ENRON,* the musical comedy, depicts a champagne celebration on receiving the approval from the SEC.[11] Fair value accounting, short-term profits, champagne bonuses, long-term disaster. Upside for management, downside for shareholders.

Fair value accounting was presumably not the primary cause of the 2008 banking crisis, but it probably did supply the grease for the wheels. We do understand that price speculation was at the core of the problem. Some of the commentary above is conjectural, but one does have to ask: Would things have been different if profits from mortgages (and the derivatives built on them) had not been recognized until loans were deemed to be long-run performing—until the customer delivered? A 2008 IMF (International Monetary Fund) report on global financial stability, published in the midst of the crisis, recommended delinking capital adequacy requirements from fair value accounting reports in order to counter the procyclicality effects.[12] If the IMF sees fair value capital as inappropriate, why should not the shareholders? It is, after all, their capital. Curiously, those who dismiss the role of fair value accounting in the financial crisis point to the fact that more than 50 percent of banks' assets were in loans and leases not subject to fair value accounting.[13] Is this to imply that we are protected by not using fair value accounting?[14]

When Is Fair Value Accounting Appropriate?
The One-to-One Principle

Mark-to-market accounting has an appeal; it is a timely, early warning system. Fair value accounting pulls the information in prices into the accounts immediately. The point presumes market efficiency. This, of course, is a doubtful presumption on which to ground accounting, as the credit default swap market did not forewarn of the financial crisis until it was upon us. But there is another, more fundamental misconception.

For purpose of demonstration, let's suppose that efficient market prices are available that aggregate all available information about the value of an asset. With no need to make estimates, would fair value accounting then be acceptable? To answer this question suppose a firm holds a bond in which it has temporarily invested its excess cash. The bond price goes up. Is the shareholder better off? The answer surely is "yes." The shareholder has benefited from the appreciation (the bond now yields more cash). Now suppose the firm has a pile of coal that goes into a blast furnace for making steel. The exit price of coal—what the firm can sell the coal for—goes up. Is the shareholder better off? Well, probably not, for the coal is an input to the business of making steel, finding customers, and selling steel. The selling price for the coal is what others think the coal is worth for their purposes, which may be quite different from the value in steel making. Indeed, the higher coal price may mean lower profits from steel making. The coal price is timely, but not an indicator of value to a steel maker.

The two examples serve to delineate when fair value accounting is appropriate. If shareholder value moves one-to-one with the market price (like the bond), mark-to-market accounting indicates shareholder value (the bubble problem aside). Call it the one-to-one principle. However, when value comes not from exposure to market prices but from employing assets (like coal) in a business that transforms them into products for sale to customers, market prices do not indicate value. That, of course, is the case with most business. A coal speculator wins or loses with the movement of market prices, one-to-one, and those market prices inform about success. But a steel producer holds coal to add value in steel production, and value is added by success in selling steel rather than one-to-one with the price of coal. A share trader might mark his or her stock portfolio to market, for success is determined by movements in market prices, but not Cisco, Intel, and Microsoft in exhibit 8.1 if their share investments represent investments in other technology companies as part of their operational model of acquiring technologies that complement their own.[15] A hedge fund betting on the price of securitized mortgages or the synthetic derivatives attached to them appropriately marks to market as a measure of success (as does a bank that purely trades mortgages or mortgage-backed securities). These people are betting on price. But a mortgage lender adds value from carefully evaluating mortgagees' credit quality, attracting deposits, and sustaining the operation in the long term. It adds value from the spread between borrowing and lending rates, net of default losses (in the income statement), not from the market price of mortgages (in the balance sheet) or the self-identified "fair value" of core deposits.[16]

As exit prices, fair values are liquidation values, typically reported when a firm is failing. Going-concern value is quite different; the exit price for an ongoing business is the price it can sell its product for after adding value through the business process—revenues in the income statement. It is not the exit price for assets and liabilities used to produce the revenues, for the firm is not in the business of selling those assets and liabilities. The equity analyst is mystified as to why one would shift to liquidation values for the going concern. Why would one record warranty liabilities, for example, at fair value (as has been proposed)? For Whirlpool, the household appliance manufacturer, the exit price is the amount that Whirlpool would have to pay someone else to service the firm's warranties. But manufacturing appliances and servicing warranties on them is Whirlpool's comparative advantage, or how they add value. That's their business. What it would cost someone else to do so, presumably less efficiently, is irrelevant. Indeed, with fair value accounting we lose our ability to understand how a firm makes money.

The one-to-one principle very much constrains fair value accounting. Add the possibility that markets may misprice, or mark-to-estimates are substituted for market prices, then fair value accounting must come with a large, bold-type product warning label.[17] The fundamentalist has the label ready: *When calculating value to challenge price, beware of putting price in the calculation.*

There are additional issues, however. One cannot fair value an asset without also fair valuing matching liabilities, otherwise gains on assets are recorded without offsetting losses on the associated liability (and vice versa). If a bank fair values mortgage loans for changes in interest rates, it must also fair value the matching core deposits, but these are typically not traded. Their value (to the shareholder) comes from the intangibles built with customer relationships (which can be a function of interest rates), not from a hypothetical "exit value." Fair value accounting is thus limited to cases where a business works on a matched book, both sides of the book have a one-to-one relationship of price to value, and both sides of the book can be marked to efficient market prices. Where the customer is the top line, fair value accounting is not accounting for value.

Which accountant could guess at the value of the intangible assets involved in servicing core deposits? The answer is "the FASB." At the time of this writing, the board had concluded that

> Core deposit liabilities would be initially and subsequently measured at the present value of the average core deposit liability amount discounted at the rate differential between the alternative funds rate and the all-in-cost-to-service rate over the implied maturity (the "remeasurement amount"). In calculating the present value of the average core deposit liability amount, entities should consider future core deposits. This would result in an intangible asset being reflected in the valuation.
>
> —FASB, Accounting for Financial Instruments:
> Summary of Decisions Reached to Date, as of
> March 31, 2010, FASB website at www.fasb.org.

The FASB is inviting banks to add value based on their forecast of future transactions with customers. That's booking profits without actually having a customer. That's what we put people in jail for. And that's very speculative accounting. A bank can now report their liability to you, the depositor, at less than what they owe you. (Complaints at the teller window will not be entertained, however.)

Fair Value Accounting and Risk

Historical cost accounting defers the recognition of value on the balance sheet until there is resolution of uncertainty (by finding a customer who pays). In the parlance of modern finance, value is not booked to the balance sheet until the firm has a low-beta asset like a receivable or cash from the customer. The resulting balance sheet is thus a "hard" balance sheet on which the investor can anchor. This suits the investor who is accounting for value, for uncertain, speculative outcomes are excluded from the accounting.

In contrast, fair value accounting, by booking value up front, presents a risky balance sheet. Whether based on prices or estimated fair values from future cash flow streams, fair values are expectations of risky outcomes. Value on the balance sheet, but value at risk. This has two implications.

First, leverage—the amount of borrowing relative to assets—is no longer leverage against hard assets, but leverage against expectations. An increase in fair value lowers reported leverage and the appearance of risk from leverage, even though added value always has variance around it. (Risk-weighted leverage measures and capital ratios ameliorate.) The situation is made worse when the firm's debt is fair valued on declining estimates on credit worthiness. That results not only in lower carrying amounts for debt but also reported gains on the deterioration of the firm. Treating debt as if it is something owned by the shareholder and to be sold on whim—something from which gains can be made—conflicts with the standard view of a financing position: Debt is something to be repaid, and reporting that there is less to be repaid when the firms runs into difficulties goes against the idea of a hard balance sheet. Effectively the firm is pushing forward the obligation to repay the face value of the debt to future years.[18]

Second, the accounting invites distributions from (unrealized) profits that may not eventuate, increasing leverage and risk. Those distributions may be in bonuses paid out of fair value profits or dividends paid to shareholders in violation of the principle that dividends are not paid until earnings are earned. Paying dividends without profits reeks of a Ponzi scheme and paying bonuses before earnings are earned looks like a compensation Ponzi scheme. Accounting is supposed to cut across Ponzi schemes, not promote them. Accounting for value (in Chapter 2), builds this in, for it sees book value as something from which dividends can be paid, not to be affected by fair value profits that are still contingent. Financial institutions paid both large bonuses—50 percent of profits seemed to be the standard for investment banks—and large dividends out of imaginary wealth that was not subsequently realized, weakening them for the crisis that followed. The dividend scheme echoes the old scam that every bond trustee is aware of: Pay out the loot to shareholders and leave the creditors holding the bag. The bonus scheme paid managers well, as Ponzi schemes do, but left shareholders holding the bag, not to mention outraged taxpayers left to bail out the banks that paid the "fat bonuses." There is a vicious circle here: As fair value earnings are just accounting journal entries (with no cash from revenues), a firm has to borrow to make these distributions, increasing leverage and risk.

A Lesson from Free Markets

Hedge funds apply fair value accounting. As they are betting on prices with a matched book (and the one-to-one principle applies), this is appropriate. And, by contract with investors, they must price the net asset value at which investors enter and depart the fund. However, when the outcome of investments are particularly uncertain or there are no available liquid prices, these funds lock up or create side pockets until they have some resolution about the ultimate value of investments (as do private equity funds). They do this because they fear a transfer of wealth between current and future investors similar to that we saw with banks paying dividends out of fair value profits prior to the financial crisis. Lessons from behavior in free markets (without regulation) might well be taken to heart in considering the imposition of accounting by regulation; lock up earnings until there has been resolution of uncertainty. Don't book earnings from which dividends can be paid until there are sales to customers. Such accounting locks up bonuses until uncertainty is resolved.

The Misconception About Historical Cost Accounting

Advocacy for fair value accounting is based on a misconception that historical cost accounting is a poor conveyor of value to the shareholder. The misconception is tied to the view that accounting is remiss if it does not get the balance sheet right. This view is shared by those who maintain that accounting fails by not putting intangible assets on the balance sheet. They ask: How can accountants leave important assets off the balance sheet, assets such as a firm's 'knowledge capital,' its 'human capital,' the 'organization capital' in its customer and supply-chain relationships, and its R&D assets? Why in this 'information age' do we still have a balance sheet more suited for the 'industrial age' when value came primarily from tangible assets rather than intangible assets? Let's get value back on the balance sheet!

This is an alluring proposal. The fundamentalist, of course, shudders. He or she sees the term, "intangible asset," as an excuse for speculation, for putting water in the balance sheet. The cry for more intangible asset accounting and more "value reporting" reached a pitch in the bubble of the 1990s when technology firms traded at 10 times book value and more. Those "intangible assets" subsequently vaporized.

Anyone drilled in the methods of accounting for value sees the fallacy in the notion that the balance sheet is remiss if it does not indicate asset values; there is also an income statement and accounting for value employs both the income statement and the balance sheet. If value is missing from book value, it can be plugged with earnings from the income statement. That's what residual income valuation does. A final accounting principle, *Accounting Principle 7*, highlights the idea:

Accounting Principle 7

The stock return is always equal to earnings plus the change in the price over book value for the earnings period

$$\text{Stock return}_t = \text{Earnings}_t + (\text{Price}_t - \text{Book value}_t)$$
$$- (\text{Price}_{t-1} - \text{Book value}_{t-1}).$$

This principle is an important one for linking accounting to value. Price minus book value is the error in the balance sheet that fair value accounting and proponents of intangible asset accounting maintain is a failure of accounting. But this principle says that omission of value from the balance sheet does not matter if the error on the balance sheet at the end of the period ($\text{Price}_t - \text{Book value}_t$) is the same as that in the beginning ($\text{Price}_{t-1} - \text{Book value}_{t-1}$); the errors cancel.[19] Valuation tolerates accounting error in the balance sheet if that error is constant. The canceling error property is taught in introductory accounting courses by pointing out that it does not matter whether one capitalizes R&D expenditure (and subsequently amortizes it) or expenses it immediately, provided there is no growth in R&D expenditure. Even though it is perceived to be "wrong" to leave R&D investment off the balance sheet, the balance sheet errors from expensing immediately cancel, leaving earnings unaffected. More generally, the omission of assets from the balance sheet is mitigated by the income statement and canceling errors.

In other words, it does not matter if intangible assets are missing from the balance sheet if earnings from those intangible assets are flowing through the income statement. Indeed, given that earnings from intangible assets are reported, one does not have to identify (or speculate about) the existence of intangible assets. The R&D accounting example shows that this is strictly so only if there is no growth in R&D expenditure. But, as it turns out, this is the case of the no-growth valuation on which the fundamentalist anchors. Growth possibly adds value, but it is the valuation of growth that the fundamentalist wants to separate from the accounting. The fundamentalist says, "Please do not bring the speculation about growth from intangible assets onto the balance sheet; leave the speculation to me (and let me add the value of speculative growth to the no-growth valuation)."

To see how valuation works for "intangible asset" firms using historical cost accounting, consider Microsoft and Dell Computer. These firms both trade at high multiples of book value, indicating considerable value missing from the balance sheet. To what extent is that missing value a problem for the equity analyst? What issues does the analyst run into when trying to incorporate the value of intangible assets?[20]

Microsoft Corporation

Microsoft is said to have value in its network externalities, the dominance of Windows, its brand, and its product R&D. None of these assets are on its balance sheet. After publishing its annual report for fiscal year ending June 2008, Microsoft traded at $25 per share or $228,775 million. With a book value of $36,286 million, the market saw a considerable value, $192,489 million, missing from the balance sheet (the price-to-book ratio is 6.3). The book value of $36,286 million was made up of a mere $12,624 million of net operating assets (enterprise book value) and $23,662 million of cash and near-cash investments (and no financing debt). The income statement for 2008 reported interest income on the cash and near-cash assets of $846 million (after an allo-cation of tax) and after-tax operating income from the business of $16,835 million, for a total net income of $17,681 million.

With just these few summary numbers from the financial state-ments, we can take considerable steps toward challenging the market price. Applying a residual earnings no-growth valuation (as in earlier chapters),

$$
\begin{aligned}
\text{Equity value} &= \text{Enterprise value} + \text{Value of cash} \\
&= \text{Net operating assets}_{2008} \\
&\quad + \frac{\text{Residual operating income}_{2009}}{r} + \text{Cash}_{2008}.
\end{aligned}
$$

This no-growth valuation is the valuation that is appropriate if balance sheet errors cancel. Let's give Microsoft a required return, r, of 9 per-cent. The no-growth equity value on which the analyst anchors is thus (in millions of dollars):

$$
\begin{aligned}
\text{Equity value} &= 12,624 + \frac{16,835 - (0.09 \times 12,624)}{0.09} + 23,662 \\
&= 210,718, \text{ or } \$23.03 \text{ per share.}
\end{aligned}
$$

Note that the valuation forecasts 2009 enterprise income as being the same as that reported for 2008. Thus we are only using information in the summary numbers, ignoring all other information (including considerable more information in the financial statements) that might get us a better anchor for 2009 earnings. One can quibble about the appropriate required return, but the point is clear; although consider-able value is missing in the balance sheet, the accounting that includes earnings explains almost all the value that the market sees in its $25 price. We have a no-growth valuation that anchors us for the question of whether value should be added for speculative growth. We have an anchor for asking whether the market's additional value for growth, $1.97 per share, is appropriate.

To the point, we would not want this anchoring accounting for value to be messed up by fair value numbers in the balance sheet or numbers that speculate about the value of intangible assets. History would suggest that this no-growth accounting for value would have provided a strong challenge to mispricing. In the bubble years of the late 1990s when Microsoft was trading up to $60 (on a post-split basis) and at very high multiples, the accounting valuation was much lower than the market price. Rather than the market price suggesting that the accounting was ignoring intangible assets, the accounting (which reflected the value of intangible assets through earnings) would have suggested that the market was mispricing those assets. Subsequent experience suggests that investors who shunned intangible asset stocks such as Microsoft, Cisco Systems, Intel, Dell, and the like in the late 1990s fared considerably better than those who purchased the stocks because they had "intangible assets." Accounting serves us well if it is designed to challenge speculation about intangible assets rather than incorporating them.

Dell Computer

Dell, the computer manufacturer, is said to have valuable "organization capital." Exhibit 8.2 displays the balance sheet for Dell for fiscal-year 2008, reformulated to separate net operating assets in the business from the net financial assets consisting of cash and near-cash assets less financing debt.

Trading at $20 per share at the time (giving it an equity market capitalization of $41,200 million), the market attributed considerable value to Dell over the book value of $3,735 million (a P/B of 11). The missing value in the balance could readily be attributed to the enterprising way Dell organizes its business (direct-to-customer delivery, just-in-time inventory, outsourcing of production, and innovative supply chains). Far from ignoring it, this "organization capital" is actually evident on the balance sheet. Relative to $61.1 billion in sales, accounts receivable is low (direct-to-customers yields cash in advance); inventory is low (just-in-time); and property, plant, and equipment is low (outsourcing production). The low operating asset values mean that shareholders need invest less to get value. But the big feature of the balance sheet is the negative net operating assets, a negative $5,076 million in 2008. This negative number is due not only to the low investment in assets,

EXHIBIT 8.2 Comparative Balance Sheet for Dell Inc. for 2008, Reformulated to Distinguish Operating Activities from Financing Activities (in millions of dollars)

	2008		2007	
Enterprise Book Value:				
Operating Assets				
Working cash		40		40
Accounts receivables		5,961		4,622
Financing receivables		2,139		1,853
Inventories		1,180		660
Property, plant, and equipment		2,668		2,409
Goodwill		1,648		110
Intangible assets		780		45
Other assets		3,653		3,491
		18,069		13,230
Operating Liabilities				
Accounts payable	11,492		10,430	
Accrued liabilities	4,323		5,141	
Deferred service revenue	5,260		4,221	
Other liabilities	2,070	23,145	647	20,439
Net Operating Assets		(5,076)		(7,209)
Net Financial Assets				
Cash equivalents	7,724		9,506	
Short-term investments	208		752	
Long-term investments	1,560		2,147	
	9,492		12,405	
Short-term borrowing	(225)		(188)	
Long-term debt	(362)		(569)	
Redeemable stock	(94)	8,811	(111)	11,537
Common Shareholders' Equity		3,735		4,328

but also to the large operating liabilities. In managing its supply chain, Dell is able to get suppliers to accept deferred payment (such that accounts payable and accrued expenses are high), and attracts customers to pay in advance (producing deferred revenues).

The negative net operating assets means that there is even more value (from the business) missing from the balance sheet than the levered P/B ratio of 11 would suggest; the shareholders' equity is positive only because Dell holds $8,811 million in net financial assets. Does this make the accounting even more deficient? No; because there is also an income statement. That statement reported operating income (after-tax) of $2,618 million for 2008. Calculating residual operating income from the enterprise for 2008 (in millions of dollars), using a required return of 10 percent for the more risky firm:

Residual operating income $= 2,618 - (0.10 \times -7,209) = 3,338.9$.

Dell's residual income is actually larger than its income! This is because Dell adds value with income of $2,618 million in the income statement, but also from organizing its business with negative net operating assets. The value of the organization asset is reflected in the accounting and in the residual income calculation with that accounting; the organizational asset indeed adds value. That organization means that Dell effectively runs a float and that float means that shareholders, rather than investing in the business, can withdraw from the business and invest elsewhere. Rather than investment being charged at the required return to reduce residual income, the component of the residual income calculation, $720.9 = - (0.10 \times -7,209)$ million, is the value that shareholders add from investing the float at 10 percent. (Dell's large, yearly stock repurchases are the flow to shareholders out of this float.)

Applying the residual income in a no-growth valuation,

$$\text{Equity value} = 8,811 - 5,076 + \frac{3,338.9}{0.10}$$
$$= 37,124 \text{ million, or } \$18.02 \text{ per share.}$$

This is somewhat lower than the market price of $20, but the point is that much of the value of "organization capital" is in the accounting; the accounting is not missing the intangible asset, and adding an intangible asset to the balance sheet would be redundant. So it is with a brand asset, for a company like Coca-Cola, for example. Further, the accounting gives us the insight for challenging speculation about added value for growth. That value must come from growth in residual income, and growth in residual income must come from growth in operating income (sales and margins) or growth in the float from the way the business is organized.

To move to fair value accounting and destroy these anchoring valuations would be a shame. Information would be lost. Earnings would now be the change in the (fair) market prices in the balance sheet, and economics tells us that such changes in prices do not forecast the future; prices follow a "random walk" (they fluctuate randomly) so earnings become uninformative, a useless anchor. Add the possibility that firms would estimate (Level 3) fair values with error (and bias), and earnings become just a change in an estimate, compounding the error in the balance sheet rather than correcting it, and a fair value house of cards is built. Adding volatility and randomness while losing the ability to forecast the future is no improvement.

Accounting for Value: A Balance Sheet Versus Income Statement Focus

Fair value accounting sees value being communicated through the balance sheet. The FASB and IASB, in developing their Conceptual Framework for accounting, appear to be taking this balance sheet focus: Measure value in the balance sheet and let earnings fall out as just the change in balance sheet measurement.[21] For valuation, the approach is misguided. Accounting for value recognizes that value is missing from the balance sheet (appropriately) but is added in the income statement, so valuation is a matter of using the income statement and balance sheet together.

Fair value accounting is not accounting for value. Apart from the case of a matched asset and liability trading book, an accountant cannot hope to capture value by listing assets and liabilities at their fair value. Value in business arises from using assets and liabilities jointly, and deploying them in an innovative way, as the Dell example vividly illustrates. Indeed, business is all about entrepreneurial ideas to deploy assets together with people, relationships, and a myriad of other "intangibles" to get an edge and add value. Individual assets and liabilities cannot have stand-alone fair values, nor can the sum of fair values express the value of using assets together. In economist-speak, fair value accounting works only with frictionless markets where (efficient) prices indicate the value of an asset in every use (and there is no need for accounting). That, of course, is a fantasy world. Dealing with market frictions is what business is all about: Business is designed to exploit differences between input and output prices, and to add value on the spread. Business, in effect, arbitrages the frictions between input and output prices. In the ideal, pure competition model of the economist, the business earns just a normal return, for the opportunity to arbitrage is priced away. The entrepreneur seeks to get an edge, if ever so temporary. In this real world, we require an independent accounting, and an accounting for value, to ascertain the success in doing so.

The remarkable feature of accounting is that it does produce one number for deploying assets together. That number is earnings. Earnings are the summary number from the deployment of assets in the balance sheet (jointly). Indeed, earnings incorporate the value added from "intangible" assets not on the balance sheet. Accordingly, the earnings number serves to correct a balance sheet that cannot hope to recognize business value. But it is historical cost accounting earnings that capture the value added. Fair value accounting earnings obscure it.

Accordingly, the search for better accounting should abandon the notion of fair value accounting and focus on improving historical cost accounting. Historical cost accounting, appropriately applied, serves the equity analyst well. Its conservatism in adding value only when there are transactions with customers provides the analyst with a powerful tool for challenging speculation about growth.[22] Based as it is on actual transactions, it is objective, based on the facts. The name "historical cost accounting" is unfortunate; it does sound like accounting as history. Let's call it historical *transactions* accounting.

The impressive feature of historical transactions accounting is that, contrary to popular opinion, it is forward looking rather than backward looking. Understanding a firm's core profitability from its transactions with customers, one has a good starting point for forecasting and valuing the future, as the Microsoft and Dell examples in this chapter indicate. Sales beget sales and core profit margins are typically a good starting point for a forecast of margins from future sales. To the extent that this is not the case, the accounting also works well: Speculation about the future is excluded from the accounting, so that the analyst is provided with an anchor with which to develop speculation about the future and to challenge speculation in the market price.

It thus remains to discuss what good forward-looking historical transactions accounting might look like. That is the subject of the next chapter of the book. Evidence suggests that the forward-looking ability of earnings has declined over the last forty years: while earnings volatility has more than doubled during the period, earnings persistence has fallen.[23] These are characteristics one would expect from the increasing application of fair value accounting, but also from the decline in the quality of historical transactions accounting.

CHAPTER NINE

Adding Value to Accounting

THE LAST CHAPTER EXPLAINED how historical transactions accounting works for valuation. What remains is to flesh it out. What should historical transaction accounting look like if it is to anchor the investor and challenge speculation? What is the appropriate accounting for valuation? Fear not, I will not bog us down in accounting minutia; the purpose is to paint a picture in broad strokes, outlining core principles rather than a detailed code.

Returns to Penetrating the Accounting

The humdrum of accounting may not sound very exciting to the investor. The yearly mailings of annual reports are tedious (thank heaven for the paperless world!). You might be tempted to check out at this point; leave this matter to the bean counters. That might be a mistake, for failure to understand accounting and where it can go wrong is to take on accounting risk. The defensive investor protects against bad accounting and the active investor exploits it. See this chapter as a letter to accounting regulators on behalf of you, the investor, but a correspondence that highlights deficiencies in GAAP about which you might wish to be aware. That having been said, this chapter is not a manual on how to deal with the imperfections of GAAP in detail. A "quality of earnings" analysis, applied to GAAP, is available in many financial analysis texts.[1]

To whet your appetite for accounting, let's look at the historical returns from analyzing financial statements. The first set of returns, in figure 9.1, comes from a financial statement analysis that utilizes information in the line items of financial statements—sales growth, core profit margins, asset turnovers, net operating asset growth, among other measures—to forecast the forward return on net operating assets (RNOA). The forward RNOA is of course an important number for the investor to anchor on in a residual income valuation. The analysis produces a score, the S-score, which indicates the probability, ranging between zero and one, that future RNOA will be higher than current RNOA (with a score of 0.5 indicating that forward RNOA will be the same as the current year). Figure 9.1(a) tracks RNOA for five years before and after the scoring year for high and low S-scores. Figure 9.1(b) reports annual returns to a trading strategy that goes long on high S-scores and short on low S-scores, for a zero-net investment (before transactions costs). Returns are size adjusted to take out the component attributable to the well-known "size effect."

It is clear from the first panel that digging deeper into the financial statements is productive; the RNOA spread between high and low S-score firms in the forward year is 4.1 percent, implying significant differences in forecasts of forward residual operating income. The differences persist over the five years. And the returns in the second panel from utilizing the financial statement scoring are also significant; the trading strategy yields positive returns in all but four years. The average return from the strategy for all years is 15.5 percent (before transactions costs). Returns to zero investment should of course be zero—otherwise there is an arbitrage opportunity—so it appears that the market does not penetrate the accounting information as it should. Indeed, exploiting the mispricing of accounting information in this way is called account-

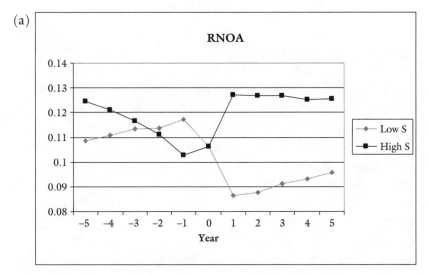

(a)

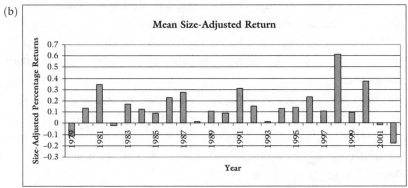

(b)

FIGURE 9.1   (a) Path of RNOA for Firms with High and Low S-Scores for Five Years Before and After the Scoring Year (Year o), and (b) Annual Returns to a Trading Strategy Based on S-Scores, 1979–2002.

The S-score is the estimated probability that RNOA will increase in the forward year, elicited from financial statement information. RNOA is based on operating income before special items, extraordinary items, and discontinued operations. In figure 9.1(a), the high RNOA group consists of stocks with S-scores in the top third each year, and the low RNOA group consists of stocks with S-scores in the bottom third. The RNOA is initialized to be the same for both groups in year o. In figure 9.1(b), the trading strategy involves going long on stocks with the top 10 percent of S-scores each year and short on those with the lowest 10 percent of scores, for a zero-net investment. Each annual return is the sum of returns from the long and short positions. Source: Stephen H. Penman and Xiao-Jun Zhang, "Modeling Sustainable Earnings and P/E Ratios with Financial Statement Analysis," Columbia University and University of California, Berkeley (2004), available at www.ssrn.com/abstract = 318967.

ing arbitrage. (The negative returns in four of the years indicate that this arbitraging is not entirely risk-free, however).

The second set of returns, in figure 9.2, is that from the so-called "accrual anomaly." Earnings are comprised of cash flow and accrual components, and the first panel in figure 9.2(a) (from the original paper on the anomaly) shows that firms with high accrual components of earnings (measured in year 0) exhibit increasing earnings up to that year but considerably lower earnings subsequently, and vice versa for firms with low accrual components. The pattern contrasts with that for high and low cash-flow components in the second panel in figure 9.2(a) where the reversion in earnings is not nearly as strong. The two panels draw a picture of firms with high accruals increasing their earnings via those accruals, but those earnings cannot be sustained; in the parlance of forecasting, accrual-intensive earnings are less persistent, that is, less sustainable. Does the market understand this? The answer appears to be "no." The final panel, in the figure 9.2(b), reports zero-net investment returns, like those in figure 9.1, from investing long in low-accrual firms and short in high-accrual firms. From 1962 to 1991, there are only two years with a negative return to this strategy. The average return to the strategy over all years is 10.4 percent. It appears that the market does not understand the accounting, and its implications for the future. Thus the term, "accrual anomaly."

These returns come with the standard warning that past returns are not indicative of the future. Indeed, the returns here are not in real time, but rather from back testing. (Street talk says the accrual anomaly has gone away, something one might expect for such a well-publicized trading strategy). One cannot rule out that the trading strategies here are just loading up on risk, although the papers reporting these returns go to pains to test for this. Nevertheless, these returns and those of many other studies call into question the efficiency of the stock market in drawing out the full implications of accounting information.[2] Perhaps surprisingly, research has also shown that analysts' forecasts on which the market relies for its information do not reflect information about future earnings that can be elicited from current and past financial statements.[3]

The investment returns in figures 9.1 and 9.2 suggest that the market extrapolates naïvely from current earnings, ignoring the deeper

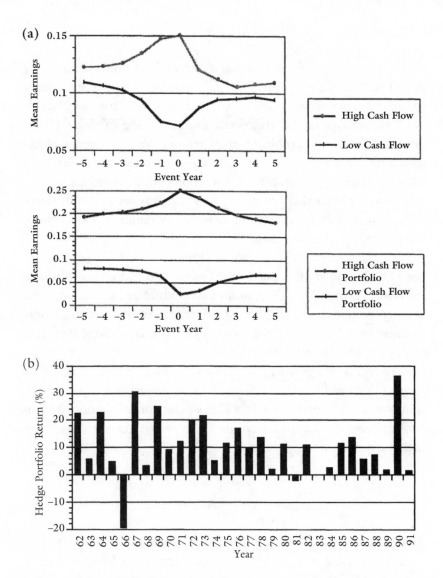

FIGURE 9.2 (a) Path of Earnings for High- and Low-Accrual Firms and High and Low Cash Flow Firms for Five Years Before and After Firms Are Identified by Their Accrual and Cash Flow Components of Earnings, and (b) Annual Returns to a Trading Strategy Based on the Accrual Component of Earnings, 1962–1991.

Earnings are income from continuing operations divided by total assets (and accruals and cash flows are similarly scaled). Cash flow is the difference between earnings and accruals. High-accrual firms are those with the top 10 percent of accruals in each year, and low accruals are firms with the lowest 10 percent (and similarly so for cash flows). Returns are size-adjusted returns on a zero-net investment (hedge) portfolio from taking a long position each year in stocks with the lowest 10 percent of accruals and a short position in stocks with the highest 10 percent of accruals. Source: Richard G.. Sloan, "Do Stock Prices Fully Reflect Information in Accruals and Cash Flows About Future Earnings?" *Accounting Review* 71 (1996), 289–315. Copyright and with permission of the American Accounting Association.

financial statement information that indicates that future earnings may be different from current earnings. Behavioralists refer to the tendency to latch onto one object in a habitual, routine way as "functional fixed-ness" (sometimes called "functional fixation"). The fixedness blocks out other aspects of a problem that are relevant. We see it with analysts who apply a standard multiple to earnings irrespective of the quality of those earnings. Perhaps this is what we should expect of humans, given our limited information processing ability; that is, we find complexity difficult to handle so we latch onto summary numbers, like bottom-line earnings, as a convenience.

If so, the returns here point to something else: GAAP earnings are not a good summary number for the limited information processors of the planet. If higher earnings mean lower future earnings, that is not satisfactory. If firms can add accrual estimates to increase earnings, only to report lower earnings in the future, that is not satisfactory. If current earnings are not a good forecast of the forward earnings on which we hope to anchor our growth expectations, then we are lost. If the difference is due to real business activity, so be it, and we may expect profitability to decline over time as a firm's competitive position is challenged. But if it is due to the accounting employed, then we have issues with the quality of the accounting.

What Is Good Accounting?

Earnest accounting standard setters wrestle with this question continually. To resolve it, they appeal to abstract accounting concepts: definitions of assets, liabilities, and income; "measurement attributes"; and "recognition principles." Though not final, the FASB's and IASB's evolving Conceptual Framework appears to revolve around these types of concepts.[4] Foundational principles are important, of course, but determining accounting on the basis of how it conforms to accounting definitions can lead to accounting standards that read much like a thesaurus: accountants referencing themselves. Fair value accounting is prescribed because it fits a prescribed measurement principle, a balance sheet focus is adopted because it fits a Hicksian concept of income, and "matching" in the income statement is rejected because it results in assets and liabilities that do not fit definitions of assets and liabilities. This is not how an investor thinks.

The thesaurus approach leads to standards that rest on language rather than concrete fundamentals. The language is often appealing, evoking the highest virtues, but vague as to the practical accounting consequences. This approach means a continual revision of accounting standards on fine points of language—as with the over 200 pieces of literature in U.S. GAAP on revenue recognition, much of it revolving around the notion of an "earnings process" and when it is "complete."[5] The most recent proposals for revenue recognition center around estimating revenue for satisfying a "performance obligation," a vague notion that will be difficult to apply in practice, leaving room for judgment and even manipulation.[6] Accounting standards promulgated in this way become a cobweb of accounting minutiae, which is then applied legalistically. Complexity becomes a dominating characteristic. The approach entangles well-meaning CFOs in the cobweb, opening them up to SEC review and litigation if they make a false step (on revenue recognition in particular). It requires follow-up "guidance" by regulatory staff and subboards, adding more detail to weave the web. But still accounting issues are rarely finally settled. Most important, the approach is in danger of producing accounting that does not work in practice (and we have seen a number of failures of accounting standards).[7]

Basing accounting standards on concepts whose practical implications are not immediate is a pain for those have to prepare financial statements as a practical matter. But, more importantly, the approach misses out on what accounting is all about. Accounting is utilitarian, so the accounting design problem is about serving the user, rather than obedience to accounting precepts. The appropriate criterion is: How can accounting aid users in the task before them? Good accounting aids the task, bad accounting frustrates it. Simply put, accounting is a product, and the understanding of good or bad accounting is a matter of understanding its product features from the point of view of its customers. Pharmaceutical research goes straight to the question: What are the benefits of a drug and what are its possible side effects? If the issue of special purpose vehicles—special investment vehicles and other names given to off-balance sheet concoctions—had been addressed from this point of view rather than with bright-line accounting criteria, the now-evident side effects might have been anticipated.

Accounting can serve a variety of purposes, so the accounting may well differ for different tasks. Our interest in this book is in accounting for the equity investor, the shareholder or prospective shareholder, so we will evaluate accounting from that point of view. That is not a radical perspective, of course. Financial statements are formally presented to shareholders at the annual meeting—the statements are *their* statements—and auditors report to the shareholders, as do the directors in discharging their fiduciary duty. Indeed, the accounting apparatus is specifically tailored to reporting to shareholders; each period, accounting starts with the balance sheet, calculates earnings, then adds those earnings to shareholders' equity with the final (closing) entry of the process. In short, accounting, nominally at least, is a process for updating shareholders' equity. A number of the problems with GAAP arise simply because it does not faithfully report to shareholders (as we will see).[8]

With a focus on serving the shareholder, accounting solutions surface fairly readily and straightforwardly. Accounting for value in this book has that focus. Indeed, the discerning reader will have appreciated many implications for accounting from the valuations in the preceding chapters. Accounting serves the shareholder well if it facilitates a no-growth valuation on which the investor can anchor. That involves anchoring on the balance sheet and then adding value from forecasts of near-term earnings. Accordingly, the investor seeks a balance sheet that he or she can accept without reservation and an income statement from which to securely forecast the future. The implications for accounting are immediate:

First, the balance sheet that anchors the valuation must be "hard." That is, the balance sheet rests on facts and eschews speculation. Accordingly, the investor is assured that balance sheet accounting cannot come back to hit him or her later; shunting liabilities off-balance sheet, with repercussions to follow, is not acceptable. "Soft," speculative intangible assets are not booked to the balance sheet. Fair values that include anticipation of gains that may or may not be realized are not on the balance sheet. Fair value accounting is restricted to the case where the one-to-one principle of the previous chapter applies. Historical transactions accounting broadly applies, and desirably so for transactions are hard facts, not conjecture. To the extent that estimates must be used (for bad debt provisions, warranty liabilities, and the like), they are based on the evidential history (of actual bad debts and warranty claims), not conjecture.

Second, the income statement must anchor the forecasts of near-term earnings, which, when added to the hard balance sheet, complete the anchoring valuation. That involves two things. First, revenues are based on actual trading with customers, not expectations of future revenues. Past sales are typically an indication of the ability to generate future sales, but speculation about future sales is left to the analyst. Second, expenses are matched to revenues to calculate a measure of valued added from sales (operating income) that informs about the profitability of sales under current conditions. Thus, if the analyst forecasts no sales growth in the near term, current operating income is a good indicator of future income. And, if the analyst forecasts that sales will be different, a reliable income forecast is made by applying the (sustainable) profit margin to those sales. The analyst might use other (hard) information (besides accounting information) to forecast a change in the profit margin, but a forecast of a change in profit margin should not be affected by the way that the accountant currently calculates it; that is, there should be no earnings reversals in the future simply because of the way the accounting is done.

Third, both the income statement and balance sheet must distinguish between operating activities and financing activities (as in Chapter 4). The distinction recognizes that value added in business operations is very different from financing activities. This is one of the principles of modern finance that is widely endorsed, and financial statements should align with it. Confusing the two blurs the value creation, so the analyst becomes frustrated in discerning the profitability of the business, and the investor is led into paying too much for profitability and growth generated by leverage.

Fourth, conservatism applies: When in doubt about the hardness of the anchoring balance sheet, be conservative about the carrying value. The effect is to reduce book values and defer value recognition in earnings to the future, with the uncertainty now a part of risky earnings growth (as in Chapter 5). That, of course, suits the investor who treats growth as the risky part of a valuation.

Fifth, "below the line" disclosures focus on information, excluded from the accounts, that assists investors in their speculation. That information is particularly helpful if it provides a check on speculation. Thus the formal disclosures (in financial statement footnotes) pertain to observations in fact rather than conjecture. Accordingly (for example), order backlog is footnote information, but management forecasts of future sales are part of management discussion and analysis; the former serves to check the latter.

These prescriptions rest on the same fundamentalist principles as those for valuation, the 10 principles laid out in Chapter 1.[9] That is how it should be, for valuation is essentially a matter of accounting. Some may claim that the insistence on being concrete excludes some relevant information. Indeed it does, but that is how it should be; the quality of accounting is judged not only by what it includes but also by what it excludes, and speculative information falls in the exclusion zone. The accounting for the balance sheet should be nonspeculative. The accounting for the income statement should be forward-looking, as in the second principle, but not too forward-looking. Those attempting to put more information into the accounting may be well intentioned but are misguided. Says the fundamentalist: *Don't mix what you know with speculation; tell me what you know and leave the speculation to me.* Help my speculation with disclosures by all means, but don't put speculative information above the line. The below-the-line designation directs me to treat this information with caution.

Caveat Emptor: What's Wrong with GAAP?

GAAP exhibits many of the features we require for accounting for value, largely because it still retains some of the conservative properties imposed on it by fundamentalist thinking of yesteryear. Fundamentalists always demanded accounting be based on "objective and verifiable evidence." Modern regulation has served to increase transparency with disclosure (considerably) but the influence on the actual accounting numbers has been more mixed. Important issues, like lease accounting and pension accounting, have been tackled (though still a work in process) and a number of accounting abuses have been confronted (with some success), but the dalliance with fair value accounting is a real concern. Accounting regulation might well concentrate on improving historical transactions accounting. Here I will elaborate upon the ideal accounting for equity valuation, as outlined in the five points above, and contrast it with GAAP. The contrast illuminates the accounting quality issues that investors face under GAAP.

The Balance Sheet

THE EYE IS NOT ON THE SHAREHOLDER. Unfortunately, the balance sheet under GAAP does not respect the common shareholders' property rights, for it does not distinguish cleanly between debt and equity. Nor does it report the full cost to shareholders in borrowing. The troublesome area is the accounting for contingent equity claims such as options, warrants, employee stock options, and convertible debt and preferred stock. These claims are typically settled with shareholders' paper (their shares) rather than cash, and that incurs a cost to the shareholder; the issue of shares at less than market value on conversion is a loss of shareholder value (through dilution). That loss is not recorded under GAAP or IFRS. So we have the specter of firms borrowing by issuing warrants, options, or convertible preferred stock with no dividends, but with the cost of borrowing "paid" on conversion not recorded; that is, the firm appears to be borrowing at no cost. The borrowing cost from issuing convertible debt is understated. We even have the prospect of firms paying for operating costs with options, with the full cost not recorded. It is no wonder that the financial engineers have a field day with these instruments to create form over substance in order to achieve a "desired accounting."[10]

GAAP compounds the problem by classifying some of these claims as equity and often leaves the amount of other claims off the balance sheet. Consequently, the indebtedness of shareholders is understated. Clearly, from a shareholder's point of view an obligation to pay out on an option or warrant claim, classified by GAAP as equity, is not equity at all, but a liability; it is a claim on the equity holder to give up value should the instrument be exercised. The balance sheet reports convertible debt as a liability, but a portion of the liability is left off the balance sheet; that is, as the claim goes into the money, GAAP does not report the increased liability for the shareholders to issue more of their paper to settle the claim. To account for value, the analyst must bring these liabilities onto the balance sheet, including the option overhang for unexercised employee stock options. Otherwise, one is not anchoring on the appropriate equity number for book value. If GAAP accounting were so corrected, the structural engineering business (adding little value) would take a big hit.[11]

CONFUSING OPERATING AND FINANCING ACTIVITIES. The GAAP balance sheet distinguishes current and noncurrent assets and liabilities. Although relevant to a creditor, this is not the distinction the equity analyst is looking for. Rather he or she seeks a distinction between operating and financing activities, as in the accounting for value of Chapter 4. Fortunately, the two accounting boards are currently engaged in a project to radically change the way that financial statements are designed, and the issue of operating versus financing activities is central to the redesign.[12] This is a very helpful innovation.

THE "HARD" BALANCE SHEET. The idea that a balance sheet must be "hard" means that it cannot come back to hit you significantly. That means historical cost rather than fair values, but also impairment of carrying values when future losses are forecast. This conservatism means that the investor can anchor to the balance sheet securely, without fear of adverse consequences[13] imbedded in uncertainty about the quality of the balance sheet. Debt must, of course, be on the balance sheet. With respect to off-balance sheet vehicles—special purpose entities (SPE), variable interest entities (VIE), special investment vehicles (SIV), and operating leases are just a few of the names that financial engineers come up with—the FASB has continually tried to impose bright-line requirements for consolidation onto the balance sheet (that the engineers then go around). The hard balance sheet requirement asks: Is there a chance of taking a hit from these things? As the investor is particularly concerned with tail risk, that includes events with relatively low probability but large effects, like those an SIV can deliver.

FOCUS ON TRANSACTIONS. It is the principle of referring to transactions that makes the balance sheet hard, for transactions are concrete. As receivables are not booked until there are transactions with customers, the receivable (discounted for risk of nonpayment) is solid: you can take it to the bank. Inventory and other assets are recorded at their acquisition transactions cost. This yields not only a hard number, but also the input cost for determining value added from transacting with customers; when sold, inventory cost becomes the cost of goods sold for the determination of profit, and plant cost becomes depreciation. Accordingly, the balance sheet, accounted for at input cost, indeed serves to indentify value added (but not with fair values).[14] Needless to say, transactions accounting minimizes the ability to manage and manipulate the numbers. There is a qualification: Transactions must be at arm's length, without self-dealing. The problem with an SIV or the off-balance sheet vehicles set up by Enron is that they were not at arm's length; the firm itself sets these up, a warning sign indeed. So for banks using repo sale accounting to window-dress financial statements (as charged by the Lehman bankruptcy examiner): Forget the bright lines for a sale versus collateralized borrowing; these are simply not arm's-length transactions.

To highlight how a conservative balance sheet might serve the investor, consider the accounting for mortgage loans, discussed in the last chapter. As we saw there, fair value accounting marks these bank liabilities to market, possibly admitting price bubbles to the financial statements, or would "fair value" them with their (Level 3) estimated value based on assumptions about default rates, prepayment rates, interest rates, and so on. Both versions of fair value accounting anticipate the payoffs to the loan, some of them thirty years in duration. Here is an alternative to such speculation: Book the loan at the (transaction) amount lent to the borrower and then, for a few years until the borrower has established his or her good-credit credentials, record interest income on the loan only at the risk-free government rate. After creditworthiness has been established (with a payment history by the borrower and his or her increased equity in the property), amortize the cumulated credit spread on the loan (the difference between the lending rate over the government rate) into subsequent earnings.[15] This accounting is conservative, excluding speculation as to whether the loan will be paid and when. It recognizes that the bank has not earned the return for taking on credit risk until the borrower is deemed creditworthy. Note that this differs from standard "historical cost accounting" for loans that require estimates (that look very much like Level 3 fair value estimates) to discount the loan for risk. The standard accounting does have some transactional features—incurred losses and nonperformance are referred to—but it focuses on estimates of losses rather than demonstration of ability to pay. The alternative proposed here delays the recognition of value for an individual loan, but for a portfolio of old and new loans the effect on earnings is small (due to averaging) if there is no growth with new business. (In short, the canceling error property of the previous chapter applies.) Only with growth in the mortgage business is earnings depressed, creating future earnings growth. This is anchoring accounting that the investor likes; new mortgage business is risky, so accounting that defers earnings and introduces risky growth is appropriate. One must ask: Had this accounting been in place, would we have had the subprime financial crisis? A very important question indeed.

The Income Statement

TRANSPARENCY. Some see the balance sheet as deficient, because it is not at fair value. However, it is really the income statement that is deficient. Indeed, the U.S. income statement is somewhat of a disgrace. It is often reduced to five or six line items, with extensive annotation sprayed among copious footnotes. One line item, selling, general, and administrative expenses (SG&A) is typically in the order of 20 percent of sales but covers a multitude of sins. With a view to forecasting, the analyst seeks to identify sustainable profitability, but its source is opaque. With before-tax operating profit margins typically less than 12 percent of sales, an investor's request to report any expense greater than 1 percent of sales—along with more sensitive lesser items such as executive, director, and auditor compensation—seems reasonable.

One has to work through the cash flow statement or the footnotes to understand the extent to which income is inflated by one-time gains or deflated by one-time charges. The almost incomprehensible pension footnote must be penetrated to understand that SG&A and indeed cost of goods sold have been reduced by gains on pension plan assets, so the gross and net profit margin from the business is contaminated by these gains. When stock prices go up, so do pension gains, which then feed into earnings that are supposed to be the basis for challenging prices (and the fundamentalist has something to say about using price in the calculation!).

REVENUES. The requirement that top-line revenues be "hard" corresponds to the requirement for a hard receivable in the balance sheet; you can take it to the bank. Revenue recognition under GAAP works well for the spot trade but not so well for more complicated transactions with customers. Under GAAP, estimates are brought to the task of allocation revenues to parts of the arrangement, with the parts themselves identified with imprecise criteria such as satisfaction of a "performance obligation." This is soft, leaving plenty of room for maneuvering. GAAP recognizes deferred revenues from this treatment that many analysts treat, not as a liability, but as revenue (and indeed, an asset); there is really a sale, the accountants are just choosing not to recognize it yet. Witness the long-standing buzz around Microsoft's huge deferred or "unearned" revenues (27 percent of equity in 2010) and the complaint that Apple was required to defer revenue from the sale of iPhone because of promised software upgrades (costing little). A transactions approach remedies; customers rarely hand over cash (or take on obligations to do so) unless it is legitimate.[16]

PROFIT DETERMINATION. The difficult part of the income statement is the matching of expenses to revenue to indicate profit, the value added from trading with customers. The second principle above says that this should be done with a view to forecasting near-term earnings. The analyst would like the profit margin to be such that it is an indicator of future profit margins if current conditions prevail. One should not expect reversals, such as those in figure 9.2(a), simply because of the accounting. That, along with a hard balance sheet, defines quality accounting that the investor can rely on and operationalizes the "true and fair" and "fairly present" notions that the auditor signs off on. If you have an earnings number that is a basis for the future, you have a basis for a P/E ratio. Growth can be added (cautiously). But if you have a number that fluctuates randomly with all sorts of accounting shocks, how can one establish the P/E ratio? It is well known that the trailing P/E (based on reported earnings) is far more volatile than the forward P/E (based on analysts' forecasts). Part of the difference is due to volatile business conditions, but part also to the accounting. The expedience has been to average earnings over a number of years to get "normalized earnings." That may help, particularly for cyclical businesses. But it fails to give weight to the most important number for forecasting, the most recent earnings: What are the sales now and what margins is the firm earning from sales?

GAAP frustrates the forecaster. One-time items behind the opaque income statement are an issue of course, though these can usually be identified by a diligent search of the footnotes. But if the analyst can get to a number, say, "earnings before one-time items," his or her problems are not over. Deferred revenue accounting is known for its susceptibility to earnings management; firms can save earnings for the future by deferring revenues, and can borrow earnings from the future by dipping into deferred revenues (the proverbial "cookie jar"). Softness in the accounting for revenues permits this. But the same applies to expenses. Those one-time items—impairments, write-downs, restructuring charges, and the like—can also shift income to the future. An excessive charge now means lower expenses and higher income in the future. An excessive impairment means lower depreciation in the future (and higher profit margins), and an excessive write-down of inventory means lower cost of goods sold in the future (and higher gross margins). The phenomenon is called bleeding back income in the future. The analyst is thus faced with a problem of understanding a current profit margin: To what extent does it represent real value added or just the result of bleed-back of past impairments, write-downs, and restructurings? The truth cannot be disentangled, so one loses the anchor. With repetitive write-downs (not uncommon), one loses any sense of the underlying profitability. Analysts tend to strip out one-time charges from earnings, as with Standard & Poor's Operating Earnings so common on The Street, but it is more complicated than this. The question of "sustainable" profit margins remains elusive and it is this issue that so frustrates the analyst.

The incentives for such accounting practices are strong. New management have an incentive to write-down and restructure on arrival—"taking a big bath," it is called—blaming it on the old management but setting themselves up to look good with subsequent earnings growth from reversals and bleed-backs. Earnings growth induced by these practices is pure accounting junk. Not growth that the investor should pay for, but also not growth the management should be rewarded for. Management can always come up with a restructuring idea to push earnings into their bonus period.

FINESSING EXCESSIVE CONSERVATISM. Conservatism means that impairments are sometimes required to maintain a hard balance sheet so that the investor does not run the hazard of expected losses. However, impairments can go too far, depressing current earnings unnecessarily and producing future profits through the bleed-backs. In short, excessive conservatism creates hidden profit reserves. Excessive conservatism—sometimes called discretionary conservatism—is as much a problem as no conservatism at all.

Establishing criteria that curtail excessive conservatism might help, and the FASB has attempted to do so.[17] But the practice is probably difficult to control with such prescriptions. A presentation of how current earnings are affected by changes in estimates from prior periods would help; report amounts bled back to earnings from reversals of restructuring charges, dipping into cookie jar reserves, reducing deferred tax valuation allowances, and changing bad debt and loan loss allowances (for example). A "quality of earnings" statement by management, along with discussion by the auditor of significant accounting effects, would place responsibility for quality reporting where it belongs. That report might include an estimate of the effect on earnings of the liquidation of hidden reserves from slowing investment under conservative accounting, much like the current LIFO reserve reporting. There is another solution (once taught in accounting textbooks): For a write-down in a continuing business, capitalize the write-down on the balance sheet and smooth it into earnings over the next few years.[18] (For an impairment of a depreciable asset, one would modify the depreciation schedule.) Although this would report the balance sheet slightly higher, temporarily, the immediate shock to earnings would be avoided and charges against future earnings would cancel bleed-backs. Earnings would be smoothed, and smooth earnings help forecast future earnings. One-time charges to earnings would be warranted only on discontinuity of the business itself or, in the case of inventory, when the inventory is essentially worthless (so cannot be sold in the future).

The condemnation of historical cost accounting as backward-looking is very much misplaced. Indeed, it is quite impressive how something based on recording transactions can aggregate to provide forward-looking numbers for the investor to embrace in dealing with the future and its uncertainty. However, that accounting must be constrained such that those forward-looking attributes can operate. Note, in this regard, that fair value accounting continually shocks the income statement with asset and liability revaluations, producing earnings volatility and destroying the ability of earnings to forecast the future.

EARNINGS SMOOTHING. The idea that earnings should be smooth (less volatile) simply facilitates forecasting. However, it should not be confused with "discretionary earnings smoothing" where firms, in anticipation of future earnings, modify current earnings. They increase earnings when they see those earnings are low against expectation of future earnings (filling the valleys by advancing sales and recognizing gains for asset sales, for example), and decrease earnings (shaving off the hills) when they see earnings will be lower in the future. This is plain earnings management and it presents a danger to the analyst; that is, changing current earnings against expectation of future earnings is based on speculation. It is speculative accounting that can turn on you: If one increases current earnings in a bad year on the expectation of higher future earnings, a large earnings shock awaits if those future earnings do not materialize.

Simplicity Is a Virtue, Complexity Is a Warning

The cry for simpler accounting is perennial. How can one expect even the accomplished investor to wade through scores of footnote pages to understand (perhaps) the accounting? On the preparers' side, reporting firms decry the detail that can entrap them. Standard setters hear the cry but don't seem to be able to respond, generating more and more complexity each year. The usual excuse is that the world is becoming more complex, with more complicated contracts and instruments, so accountants must be accommodating—particularly if those complexities are designed to present form over substance. This observation is fair enough. But we do need to step back and appraise the situation before we drown in the bog.

First, appreciate that complexity is a warning. History shows that complexity foreshadows trouble. Enron's accounting was enormously complex. Those off-balance sheet arrangements that ultimately blew up were so difficult to penetrate. And so with banks during the financial crisis; understanding the accounts of all but the simplest bank is a challenge. The investor is warned: When you see complexity, run. SIV, SPE, QSPE, CDO, CDO-squared, VIE, CMBS, ABCP, RMBA, CLO, and CoCo is a dizzying list of acronyms that should turn you away. They are a cover for complexity. Have you noticed that it is always an acronym that turns up as a culprit in a financial disaster? Have you noticed that it is often an acronym that stings you?

Second, appreciate that complexity is not just a necessity of the times. It's also a product of the accounting. The protagonists at Enron used complex accounting to structure complex instruments to obscure, as do those who design the fancy instruments and special investment vehicles in which banks indulge. Indeed, it is to these "financial instruments" that fair value accounting is applied, so complex "financial instruments" can be structured to exploit fair value accounting and obscure.

Third, recognize that there is a simple accounting solution: When a business is wrapped up in all sorts of complex arrangements, accounting standards should require transactions accounting. That is, don't recognize earnings until there is a settling-up on these arrangements (but with the conservative accounting proviso to recognize any expected losses). Fair value accounting combines with these complex arrangements to report mysterious income (as with Enron). The gain or loss from closing out a structure or an instrument is about as transparent as one can get. It is at that point we understand if and how a firm makes money. It is as simple as that.

CHAPTER TEN

The Intelligent Investor and the Intelligent Accountant

BENJAMIN GRAHAM SAW INVESTING more as a matter of good thinking than technique, with the fundamentalist principles of Chapter 1 supplying the thinking for his intelligent investor. Accounting for value in this book, based on those same principles, is in the same vein. Although accounting for value lends itself to concrete technique, it is not the technique that is most important. First and foremost, accounting for value supplies a way of intelligently thinking about valuation; it supplies the mental thinking for the intelligent investor. Insights from intelligent investing in turn provide insights into intelligent accounting.

The intelligent investor understands that the risk in investing is the risk of paying too much, so seeks to understand the difference between value and price (Chapter 1). The intelligent investor seeks to determine value in a way that not only upholds prudent, fundamentalist principles but also honors principles of modern finance (Chapter 1). The intelligent investor sees the investing problem as one of handling uncertainty, but finds many of the risk-analysis tools of modern finance are not suited for the task. Rather, the problem is one of parsing out uncertainty, understanding what is known and separating this from speculation (Chapter 1). The intelligent investor accordingly distinguishes accounting value from speculative value; the investor accounts for value, so thinks of valuation as an accounting problem and adopts an accounting model that imbeds this view (Chapter 2). The intelligent investor thinks in terms of accrual accounting rather than cash accounting, for cash is not necessarily value added (Chapter 2). The intelligent investor sees value in terms of where book value will be in the future and what will be the return on book value (Chapter 2). The intelligent investor understands that speculation revolves around growth prospects and is apprehensive about paying for growth (Chapter 2). The intelligent investor will not pay for sales growth, asset growth, or even earnings growth, but only for residual earnings growth (Chapter 4). The intelligent investor focuses on accounting for the business, abstracting from leverage, and so avoids paying for growth that is added with leverage but is not to be valued (Chapter 4). The intelligent investor thinks like a conservative accountant, understanding that conservative accounting adds growth that is risky, but also with an understanding of how accounting for value protects from paying too much for risky growth (Chapters 5 and 7).

With this intelligence, and with an understanding that investing is not a game against nature but against other investors, the intelligent investor then goes active to challenge the market price set by other investors, applying an anchoring valuation supplied by the accounting (Chapter 3). With an appreciation of the risk of paying too much for growth, the accounting is employed to elicit the market's forecast of growth, and then to challenge it (Chapters 3 and 6). The intelligent investor is honest about not knowing the cost-of-capital so focuses instead on the expected return to buying at the market price (Chapter 6). The intelligent investor analyzes uncertainty intelligently, not through simple, too-easy risk metrics, but by thinking in terms of a lattice of alternative accounting outcomes through which uncertainty is resolved (Chapter 6). The intelligent investor understands the difference between growth versus value investing and which is the more risky engagement (Chapter 7). At all times, the intelligent investor refuses to book value until there has been some resolution of uncertainty, for such a fair value accounting approach is speculative (Chapter 8).

Although accounting for value supplies an intelligent way of thinking about investing, it also lends itself to technique, facilitating engineering and quantification, those mantras of modernism. While retaining many of the principles of modern finance, but with an accounting overlay, the apparatus is more grounded than many of the products of modern finance. Among the tools the intelligent investor employs are no-growth valuations (Chapter 2), reverse-engineering growth forecasts and earnings per share paths (Chapter 3), benchmark growth valuations (Chapter 3), unlevered accounting valuations (Chapter 4), the weighted-average return formula that yields an expected return to investing and growth-return profiles (Chapter 6), and accounting for risk to handle uncertainty (Chapter 6).

With the appreciation that valuation is essentially a matter of intelligent accounting, the intelligent investor gives a lot of thought to how accounting should be done, and is prepared to ask accounting regulators for accounting that serves the purpose. Chapter 9 communicated that request. The intelligent investor wants accounting that eschews speculation, for only that type of accounting can serve as an anchor to challenge speculation in the market price. The intelligent investor has a serious distaste for fair value accounting with its speculation about the future. Rather, he or she demands a nonspeculative balance sheet on which to build a valuation, supplemented by an income statement that serves as a basis for forecasting, based on hard transaction data rather than value estimates. And the accounting must be conservative, booking risky earnings later rather than sooner, so risk is in growth that the intelligent investor treats with care.

With this intelligence, with these techniques, and with the appropriate accounting, the investor is equipped to determine the difference between value and price. In Benjamin Graham's words, the intelligent investor is ready to negotiate with Mr. Market. In more modern terms, the investor is ready to test whether the market is efficient. If investors more generally embraced the fundamental approach, perhaps we might have more efficient markets, without the bubbles and crashes that are so damaging to our savings and to the efficiency of the economy more generally. That, however, calls for sound accounting. One accounts for value, and a valuation is only as good as the accounting that underlies it.

Notes

1. Return to Fundamentals

1. There are at least 310 million of you in the world who own equity shares directly, 173 million in countries with developed stock markets, and 137 million in countries with emerging markets. In addition, at least 503 million of you own shares indirectly through pension fund holdings. As reported in Paul A. Grout, William L. Megginson, and Ania Zalewska, "One Half-Billion Shareholders and Counting—Determinants of Individual Share Ownership Around the World" (2009), at http://ssrn.com/abstract=1457482.

2. The S&P 500 index subsequently dropped from 1499 at the beginning of 2000 to 815 by mid-2002. By mid-2002, Cisco Systems traded at $14, down from $77 in early 2000. Dell Computer dropped from $50 in 2000 to $26 by mid-2002. For an analysis of the 1990s bubble, see Carl Haacke, *Frenzy: Bubbles, Busts, and How to Come Out Ahead* (New York: Palgrave Macmillan, 2004).

3. By the end of 1989, the Nikkei 225 index of Japanese stocks stood at 38,957, 238 percent above its level five years before. Twelve years later in 2001, the Nikkei 225 fell below 10,000, for a loss of over 75 percent from the 1989 high. The "Nifty-Fifty" stocks refer to the so-called glamour stocks of the early 1970s: the likes of Coca-Cola, Johnson & Johnson, Burroughs, Digital Equipment, IBM, Polaroid, Eastman Kodak, and Xerox. The S&P 500 P/E ratio declined from 18.4 at the end of 1972 to 7.7 at the end of 1974, and was at 7.3 at the end of that decade.

4. See Benjamin Graham, *The Intelligent Investor*, rev. ed. (New York: Harper & Row, 1973). The first edition was published in 1949, and a reprint in 2005 with a preface by Warren E. Buffett. The other classic, with considerably more on technique, is Benjamin Graham, David L. Dodd, and Sidney Cottle, *Security Analysis: Principles and Technique*, 4th ed. (New York: McGraw-Hill, 1962). The first edition, authored by Graham and Dodd, was published in

1934. A later incarnation is Sidney Cottle, Roger F. Murray, and Frank E. Block, *Graham and Dodd's Security Analysis*, 5th ed. (New York, McGraw-Hill, 1988). A more recent book in the same vein (of what has become known as "value investing") is Bruce C. N. Greenwald, Judd Kahn, Paul D. Sonkin, and Michael van Biema, *Value Investing: From Graham to Buffett and Beyond* (New York: Wiley, 2001).

5. The yearly trading volume on the world's stock markets increased from $1.22 trillion in 1983 to $111.2 trillion in 2007 (as reported in Grout, Megginson, and Zalewska, "One Half-Billion Shareholders and Counting").

6. The Warren Buffett quip is often quoted: he observes that beta implies that "a stock that has dropped very sharply compared to the market . . . becomes 'riskier' at the lower price than it was at the higher price." As quoted in Lawrence A. Cunningham, *The Essays of Warren Buffett: Lessons for Corporate America* (New York: Cardozo Law Review, 1997), p. 14.

7. Another of Keynes's oft-cited sayings warns that the market can stay irrational longer than you can stay solvent. Although the price of patience may be relatively low for individual investors, not so for investment fund mangers who face redemptions when their short-term returns fall below market benchmarks. Many of these managers increased their investment in technology stocks as prices rose to high multiples in the 1990s. In the words of Chuck Prince, CEO of Citigroup to the *Financial Times* on July 9, 2007 (before the financial crisis), "as long as the music is playing, you've got to get up and dance." He also had foresight in saying, "when the music stops, in terms of liquidity, things will be complicated" (as they indeed were for Citigroup). The problems the fundamental investor faces with irrational markets are posed as "limits to arbitrage" in Andrei Shleifer and Robert Vishny, "The Limits of Arbitrage," *Journal of Finance* 52 (1997), 35–55. But note that confidence that fundamentals will be revealed in financial reports mitigates limitations on arbitrage (and belief that the accounting cannot be relied upon exacerbates).

8. Reviews of modern finance are in Peter L. Bernstein, *Capital Ideas: The Improbable Origins of Modern Wall Street* (New York: Wiley, 1992), Peter L. Bernstein, *Capital Ideas Evolving* (New York: Wiley, 2007), and Mark Rubinstein, *A History of the Theory of Investments: My Annotated Bibliography* (Hoboken, NJ: Wiley, 2006).

9. The formal statement of the efficient market hypothesis is in Eugene Fama, "Efficient Capital Markets: A Review of Theory and Empirical Work," *Journal of Finance* 25 (1970), 383–417, though the idea has its origins in earlier rational expectations theory and indeed in Hayek's insight on the informativeness of the price system. See also Paul Samuelson, "Proof That Properly Anticipated Prices Fluctuate Randomly," *Industrial Management Review* 6 (1965), 41–49 and, for the practical implications, Burton Malkiel, *A Random Walk Down Wall Street* (New York: W. W. Norton, 1973), now in its ninth edition.

Fama provides an update on the hypothesis in "Efficient Capital Markets: II," *Journal of Finance* 45 (1991), 1575–1617. For a history of the efficient markets debate, blow by blow, see Justin Fox, *The Myth of the Rational Market* (New York: HarperCollins, 2009).

10. This is the point in the so-called Grossman-Stiglitz paradox: if the market were informationally efficient, then no one would have the incentive to acquire the information on which prices are based. See Sanford J. Grossman and Joseph E. Stiglitz, "The Impossibility of Informationally Efficient Markets," *American Economic Review* 70 (1980), 393–408.

11. Efficient market advocates do have some answers, however: the supposed bubble prices are due to a decrease in investors' risk premiums.

12. The early empirical work on the statistical properties of stock returns, including Fama's own work, largely supported the hypothesis. But when information other than stock prices was introduced, the picture became considerably murkier. Although "event studies" showed that market prices typically adjusted quickly to the arrival of new information, later studies increasingly reported that one could predict stock returns with information, most notably accounting information (at least in the data, if not in real time). The study of so-called "anomalies" was heralded by a special issue of the *Journal of Financial Economics* in 1978 with an introduction by Michael Jensen (editor), "Some Anomalous Evidence Regarding Market Efficiency," pp. 95–111. Subsequent research has documented many "anomalies," too many to list, that appear to be inconsistent with rational pricing of risk. Many of these involve trading strategies based on accounting information. For a recent overview, see Scott A. Richardson, İrem Tuna, and Peter Wysocki, "Accounting Anomalies and Fundamental Analysis: A Review of Recent Research Advances," *Journal of Accounting and Economics* (2010), forthcoming.

13. The inability of experts to "beat the market" on average was documented even before the formal statement of the efficient market hypothesis. See Alfred Cowles 3rd, "Can Stock Market Forecasters Forecast?" *Econometrica* 1 (1933), 309–324. The paper by Michael Jensen, "The Performance of Mutual Funds in the Period 1945–1964," *Journal of Finance* 23 (1968), 389–416, heralded a long line of investigations indicating that investment fund returns, on average, are little different from those on broad market indexes, after costs. The point was appreciated by Benjamin Graham. He saw that as professional investors emerged, employing his principles, they became the market, trading with one another (just as hedge funds today, trading with each other, make up a good slice of the market); the average player cannot beat the average for the market if he or she is the market. See Benjamin Graham, "The Future of Financial Analysis," *Financial Analysts Journal* 16 (May-June 1963), 65–70. Graham's statement in this paper is matched with his continued warning to separate "minimum true value" from speculative value, for that is where the

analyst is likely to get an edge. In "A Conversation with Benjamin Graham" in the *Financial Analysts Journal* (September-October 1976), 20–23, Graham also distinguishes "investment characteristics" from "speculative characteristics" of stocks, but also says (in recognition of the large amount of stock research going on) that "to that very limited extent, I'm on the side of the 'efficient market' school of thought now generally accepted by the professors."

14. Friedrich von Hayek, "The Use of Knowledge in Society," *American Economic Review* 35 (1945), 519–530.

15. Robert E. Lucas Jr., "Expectations and the Neutrality of Money," *Journal of Economic Theory* 4 (1972), 103–124.

16. The model is attributed to John Burr Williams, *The Theory of Investment Value* (Cambridge, MA: Harvard University Press, 1938), though the idea of present value as a measure of wealth is due to Irving Fisher earlier. The model is essentially a statement of the no-arbitrage idea: present value must bear a no-arbitrage relationship to expected future cash flows, such that value must be the price at which one expects to earn the required return for the risk assumed; no more, no less.

17. The property is best seen with a bond: treat the liquidating price as the maturity payment of the bond and the dividends as the coupon payments. Given the discount rate, the value of a bond does not depend on the coupon.

18. Merton H. Miller and Franco Modigliani, "Dividend Policy, Growth, and the Valuation of Shares," *Journal of Business* 34 (1961), 411–433.

19. As with all economic theory, the proposition comes with assumptions and thus serves as a benchmark to identify conditions where the general principle may not apply. The main one is the assumption of perfect capital markets. Dividends provide liquidity, and investors may demand liquidity as well as value. If there are liquid debt and equity markets, investors can sell some shares if they require more dividends than the firm pays (and leave themselves just as well off in value terms); if the firm pays dividends they do not want, they can just buy the stock with the dividend (and leave themselves just as well off in value terms). This is the idea of homemade dividends: irrespective of the firm's payout policy, shareholders can create any payout they wish. As to the firm, it does not need to sell off profitable investments if its shareholders require cash dividends: with available debt markets, it can just borrow against the value in the business to pay dividends. These insights, of course, point to situations where dividends might matter: for a private firm for which there is no liquid market for its shares (or no bank is willing to lend to pay dividends), dividends might matter if shareholders—family owners—need cash. Accordingly, shares of private firms tend to be priced with a "liquidity discount," but not so for firms with shares that are regularly traded on public exchanges. It is also understood that firms should pay out dividends if they do not have invest-

ments to make with their cash (but that does not affect shareholders' cum-dividend value). If management makes bad investments (in the corporate jet) instead of paying out dividends, value is lost, but that is a matter of investment policy, not dividend policy.

20. Graham, Dodd, and Cottle, *Security Analysis,* 4th ed., pp. 515–518 put weight on dividends in their valuation methods.

21. Harry M. Markowitz, "Portfolio Selection," *Journal of Finance* 7 (1952), 77–91. The idea is also credited to Andrew D. Roy, "Safety First and the Hold-ing of Assets," *Econometrica* 20 (1952), 431–449.

22. Warren Buffett counters the diversification idea by quoting Mark Twain's advice from Pudd'Nhead Wilson: "Put all your eggs in one basket—and watch the basket" (as quoted in Cunningham, *Essays of Warren Buffett,* p. 14).

23. As quoted in Bernstein, *Capital Ideas: Improbable Origins.*

24. Franco Modigliani and Merton H. Miller, "The Cost of Capital, Cor-poration Finance and the Theory of Investments," *American Economic Review* 48 (1958), 261–297.

25. Rubinstein, *History of the Theory of Investments,* p. 79 notes that Williams also stated the principle in 1938 in *Theory of Investment Value,* pp. 72–73. As with the M&M dividend irrelevance notion, some caveats apply. First, if the government subsidizes debt with a favorable tax treatment, issuing debt is a means to apply for this subsidy. (This point is controversial, for the firm may receive a tax deduction for interest on debt, but investors receiving the interest income must pay taxes. So the firm has to raise the interest payment to com-pensate the investor for the taxes. Miller makes the point in Merton H. Miller, "Debt and Taxes," *Journal of Finance* 32 (1977), 261–275. Further, all else being equal, issuing debt to capture the subsidy means higher payout to sharehold-ers, and shareholders may pay taxes on those payouts.) Second, in issuing debt, the firm increases the risk of bankruptcy, and thus may incur bankruptcy costs that would otherwise be avoided. Third, if financing (or financing con-straints) affect investment in the business, the value of the business will also be affected. Fourth, if a firm can issue debt for more than it is worth or repur-chase debt cheaply, it adds value for shareholders. That, of course, presumes inefficiency in the debt market.

26. For a discussion on a product focus in both accounting and finance re-search, see Stephen Penman, "Eye of the Prize: Directions for Accounting Research," *China Accounting Review* 6 (2008), 465–476.

27. As reported in the *Financial Times* (U.S. edition), November 3, 2009, p. 1.

28. The historical analysis to support this investment advice is in Jeremy Siegel, *Stocks for the Long Run,* 2nd ed. (New York: McGraw-Hill, 1998).

29. This point of ex post bias in historical stock returns is made in Stephen Brown, William N. Goetzmann, and Stephen Ross, "Survival," *Journal of*

Finance 50 (1995), 853–873. In any case, if one compares the average historical return to the variance of return, one has to have quite a long history to show that the average return over the risk-free return is significantly different from zero. A more recent paper questions the whole notion of comparing historical average returns to historical volatility. Focusing on forward-looking volatility, one has to be concerned not only with volatility of returns but also the variance in average returns, making average return less predicable in the long run. Indeed, the paper estimates that uncertainty about returns increases with distance into the future: the annualized variance of 30-year returns is estimated to be 1.5 times that of the one-year return variance. See Lubos Pastor and Robert F. Stambaugh, "Are Stocks Really Less Volatile in the Long Run?" (2009) at http://ssrn.com/abstract=1136847.

30. For a tabulation of historical returns from around the world, see Elroy Dimson, Paul Marsh, and Mike Staunton, *Triumph of the Optimists:101 Years of Global Investment Returns* (Princeton, NJ: Princeton University Press, 2002).

31. With the yearly standard deviation of returns for the S&P 500 of about 20 percent and a risk premium of 6 percent (to be generous), one can, with reasonable probability, have periods of 25 years or more where stock returns are less than those for safe bonds.

32. The phenomenon is investigated in François Longin and Bruno Solnik, "Extreme Correlation of International Equity Markets," *Journal of Finance* 56 (2001), 649–676, and Andrew Ang and Geert Bekaert, "International Asset Diversification with Regime Shifts," *Review of Financial Studies* 15 (2002), 1137–1187. Fads and fashions or just common investment strategies (in hedge funds) cause investors to crowd into certain assets and induce correlation in returns among investors, leading to large swings in prices when they move together. See Amir Khandani and Andrew Lo, "What Happened to the Quants in August 2007?" Working paper, Sloan School, MIT (2007) for an account of cascading hedge fund losses as investors unwound positions. The same phenomenon was seen in the unwinding of the carry trade and the rush from mortgage-backed securities in 2007–2008.

33. Eugene Fama and Kenneth French, "The Cross-Section of Expected Returns," *Journal of Finance* 47 (1992), 427–465; "Common Risk Factors in the Returns of Stocks and Bonds," *Journal of Financial Economics* 33 (1993), 3–56; "Multi-Factor Explanations of Asset Pricing Anomalies," *Journal of Finance* 51 (1996), 55–84.

34. Asset-pricing researchers are considering a "a conditional CAPM" to replace the CAPM and confront the Fama and French model. They are breaking up beta into "bad beta" (associated with the arrival of cash flow news) and "good beta" (associated with changes in the discount rate). They are attempting to model why book-to-price might pertain to risk and are introducing other conjectured risk factors to explain the data.

35. For a critical review of financial engineering models, see Riccardo Rebonato, *Plight of the Fortune Tellers: Why We Need to Manage Financial Risk Differently* (Princeton, NJ: Princeton University Press, 2007).

36. For more reflections along these lines, see Hans J. Blommestein, "The Financial Crisis as a Symbol of the Failure of Academic Finance? (A Methodological Digression)" at http://ssrn.com/abstract=1477399.

2. Anchoring on Fundamentals

1. Interest rates may change in the future, but will not affect the value of the savings account because earnings in a savings account also change with the interest rate such that changes in the discount rate are offset by changes in earnings (similar to a variable-rate bond).

2. One can apply the dividend discount model of the previous chapter in this case; the present value of a $5 dividend, continuing indefinitely, is $100. Stated using the perpetuity formula,

$$\text{Value}_0 = \frac{\$5}{0.05} = \$100,$$

where the 5 percent for the capitalization factor is the required return for the savings account.

3. The accounting must also work for the second savings account where dividends are paid out:

$$\text{Future book value} = \$100 + \$25 - \$25 = \$100.$$

For an equity, the dividends are net dividends (or net payout), that is, Cash dividends + Share repurchases – Share issues.

4. See Peter D. Easton, Trevor S. Harris, and James A. Ohlson, "Aggregate Accounting Earnings Can Explain Most of Security Returns: The Case of Long Event Windows," *Journal of Accounting and Economics* 15 (1992), 119–142, and James A. Ohlson and Stephen H. Penman, "Disaggregated Accounting Data as Explanatory Variables for Returns," *Journal of Accounting, Auditing and Finance* (1992), 553–573.

5. In doing so, the student is taken through the gyrations of converting the "equity cost-of-capital" into the "weighted average cost-of-capital (WACC)" that pertains to firm risk rather than equity risk.

6. Graham's warnings about growth survive in modern texts of fundamental investing. See Bruce C. N. Greenwald, Judd Kahn, Paul D. Sonkin, and Michael van Biema, *Value Investing: From Graham to Buffett and Beyond* (New

York: Wiley, 2001), p. x, pp. 31–35, and pp. 42–43. Note that Benjamin Graham, David L. Dodd, and Sidney Cottle, *Security Analysis: Principles and Technique* 4th ed. (New York: McGraw-Hill, 1962), proposes, in Chapter 39, some (rather ad hoc) methods for dealing with growth that place limits on growth multipliers, as does Sidney Cottle, Roger F. Murray, and Frank E. Block, *Graham and Dodd's Security Analysis*, 5th ed. (New York, McGraw-Hill, 1988), pp. 542–546.

7. Wal-Mart, Home Depot, and GE are selected examples, but note that both the mean and median free cash flow for U.S. listed firms over the forty-five years up to 2009 were negative. The period was, of course, a time of considerable corporate investment growth.

8. Mark T. Bradshaw, "The Use of Target Prices to Justify Sell Side Analysts' Stock Recommendations," *Accounting Horizons* 16 (2002), 27–41 finds that 76 percent of equity analysts use P/E multiples and only 5 percent use cash-flow multiples.

9. Investment + added accruals is sometimes referred to as total accruals, for investment is also an accrual; recorded investments are part of accrual accounting that distinguishes it from cash accounting.

10. Those familiar with "economic value added," "shareholder value added," and "economic profit" metrics will recognize residual earnings by another name. But note that it is not necessarily economic profit; it is just an accounting measure and so depends on how the accounting is done. Note that ROCE for the future is expected earnings divided by expected book value, not expected earnings divided by book value (the two are different, by Jensen's inequality).

11. The mathematical proof involves substituting Dividends = Earnings – Change in book value (from *Accounting Principle 1*) into the dividend discount model. Boundary conditions, like those for the dividend discount model, require that book value should not grow too fast in the long run. The valuation is also consistent with the DCF model for forecasts made over very long forecast horizons. See Wolfgang Lücke, "Investitionsrechnung auf der Grundlage von Ausgaben oder Kosten?" *Zeitschrift für Betriebswirtschaftliche Forschung* 7 (1955), 310–324.

The residual earnings model has had a long history. In the early part of the twentieth century, the idea that a firm's value was based on "excess profits" was firmly established in the United Kingdom. The model is in the German literature of the 1920s and 1930s, particularly in the writings of Schmalenbach. In the United States, Gabriel Preinreich, an accounting and valuation theorist associated with Columbia University in the 1930s and 1940s, wrote extensively on the model, including "The Fair Value and Yield of Common Stock," *The Accounting Review* (1936), 130–140 and "Annual Survey of Economic Theory: The Theory of Depreciation," *Econometrica* 6 (1938), 219–241. In a 1941 paper,

Preinreich recognizes the model in a prize essay by a student, J. H. Bourne in *Accountant*, London, September 22, 1888, pp. 605–606 (as referenced by Preinreich). Strangely, the model was ignored for many years. John Burr Williams's *The Theory of Investment Value* (Cambridge, MA: Harvard University Press, 1938) promoted dividends as the fundamental for equity valuation, and academics have followed that tradition. U.S. texts have modified the dividend discount model to focus on free cash flows within the firm rather than cash flows to shareholders (dividends), and discounted cash flow analysis was the premier valuation technique in investment houses for many years (less so in Europe). Some relatively recent expositions of the residual earnings model are in Edgar O. Edwards and Philip W. Bell, *The Theory and Measurement of Business Income* (Berkeley: University of California Press, 1961), 48–54 and 66–69, and Ken Peasnell, "Some Formal Connections Between Economic Values and Yields and Accounting Numbers," *Journal of Business Finance and Accounting* (1982), 361–381. The residual earnings model features prominently in modern texts on financial statement analysis and valuation (less so in finance investment texts that stick to cash flow valuation). See, for example, Peter D. Easton, Mary Lea McAnally, Patricia M. Fairfield, Xiao-Jun Zhang, and Robert F. Halsey, *Financial Statement Analysis and Valuation*, 2nd ed. (Chicago: Cambridge Publishers, 2010); James M. Wahlen, Stephen P. Baginski, and Mark Bradshaw, *Financial Reporting, Financial Statement Analysis and Valuation: A Strategic Perspective* (Cincinnati: South-Western, 2010); and Stephen H. Penman, *Financial Statement Analysis and Security Valuation*, 4th ed. (New York: McGraw-Hill Irwin, 2010). For a focus on practitioners, see James English, *Applied Equity Analysis* (New York: McGraw-Hill, 2001).

12. James A. Ohlson, "Earnings, Book Values, and Dividends in Equity Valuation," *Contemporary Accounting Research* 12 (1995), 661–687 shows how valuation based on earnings and dividends is dividend irrelevant, provided that dividends are not included in earnings but rather are paid out of book value. This paper provides a foundation for accounting-based valuation, for it reconciles accounting principles to the foundational (Miller and Modigliani) principle of modern finance. Intuitively, dividend payments reduce prices one-for-one under Miller and Modigliani propositions but also reduce book value one-for-one (under *Accounting Principle 1*). GAAP and IFRS accounting follow this treatment of dividends and indeed empirical analysis demonstrates how GAAP accounting exhibits the Miller and Modigliani properties. See Stephen H. Penman and Theodore Sougiannis, "The Dividend Displacement Property and the Substitution of Anticipated Earnings for Dividends in Equity Valuation," *The Accounting Review* 72 (1997), 1–21.

13. For alternative statements of the residual earnings model and a demonstration of its equivalence to other models, including the dividend discount model, see Stephen H. Penman, "A Synthesis of Equity Valuation Techniques

and the Terminal Value Calculation for the Dividend Discount Model," *Review of Accounting Studies* 2 (1997), 303–323.

14. Accordingly valuation can be seen at buying book value and earnings for future delivery, with the current price being the market price of the futures contract.

15. See Stephen H. Penman and Theodore Sougiannis, "A Comparison of Dividends, Cash Flow, and Earnings Approaches to Valuation," *Contemporary Accounting Research* 15 (1998), 343–383, and Stephen H. Penman, "On Comparing Cash Flow and Accrual Accounting Models for Use in Equity Valuation," *Contemporary Accounting Research* 18 (2001), 681–692.

16. Indeed, if we are not willing to speculate at all, we can anchor on current book value and then forecast earnings based on the earnings we observe currently. We would then be literally anchoring on what we know from financial statements, subject to the quality of the accounting. But we would be excluding information beyond current earnings that we might be reasonably confident about and that indicates that near-term earnings will be different from current earnings.

17. The display is developed by ranking firms in a base year, year 0, on their residual earnings, forming 10 portfolios from the rankings, then tracking the median values for the portfolios over the subsequent five years. Residual earnings at all points is deflated by the book value of common equity in the base year. Residual earnings are calculated with a required return equal to the Treasury rate in the relevant year plus a 6 percent risk premium (for all firms). The ranking is done seven times, for years 1964, 1969, 1974, 1979, 1984, 1989, and 1994, that is, at five-year intervals. The figure presents the average of results from these seven replications. There is one caveat: Firms in the base year may not survive over the full five years.

18. Mathematically, we have just differenced the residual earnings model: earnings are the change in book value (dividends are irrelevant) so, rather than basing the valuation on book value and the level of expected residual earnings, this model bases it on the change in book value (earnings) and the change in expected residual earnings. See Patricia M. Fairfield, "P/E, P/B and the Present Value of Future Dividends," *Financial Analysts Journal* 50(4) (1994), 23–31 and James R. English, *Applied Equity Analysis*, p. 350. The valuation can also be applied by anchoring on trailing earnings. Forward earnings is, of course, the earnings for the fiscal year in progress.

19. See James A. Ohlson and Beate E. Juettner-Nauroth, "Expected EPS and EPS Growth as Determinants of Value," *Review of Accounting Studies* 10 (2005), 349–365. For elaboration, see James A. Ohlson and Zhan Gao, "Earnings, Earnings Growth and Value," *Foundations and Trends in Accounting* 1 (2006), 1–70.

20. See again Peter D. Easton, Trevor S. Harris, and James A. Ohlson, "Accounting Earnings Can Explain Most Security Returns: The Case of Long-Event Windows," *Journal of Accounting and Economics* 15 (1992), 119–142.

3. Challenging Market Prices with Fundamentals

1. More from Benjamin Graham and David L. Dodd, *Security Analysis* (New York: McGraw-Hill, 1934). p. 19: "An indefinite and approximate measure of the intrinsic value may be sufficient. To use a homely simile, it is quite possible to decide by inspection that a woman is old enough to vote without knowing her age, or that a man is heavier than he should be without knowing his exact weight."

2. Sell-side analysts' consensus forecasts are available under ticker symbols on finance websites such as Yahoo! Finance and Reuters. Thompson Financial Network compiles analysts' consensus earnings estimates.

3. Research indicates that forecasts developed from financial statement analysis successfully challenge analysts' forecasts and stock recommendations. For a recent example, see James M. Wahlen and Matthew M. Wieland, "Can Financial Statement Analysis Beat Consensus Analysts' Recommendations?" *Review of Accounting Studies* 16, no. 1 (2011).

4. The recovery of the implied growth rate does not work satisfactorily when residual earnings (to which growth might be applied) are negative. Negative residual earnings imply a price-to-book less than 1, which is not typical. If the accounting renders negative residual earnings, the investor is of course warned: Do not pay more than book value (there probably is no growth involved)! Indeed, one might expect these firms to write down assets under impairment rules. If one anticipates that residual earnings will be positive three or four years ahead (say), the forecast horizon can be extended, but now one is really speculating about a longer-term future. Note that analysts often provide a "five-year growth rate" with their forecasts, but these are notoriously imprecise. In a similar vein to the apparatus here, one can reverse engineer the P/E model of the last chapter.

5. The scheme is laid out more fully in Stephen H. Penman, "Handling Valuation Models," *Journal of Applied Corporate Finance* 18 (2006), 48–55.

6. John Burr Williams, *The Theory of Investment Value* (Burlington, VT: Fraser Publishing, 1997), p. 188 (an exact copy of the 1938 Harvard University Press edition) and Alfred Rappaport and Michael J. Mauboussin, *Expectations Investing* (Cambridge, MA: Harvard Business Press, 2001).

7. Consider reverse engineering GE's FCF growth rate from the market price and FCFs in Chapter 2. It is quite difficult, given the negative FCFs.

More generally, a firm on a path of growing investments may have declining FCF, yet warrant a higher stock price.

8. The calculated growth rates are ex-dividend growth rates, not cum-dividend growth rates (though for Cisco, with no dividends, they are the same thing).

9. Accounting numbers are in nominal terms and so is the required return, so this implied growth rate is a nominal (not a "real") growth rate. The benchmark growth rate will depend on the anticipated inflation at a particular point in time.

10. The correlation between the growth rates and subsequent returns in excess of the ten-year U.S. government bond yield is −0.14. (Excess returns adjust for changing interest rates.) For an analysis of value-to-price ratios for the Dow stocks, with changing discount rates and residual earnings valuation, see Charles M. C. Lee, James Meyers, and Bhaskaran Swaminathan, "What Is the Intrinsic Value of the Dow?" *Journal of Finance* 54 (1999), 1693–1741.

11. The conservative estimate recognizes that historical GDP growth in the United States has been exceptional (during "the American century") and may not persist. As a nominal growth rate, the GDP growth rate reflects anticipated inflation, so should be adjusted at any point in time for the expected inflation rate. This can be identified from yields on government inflation-protected securities (TIPS). Note that, as the required return, r is also a nominal rate. Expected inflation cancels in the $r–g$ denominator calculation in a valuation, effectively discounting for growth that comes from expected inflation.

12. Note that the Ohlson-Juettner abnormal earnings growth model of the last chapter builds in a declining growth rate for residual earnings. Expressing abnormal earnings growth as change (growth) in residual earnings,

$$\text{Value of equity}_0 = \frac{\text{Earnings}_1}{r} + \frac{1}{r}\left[\frac{\text{Change in RE}_2}{r - g}\right]$$

for a two-year forecasting horizon. The growth rate now is applied to changes in residual earnings rather than the level of residual earnings, and a constant growth in changes implies a declining growth rate in the levels.

13. The valuation is not quite the same as that for the Fed model:

$$\text{Value}_0 = B_0 + \frac{(\text{ROCE}_1 - r) \times B_0}{r_f} = \frac{\text{Earnings}_1}{r_f} - \left(\frac{r}{r_f} - 1\right)B_0,$$

in contrast to

$$\text{Value}_0 = \frac{\text{Earnings}_1}{r_f}.$$

The valuation preserves the notion that forward earnings (without growth) are at risk and thus should be charged with a required return that reflects that risk.

14. The model is associated with Edward Yardeni, an economist at Deutsche Morgan Grenfell, who found it in the back pages of a July 1977 Federal Reserve Monetary Policy Report (or so folklore has it).

15. The idea of canceling growth and risk is in the Thomas paper, the source of Figure 3.6, and in James A. Ohlson, "Risk, Growth, and Permanent Earnings," (New York: New York University, Stern School of Business, 2008). An elaboration of the Thomas paper is in Jacob Thomas and Frank Zhang, "Understanding Two Remarkable Findings About Stock Yields and Growth," *Journal of Portfolio Management* 35 (2009), 158–165. The Thomas 2005 paper reports the same pattern as in Figure 3.6 for a number of countries (Japan being an exception).

16. As reported in Stephen H. Penman and Francesco Reggiani, "Returns to Buying Earnings and Book Value: Accounting for Growth and Risk," unpublished paper, Columbia University and Bocconi Univerity (2008), at http://ssrn.com/abstract=1536618.

17. See Robert D. Arnott, Feifer Li, and Katrina F. Sherrerd, "Clairvoyant Value and the Value Effect," *Journal of Portfolio Management* 35 (2009), 12–26, and Robert Arnott, Feifei Li, and Katrina F. Sherrerd, "Clairvoyant Value II : The Growth/Value Cycle," *Journal of Portfolio Management* 35 (2009), 142–157.

4. Accounting for Growth from Leverage

1. The ROCE declines in subsequent years in this example because the leverage declines. Debt remains the same, whereas equity increases.

2. The residual earnings for equity is calculated with the required return for equity, 15 percent, that reflects the added risk to the equity holder for leverage. The required return for equity is given by the weighted average cost-of-capital formula in reverse form:

Equity cost-of-capital = Cost-of-capital for the business + [Value leverage
× (Cost-of-capital for the business
− After-tax cost-of-capital for debt)]

$$= 10\% + \left[\frac{50}{50} \times (10\% - 5\%)\right] = 15\%.$$

3. See note 2 for the calculation of the effect of leverage on the required return for equity.

4. If a firm buys back its stock at less than fair value, it will add value (for the shareholders who do not participate in the stock repurchase), and similarly so if it issues debt for more than it is worth. But business firms typically are

not bond or stock traders, trading in their own securities; they take bond and stock prices as given. Other exceptions to financing irrelevance indicated in note 25 in Chapter 1 also apply, including possible tax effects. Note that interest expense referred to in the accounting here is after-tax (effective interest), as is operating income, so the "tax shield" is accommodated in the accounting.

5. As leverage changes over time, so does the required return in future years, so the calculation typically involves a changing required return and residual earnings for each year in the pro forma. The example has been set up here so that the value calculated with constant residual earnings equals that from the more cumbersome calculation.

6. The introduction to the following paper surveys the empirical research and actually documents negative returns to leverage after controlling for other risk factors in standard asset pricing models; see Stephen Penman, Scott Richardson, and İrem Tuna, "The Book-to-Price Effect in Stock Returns: Accounting for Leverage," *Journal of Accounting Research* 45 (2007), 427–467.

7. Again, borrowing costs are after-tax (effective interest) borrowing costs.

8. The FASB and IASB are currently engaged in a project to redesign financial statement presentation to separate business activities from financing activities (among other things). For a comprehensive design, see Stephen Penman, *The Design of Financial Statements*, White Paper No. 3, Center for Excellence in Accounting and Security Analysis, Columbia Business School (2010). The mechanics of reformulating financial statements are in Stephen H. Penman, *Financial Statement Analysis and Security Valuation*, 4th ed. (New York, McGraw-Hill Irwin, 2010), chap. 9.

9. As GAAP reports only one tax number, one must allocate taxes to the two components.

10. The unlevering implicitly discards the familiar return-on-assets, ROA (Operating income/Total assets) as a measure of business profitability. Total assets include financial assets (not used in the business) and exclude enterprise liabilities, and typically result in too-low rates of return. The distinction between financing liabilities and liabilities arising from the business introduces a second type of leverage from operating liabilities—operating liability leverage—which can be analyzed as a source of value from the business, particularly those (like insurance companies) that play a float. See Doron Nissim and Stephen Penman, "Financial Statement Analysis of Leverage and How it Informs About Profitability and Price-to-Book Ratios," *Review of Accounting Studies* 8 (2003), 531–560.

11. The difference between ROCE and RNOA goes in the other direction if a firm is negatively leveraged, that is, with financial assets in excess of financial liabilities. In the last chapter, we saw an ROCE of 21.1 percent for Cisco

Systems. But Cisco has considerably more financial assets than financial debt, so its net debt is negative. Thus its RNOA of 57.1 percent is greater than the ROCE of 21.3 percent; the ROCE hides the real profitability of the business.

12. See Alon Brav, John Graham, Campbell Harvey, and Roni Michaely, "Payout Policies in the 21st Century," *Journal of Financial Economics* 77 (2005), 483–527. In the same survey, 68 percent of respondents also said that reversing the dilution effects of stock options was another important consideration, a fallacy indeed. But 86 percent also said that they repurchase when they consider their stock to be cheap.

13. None of this necessarily conflicts with the standard business school dogma that the announcement of a stock repurchase increases price because it "signals" that management thinks the stock is underpriced (less than fair value). This "signaling" conjecture has nothing to do with the mechanical increase in EPS and its relation to value, however.

5. Accounting for Growth in the Business

1. The applicable accounting is the "lower-of-cost-or-market" rule whereby inventories must be written-down to (fair) market value if that value is below cost, but carried at cost if market value is above cost.

2. The accounting here is also illustrative of LIFO (last in, first out) accounting for inventory where carrying values for inventory are lower when inventory prices are rising.

3. For an account of momentum accounting during the 1990s, see Stephen H. Penman, "The Quality of Financial Statements: Perspectives from the Recent Stock Market Bubble," *Accounting Horizons* (Suppl. 2003), 77–96.

4. This is not to dismiss the measures for the purpose for which they are designed; the accounting may provide a better incentive mechanism to reward management, for example. As there is an appropriate accounting for value (as a matter of design), so is there an appropriate accounting for incentives and performance measurement (as a matter of design). See Stefan Reichelstein and Sunil Dutta, "Accrual Accounting for Performance Evaluation," *Review of Accounting Studies* 10 (2005), 527-552.

5. The effects of conservative accounting are modeled in James A. Ohlson and Gerald A. Feltham, "Valuation and Clean Surplus Accounting for Operating and Financing Activities," *Contemporary Accounting Research* 11 (1995), 689–731; Xiao-Jun Zhang, "Conservative Accounting and Equity Valuation," *Journal of Accounting and Economics* 29 (2000), 125–149; and William H. Beaver and Stephen G. Ryan, "Conditional and Unconditional Conservatism: Concepts and Modeling," *Review of Accounting Studies* 10 (2005), 269–309. For

empirical documentation of the effects, see Stephen H. Penman and Xiao-Jun Zhang, "Accounting Conservatism, Quality of Earnings, and Stock Returns," *The Accounting Review* 77 (2002), 237–264; and Steven J. Monahan, "Conservatism, Growth, and the Role of Accounting Numbers in the Fundamental Analysis Process," *Review of Accounting Studies* 10 (2005), 227–260.

6. Note that the dividends are reduced from those without growth: Investment requires retention and retention means lower dividends. Also note that, despite the lower payout, the value is the same; dividend irrelevance in action.

6. Accounting for Risk and Return

1. Surveys of academics, analysts, and companies put estimates of the market risk premium in a range between 3 and 10 percent, although some of that is due to variation over time. See, for example, a survey conducted by Pablo Fernandez of IESE Business School at http://ssrn.com/abstract=1473225 and http://ssrn.com/abstract=1609563. See also a survey by Ivo Welch of Brown University at http://papers.ssrn.com/sol3/papers.cfm?abstract_id=1084918. For a roundtable discussion on the issue, see http://papers.ssrn.com/sol3/papers.cfm?abstract_id=234713. As the cost-of-capital is determined by multiplying the estimated risk premium by an estimated beta, the variation in the cost-of-capital is magnified by beta (and by the estimation error in beta).

2. The point was made at the time of the crisis by John Cochrane, "Is Now the Time to Buy Stocks? Here Is What the Evidence Suggests," *Wall Street Journal*, November 12, 2008, p. A19.

3. Behavioral research indicates that risk tolerance does not just vary from individual to individual (man vs. woman, for example), but depends on the context for a given individual. See, for example, Elke U. Weber, Ann-Renée Blais, and Nancy E. Betz, "A Domain-Specific Risk-Attitude Scale: Measuring Risk Perceptions and Risk Behaviors," *Journal of Behavioral Decision Making* 15 (2002), 263–290. A DOSPERT scale that has been applied in many contexts is explained on the Center for Decision Sciences website at http://www4.gsb .columbia.edu/decisionsciences/research/tools/dospert.

4. The formula works only for $RNOA_1$ greater than g, so is not a panacea. With g typically 4 percent or less, this covers most firms, but not loss firms. For loss firms, the accounting says that the firm is highly speculative; the firm could fail, so watch out. Firms often report trailing losses (temporarily); forward losses are less common. See Figure 4.1b in Chapter 4 for the typical pattern of RNOA for loss firms.

5. For a forecast horizon two years ahead (as with Cisco Systems in Chapter 3), the reverse-engineering model is

$$\text{Market price of operations}_0 = \text{Net operating assets}_0$$
$$+ \frac{\text{Residual operating income}_1}{1+r}$$
$$+ \frac{\text{Residual operating income}_2}{(1+r)\times(r-g)}.$$

from which r can be inferred for any g. The horizon year should not be a year where earnings are forecasted to be temporarily high or low, for then the no-growth valuation would not be a good anchoring point. This can be the case with the immediate forward year.

6. The forecast of 57.1 percent is obtained by unlevering the ROCE forecast of 21.3 percent in Chapter 2 based on analysts' forward earnings forecasts. One is again cautioned about using analysts' forecasts; the sustainable RNOA for the trailing year was only 40.1 percent.

7. Professional money managers have a problem defining the risk tolerance of their investors and thus the appropriate hurdle rate. This might be imputed from the style designation of the fund, with offering documents expressly detailing the risk profile adopted. The hurdle rate might also be the rate at which the manager's incentive return kicks in, for that should be set at the point where the manager is achieving returns in excess of those that compensate for the risk he or she takes.

8. On a levered basis, the weighted-average return formula is

$$r = \left[\frac{B}{P}\times \text{ROCE}_1\right] + \left[\left(1-\frac{B}{P}\right)\times g\right],$$

where the expected return is now the expected return from buying the equity (including the debt of the firm) rather than the return from buying the business without the debt, B/P is the (levered) book-to-price for the equity, and g is growth in (levered) residual earnings. For Cisco, with a book-to-price of 0.278 and a forward ROCE of 21.25 percent, the no-growth levered expected return is 5.91 percent. This levered expected return reconciles with the unlevered return of 6.97 percent according to the weighted-average cost-of-capital formula (in accordance with the financing irrelevance principle of modern finance):

$$\text{Levered } r = \text{Unlevered } r + [\text{Market leverage}$$
$$\times (\text{Unlevered } r - \text{Return on net debt})]$$
$$= 6.97\% - [0.178 \times (6.97\% - 1.0\%)]$$
$$= 5.91\%.$$

(Cisco is negatively levered and thus has a levered return less that the unlevered return.)

9. For the techies, the problem arises because formulas with discount rates in the denominator are not quite correct. Valuation theory discounts expected payoffs in the numerator (to yield risk-neutral expected payoffs), and then discounts at the risk-free rate. See, for example, Mark Rubinstein, "The Valuation of Uncertain Income Streams and the Pricing of Options," *Bell Journal of Economics and Management Science* 7 (1976), 407–425. How one makes the numerator discount in practice is not worked out, thus the textbook expediency of adding risk to the discount in the denominator. But there is no free lunch, thus the technical problem here (indeed, a fudge).

10. Fama's early work, fifty years ago, documents fat-tailed empirical distributions. See Eugene Fama, "The Behavior of Stock Market Prices," *Journal of Business* 38 (1965), 34–105. Attempts to formalize the observation in asset pricing—replacing normal distributions with (fat-tailed) stable Paretian distributions or a mixture of normal distributions, for example—have not proved successful. For a recent rendition of the "fat-tail" phenomenon, see Nassim Nicholas Taleb, *The Black Swan: The Impact of the Highly Improbable* (New York: Random House, 2007).

11. If one follows the annual Shareholder Scorecard published each February in *The Wall Street Journal*, one will routinely see returns of over 300 percent. The Scorecard gives the top and bottom 2.5 percent of returns for 1,000 larger firms, a significant cutoff because it is the point under the normal distribution where firms are supposed to have returns in excess of two standard deviations from the mean. With a mean of (say) 12 percent and a standard deviation of (say) 25 percent, relatively few firms should have annual returns less than −38 percent or greater than 62 percent. In 2007 (a poor year for stocks generally), 2.5 percent of firms had returns greater than 120 percent, with the best firm returning 795 percent. In 1998 (a good year for stocks), 2.5 percent of firms had returns less than −55 percent, with the worst firm returning −83.7 percent.

12. Frank Knight, *Risk, Uncertainty, and Profit* (Boston: Houghton Mifflin, 1921).

13. Recent research in finance has experimented with "cash-flow betas" (misnamed, for they are actually based on earnings and book rates-of-return) and find that the measures explain puzzles arising from using stock return betas. See, for example, Alexander Nekrasov and Pervin Shroff, "Fundamentals-Based Risk Measurement in Valuation," *The Accounting Review* 84 (2009), 1983–2011, and Randolph B. Cohen, Christopher Polk, and Tuomo Vuolteenaho, "The Price is (Almost) Right," *Journal of Finance* 64 (2009), 2739–2782. Years ago, Barr Rosenberg set about estimating "fundamental betas" that become the initial product of the BARRA firm. See Barr Rosenberg and Walt McKibben, "The Prediction of Systematic and Specific Risk in Common Stocks," *Journal of Financial and Quantitative Analysis* 8 (1973), 317–333.

14. Refer to Stephen H. Penman, *Financial Statement Analysis and Security Valuation*, 4th ed. (New York, McGraw-Hill Irwin, 2010), chapter 18 for elaboration.

15. In valuation formulas, growth enters as an expected growth rate (that is, the average growth rate over a number of scenarios). However, rather than pricing average growth rates, appropriate valuation averages prices for alternative growth rates. Jensen's inequality is the operational principle.

16. The outcomes (in retrospect) included second-order effects of trading partners losing faith in the firm as a whole, and the lowering of the credit rating so important to an insurer, with the resulting cascading third-order effects and effective collapse (save the taxpayers' reluctant rescue).

17. See, for example, Dirk Bezemer, "Why Some Economists Could See It Coming," *Financial Times*, September 8, 2009.

18. Two recent books are good reading here. See Riccardo Rebonato, *Plight of the Fortune Tellers: Why We Need to Manage Financial Risk Differently* (Princeton, NJ: Princeton University Press, 2007), and Kenneth A. Posner, *Stalking the Black Swan: Research and Decision Making in a World of Extreme Volatility* (New York, Columbia University Press, 2010).

19. On accounting and forecasting, see Stephen H. Penman, "Financial Forecasting, Risk, and Valuation: Accounting for the Future," *Abacus* 46 (2010), 211–228.

7. Pricing Growth

1. Standard significance tests show the return differences between high and low portfolios are statistically significant. The returns in the exhibit are from a period when investors said the strategy worked so are not an independent (out-of-sample) validation of their strategies. The returns to E/P were brought to prominence (in academic journals) in Sanjoy Basu, "Investment Performance of Common Stocks in Relation to Their Price-Earnings Ratios: A Test of the Efficient Market Hypothesis," *Journal of Finance* 32 (1977), 663–682 and Sanjoy Basu, "The Relationship Between Earnings Yield, Market Value, and Return for NYSE Common Stocks: Further Evidence," *Journal of Financial Economics* 12 (1983), 129–156. The returns to B/P were brought to the fore in Eugene Fama and Kenneth French, "The Cross-Section of Expected Stock Returns," *Journal of Finance* 47 (1992), 427–465. Benjamin Graham and cohorts had the idea firmly in mind before these academic renderings.

2. The point that E/P, as a yield, could indicate risk (as with a bond yield) was made in Ray Ball, "Anomalies in Relationships Between Securities' Yields and Yield-Surrogates," *Journal of Financial Economics* 6 (1978), 103–126.

3. The most comprehensive documentation is in Eugene Fama and Kenneth French, "The Cross-Section of Expected Stock Returns," *Journal of Finance* 47 (1992), 427–465.

4. See Eugene Fama and Kenneth French, "Common Risk Factors in the Returns on Stocks and Bonds," *Journal of Financial Economics* 33 (1993), 3–56, and Eugene Fama and Kenneth French, "Multifactor Explanations of Asset Pricing Anomalies," *Journal of Finance* 51 (1996), 55–84. Others have added additional factors to the model; a momentum factor and a liquidity factor, for example.

5. See Stephen H. Penman, Scott A. Richardson, and İrem Tuna, "The Book-to-Price Effect in Stock Returns: Accounting for Leverage," *Journal of Accounting Research* 45 (2007), 427–467.

6. Much of what follows is based on Stephen H. Penman and Francesco Reggiani, "Returns to Buying Earnings and Book Value: Accounting for Growth and Risk," unpublished paper, Columbia University and Bocconi University (2008), at http://ssrn.com/abstract=1536618.

7. The reader is reminded that the required return for operations and the required return for equity in these expressions are tied together by the weighted average cost of capital formula. See note 8 in Chapter 6.

8. IFRS accounting expenses "research" but not "development" (of products of the research), presumably because the latter is less risky.

9. In principle, one could conceive of an accounting where the growth rate corresponds to risk, one-to-one, as in James Ohlson, "Risk, Growth, and Permanent Earnings," unpublished paper, New York University Stern School of Business (2008).

10. The returns for some portfolios in exhibit 7.2 may seem to be too large to be explained as reward for risk. But the last half of the twentieth century is a period where (presumably) growth paid off handsomely.

8. Fair Value Accounting and Accounting for Value

1. Some initial proposals for the new Conceptual Framework are in an FASB Exposure Draft, "Conceptual Framework for Financial Reporting: The Objective of Financial Reporting and Qualitative Characteristics and Constraints of Decision-Useful Financial Reporting," Financial Accounting Series 1570-100 (2008), available at www.fasb.org. A similar document has been published by the IASB at www.iasb.org.

2. This chapter is based loosely on a CEASA White Paper on fair value accounting. See Doron Nissim and Stephen H. Penman, *Principles for the Application of Fair Value Accounting,* White Paper No. 2, Center for Excellence in Accounting and Security Analysis, Columbia Business School, 2008. See also, Stephen H. Penman, "Financial Reporting Quality: Is Fair Value a Plus or a

Minus?" *Accounting and Business Research* (International Accounting Policy Forum Special Issue) 37 (2007), 33–44.

3. Fair value accounting measurement is prescribed in FASB Statement of Financial Accounting Standards No. 157, *Fair Value Measurements* (Norwalk, CT: FASB, 2006). At the time of this writing, the FASB and IASB were revisiting the issue of fair value measurement (as a result of the financial crisis), with a final rule expected by late 2010.

4. In accounting terms, the holdings were part of "available-for-sale" investments. At the time, GAAP did not book unrealized gains and losses on these investments to the income statement, but added them directly to shareholders' equity (in an accounting operation called "dirty-surplus accounting").

5. For scenarios where "momentum accounting" promotes momentum pricing, see Stephen H. Penman, "The Quality of Financial Statements: Perspectives from the Recent Stock Market Bubble," *Accounting Horizons* (Suppl, 2003), 77–96.

6. For descriptions of how fair value accounting can induce feedback effects that amplify price movements, see Guillaume Plantin, Haresh Sapra, and Hyun Song Shin, "Marking to Market: Panacea or Pandora's Box?" *Journal of Accounting Research* 46 (2008), 435–460; and Tobias Adrian and Hyun Song Shin, "Liquidity and Leverage," Working Paper, Federal Reserve Bank of New York and Princeton University (2007). See also, Haresh Sapra, "The Economic Trade-Offs in The Fair Value Debate," Working Paper No. 09-35, The University of Chicago Booth School of Business at http://papers.ssrn.com/abstract=1481777, and European Central Bank, "Fair Value Accounting and Financial Stability," *Occasional Paper Series, No. 13* (April, 2004).

7. Interestingly, investment bankers (for a variety of reasons) favor fair value accounting.

8. As reported in the *Wall Street Journal,* February 26, 2009, p. A13.

9. For further exploration of the interplay between a bank's actions and the market prices of loans, see Alexander Bleck and Pingyang Gao, "Where Does the Information in Mark-to-Market Come From?" The University of Chicago Booth School of Business (2009) at http://ssrn.com/abstract=1507342.

10. For the interplay between mark-to-market accounting and liquidity pricing, see Franklin Allen and Elena Carletti, "Mark-to-Market Accounting and Liquidity Pricing," *Journal of Accounting and Economics* 45 (2008), 358–378.

11. The documentary film, *Enron: The Smartest Guys in the Room* (2005), confirms that the celebration was not fiction (thought there may be a question about the champagne). The film is based on a book of a similar title by Bethany McLean and Peter Elkind (New York, Portfolio, 2004).

12. International Monetary Fund, *Global Financial Stability Report: Financial Stress and Deleveraging, Macrofinancial Implications and Policy* (Washington, DC, IMF, 2008), chap. 3.

13. See, for example, Christian Laux and Christian Leuz, "Did Fair-Value Accounting Contribute to the Financial Crisis?" *Journal of Economic Perspectives* 24 (2010), 93–118, and Mary Barth and Wayne Landsman, "How Did Financial Reporting Contribute to the Financial Crisis?" *European Accounting Review* 19 (2010), 399–423. For another critique of fair value accounting in the crisis, see Vincent Bignon, Yuri Biondi, and Xavier Ragot, "An Economic Analyais of Fair Value: Accounting as a Vector of Crisis," at http://ssrn.com/abstract=1474228.

14. The claim is also suspect because, although bank loans (at the time of this writing) are not explicitly fair valued to exit value, they are quasi-fair valued with discounts for estimates of default. These estimates are similar to Level 3 fair values, though transactional information on incurred losses and nonperformance are incorporated in the estimate. (The issue is taken up in the next chapter.) At the time of this writing, the FASB was proposing to apply formal fair value accounting to all bank loans, applicable in 2013.

15. The point pertains to the issue (currently on the table) of whether equity investments should be fair valued or accounted for under the (historical cost) equity method or proportional consolidation.

16. The distinction points to fair value accounting being appropriate for a bank's trading book but not its bank book. Although fair value accounting is appropriate for a pure trading operation, one must be sensitive to the scam of restructuring a production operation to look like a trading operation to get the "benefits" of fair value accounting (like Enron did).

17. The warning applies even to an active investment fund that bets on market prices. An active investment manager supposedly holds or shorts investments that are mispriced, so the market price of the portfolio holdings is not fair value. And the active manager must not only find investments that will appreciate in price, but also liquidate the positions at the right time. Active investing is not about holding investments, but about execution; any schmuck can hold a stock.

18. The discussion here refers to financing debt (that finances business operations). Debt as part of a business of running a matched book (in a financial institution) would be marked to market if the assets on the other side of the book are also marked to maket under the one-for-one principle. In this case, unrealized gains and losses on debt net out against unrealized losses and gains on the assets.

19. The relation first appears in Peter D. Easton, Trevor S. Harris, and James A. Ohlson, "Accounting Earnings Can Explain Most Security Returns: The Case of Long-Event Windows," *Journal of Accounting and Economics* 15 (1992), 119–142, but accounting textbooks of old used to discuss the canceling error property.

20. These examples, as well as a wider discussion of intangible asset accounting, are in Stephen H. Penman, "Accounting for Intangible Assets:

There Is Also an Income Statement," *Abacus* 45 (2009), 359–371 and in a CEASA Occasional Paper at http://www4.gsb.columbia.edu/ceasa/research/papers/occasional_papers. See also Douglas J. Skinner, "Accounting for Intangibles—A Critical Review of Policy Recommendations" *Accounting and Business Research* 38 (2008), 191–204.

21. For a critique of the balance sheet focus, see Ilia Dichev, "On the Balance Sheet-Based Model of Financial Reporting," CEASA Occasional Paper (2007); and (with a focus on banking), Andreas Bezold, "The Subject Matter of Financial Reporting: The Conflict Between Cash Conversion Cycles and Fair Value in the Measurement of Income," CEASA Occasional Paper (2009). Both papers are available at http://www4.gsb.columbia.edu/ceasa/research/papers/occasional_papers.

22. Note, however, that the CFA Institute, the professional organization of security analysts, endorses fair value accounting enthusiastically (though some suggest that this position is in conflict with the rank-and-file analyst on the Street). See *A Comprehensive Business Reporting Model: Financial Reporting for Investors* (Charlottesville, VA: CFA Institute Centre for Financial Market Integrity, 2007).

23. See Ilia Dichev and Vicki Wei Tang, "Matching and the Changing Properties of Accounting Earnings Over the Last 40 Years" *Accounting Review* 83 (2008), 1425–1460. This study covers the 1,000 largest U.S. firms during the last forty years, and finds that earnings volatility has more than doubled during the period, whereas earnings persistence has fallen from 0.91 to 0.65, a substantial deterioration in the properties of accounting earnings. In contrast, the study finds little change in the properties of the underlying revenues, expenses, and cash flows over the same period, indicating that the bulk of the changes in the properties of earnings are due to changes in the accounting rather than changes in the real economy. Research has also shown that the relation between stock prices and reported earnings has declined over time. See, for example, Daniel W. Collins, Edward L. Maydew, and Ira S. Weiss, "Changes in the Value-Relevance of Earnings and Book Values over the Past Forty Years," *Journal of Accounting and Economics* 24 (1997), 39–67.

9. Adding Value to Accounting

1. For an analysis of GAAP accounting quality for valuation, see Stephen H. Penman, *Financial Statement Analysis and Valuation*, 4th ed.(New York, McGraw-Hill, 2010) chap. 17. See also Nahum D. Melumad and Doron Nissim, "Line-Item Analysis of Earnings Quality," *Foundations and Trends in Accounting* 3 (2009), 87–221; and Patricia M. Dechow and Catherine M. Schrand, *Earnings Quality* (The Research Foundation of CFA Institute, 2004).

2. For a review of many of these studies, see Scott A. Richardson, İrem Tuna, and Peter Wysocki, "Accounting Anomalies and Fundamental Analysis: A Review of Recent Research Advances, *Journal of Accounting and Economics* (2010), forthcoming.

3. A long line of papers document that analysts overreact to past earnings changes and underreact to other information, but on average tend to be overly optimistic in their forecasts. For a recent paper, see James A. Wahlen and Matthew A. Wieland, "Can Financial Statement Analysis Beat Consensus Analysts' Recommendations?" *Review of Accounting Studies* 16 (2011), Issue No. 1, forthcoming. On analysts failing to see the differential persistence of accruals and cash flows, see Mark T. Bradshaw, Scott A. Richardson, and Richard G. Sloan, "Do Analysts and Auditors Use Information in Accruals?" *Journal of Accounting Research* 39 (2001), 45–74.

4. The Conceptual Framework is still evolving, but some initial proposals are in an FASB Exposure Draft, "Conceptual Framework for Financial Reporting: The Objective of Financial Reporting and Qualitative Characteristics and Constraints of Decision-Useful Financial Reporting," Financial Accounting Series 1570-100 (2008), available at www.fasb.org. A similar document has been published by the IASB at www.iasb.org.

5. The 200 number is reported in Katherine A. Schipper, Catherine M. Schrand, Terry Shevlin, and Jeffrey T. Wilks, "Reconsidering Revenue Recognition," *Accounting Horizons* 23 (2009), 55–68.

6. At the time of this writing, the IASB and FASB had just published an exposure draft for a new standard on revenue recognition. See Exposure Draft of the International Accounting Standards Board, *Revenue from Contracts with Customers* (London, IASB, June 2010) and a similar document from the FASB.

7. In addition to revenue recognition, the accounting boards are currently redoing the accounting for leases, pensions, fair value measurement, financial instruments, income taxes, allowance for credit losses, and off-balance sheet vehicles, and have recently written new standards on stock option accounting, put options, and impairment accounting in response to failures of existing accounting. The FASB has made a number of attempts to deal with the accounting for off-balance sheet vehicles, including FASB Statements 125 (in 1996) and 140 (in 2000), FIN 46 in the wake of Enron, and Statements 166 and 167 in the wake of the financial crisis in 2010.

8. The FASB and IASB have accepted a mandate for "general-purpose" financial reporting, an impossible task through one set of books and a reason for some haziness in GAAP. As an example, take the simple issue of treatment of interest. Interest is an expense from the point of view of the shareholder, and dividends are a distribution. But from the bondholder's point of view, interest is not an expense but a distribution (and the bondholder is

concerned about dividends reducing the value left in the firm to cover the debt claim).

9. These principles are similar to those in a committee report of the American Accounting Association, "A Framework for Financial Accounting Standards: Issues and a Suggested Model," Financial Accounting Standards Committee of the American Accounting Association, *Accounting Horizons* 24 (2010), 471–485, for which (to be transparent) your author, along with James Ohlson, is a principal author.

10. The FASB and IFRS went some of the way in correcting the situation for employee stock options with Statement 123R in the United States and IFRS 2 internationally. They apply "grant-date" accounting; the value of the options at grant date is an expense. But the grant-date expense is not the expense to the shareholder. That happens at exercise date when the shareholder surrenders value. Indeed, the GAAP and IFRS accounting means that firms will record a grant-date expense that is never incurred if the option fails to go into the money to be exercised. In short, there is no settling up against shareholder value. Such accounting invites grant-date scheming, like backdating and choosing to issue options when prices are down; the accounting plays to the management rather than the shareholder.

11. For a layout of the appropriate accounting for shareholders, see James A. Ohlson and Stephen H. Penman, "Debt vs. Equity: Accounting for Claims Contingent on Firms' Common Stock Performance," White Paper No. 1, Center for Excellence in Accounting and Security Analysis, Columbia Business School (2005). See also Stephen H. Penman and James A. Ohlson, "Accounting for Employee Stock Options and Other Contingent Equity Claims: Taking a Shareholders' View," *Journal of Applied Corporate Finance* 19 (2007), 24–29.

12. See International Accounting Standards Board, Discussion Paper, *Preliminary Views on Financial Statement Presentation* (London: IASB, October 2008) and a paper from the FASB with the same title and date. For an alternative design that aligns closer with accounting for value, see Stephen H. Penman, *The Design of Financial Statements,* White Paper No. 4, Center for Excellence in Accounting and Security Analysis, Columbia Business School, 2010. Templates for reformulating balance sheets for equity valuation are in that document, and also in Stephen H. Penman, *Financial Statement Analysis and Security Valuation,* 4th ed. (New York: McGraw-Hill, 2010), chap. 9.

13. In their draft Conceptual Framework, the FASB and IASB have abandoned "conservatism" as a qualitative characteristic of accounting, choosing instead "neutrality" and "absence of bias."

14. The observation that balance sheet costs become expenses for profit assessment in the income statement has implications for the balance sheet treatment of transactions. The accountant might not record an investment in R&D on the balance sheet because there is too much uncertainty as to whether the

R&D will pay off : It is not hard enough. But he or she also might not do so because an amortization schedule against revenue is so speculative, for speculative amortizations ruin earnings measurement. (Uncertainty about payoffs and the pattern of payoffs for amortization are presumably highly correlated). In this regard, note that U.S. GAAP does not permit capitalization of R&D costs on the balance sheet, whereas IFRS allows capitalized development (after the research stage when products are apparent and there is less uncertainty) but not basic research (where the outcome to the research is still uncertain).

15. The suggestion, from James Ohlson, is in an American Accounting Association paper on revenue recognition. See "Accounting for Revenues: A Framework for Standard Setting," Financial Accounting Standards Committee of the American Accounting Association (2010).

16. For a transactions approach to revenue and profit recognition, see a committee report, "Accounting for Revenues: A Framework for Standard Setting," Financial Accounting Standards Committee of the American Accounting Association (2010).

17. FASB Statement No. 146, issued in 2002, restricts the ability to manipulate income with restructuring charges. Firms must now have an obligation to make specific payments under the restructuring rather than just a restructuring plan.

18. The recommendation is made in American Accounting Association, Financial Accounting Standards Committee, "A Framework for Financial Accounting Standards," *Accounting Horizons* 24 (2010), 471–485.

Index